AFRICAN IS

Somalia   Economy Without
State

AFRICAN ISSUES

Series Editors Alex de Waal & Stephen Ellis
Published in the US & Canada by Indiana University Press

Published in the US & Canada by Heinemann (N.H.)

AFRICAN ISSUES

Somalia

PETER D. LITTLE

Department of Anthropology
University of Kentucky

Economy Without State

The International
African Institute

in association with

JAMES CURREY
Oxford

INDIANA UNIVERSITY PRESS
Bloomington & Indianapolis

Btec Books
Hargeisa

The International
African Institute
in association with

James Currey
73 Botley Road
Oxford OX2 0BS

Btec Books
Maaweel Street
Hargeisa
Somaliland

Indiana University Press
601 North Morton Street
Bloomington
Indiana 47404
(North America)

British Library Cataloguing in Publication Data

Little, Peter D.
    Somalia : economy without state. – (African issues)
    1.Somalia – Politics and government – 1960-1991 2.Somalia –
    Politics and government – 1991- 3.Somalia – Social
    conditions – 1960- 4.Somalia – Economic conditions – 1960-
    I.Title
    967.7'305

    ISBN 0-85255-865-1 (James Currey paper)
    ISBN 0-85255-866-X (James Currey cloth)

Library of Congress Cataloging-in-Publication Data
A catalog record for this book is availailable from the Library of Congress

    ISBN 0-253-21648-6 (Indiana paper)
    ISBN 0-253-34362-3 (Indiana cloth)

Typeset by
Saxon Graphics Ltd, Derby
in 9/11 Melior with Optima display
Printed and bound in Great Britain by
Woolnough, Irthlingborough

DEDICATION

For the children of Somalia
who have endured so much

CONTENTS

LIST OF TABLES

LIST OF ILLUSTRATIONS

ACKNOWLEDGEMENTS

Support for this research and book has come from several sources spanning a 15-year period. I would like to thank most of all the John D. and Catherine T. MacArthur Foundation for providing a generous grant under its Global Security and Sustainability Program that allowed me to complete the research, analysis, and writing for this book. Without their support, this project would not have been possible. I also appreciate the assistance of the Institute for Development Anthropology under its Settlement and Resource Systems Analysis Cooperative Agreement that provided funding for the initial field research in southern Somalia. Field research support in subsequent years was provided by the Office of Foreign Disaster Assistance of the Agency for International Development (AID), the Broadening Access to Input Systems and Markets Collaborative Research Support Program (BASIS-CRSP) (administered at the University of Wisconsin), and the Global Livestock Collaborative Research Support Program (GL-CRSP) (administered at the University of California-Davis). It goes with saying, however, that none of the above organizations hold any responsibility for the contents of this book.

Along the way numerous individuals and other institutions have provided both moral and professional support. First, I would like to thank my colleague and student, Hussein Mahmoud, who served as my research assistant during the summers of 1996 and 1998, and helped with most of the trader interviews and their transcriptions. His help was invaluable and I am very grateful. At the University of Kentucky Barbara Cellarius and Satish Kedia also provided invaluable assistance in data entry and analysis. Secondly, I would like to acknowledge my field assistants, Ahmed Adan Abdi and Ali Mohamed Mohamoud, who worked with me in southern Somalia during 1986 to 1988, and my colleagues, Michael Cullen and Hugh Evans, who collaborated with me on an interdisciplinary research program in the region at the time. Thirdly, I would like to thank Larry Abel, Joe Carvalho, Brian D'Silva, and Ray Meyers, all of whom appreciated the importance of understanding cross-border trade and pastoralism in the Horn of Africa and helped to secure funding for parts of the study. Fourthly, Phillip Steffen, Michele McNabb, A.H. Shirwa, and Sidow Addou, Nancy Mutunga, and Nick Maunder of the

Famine Early Warning Systems (FEWS) (now called FEWS-Net) program kindly shared their Somali marketing data and reports with me. Phillip Steffen, in particular, provided encouragement and constructive input at different stages of the study. Fifthly, Abdel Ghaffar M. Ahmed and Tegegne Teka of the Organization of Social Science Research in Eastern and Southern Africa (OSSREA), who worked with me on a comparative study of trans-border trade in the Horn of Africa during 1999–2001, freely shared many of their insights on pastoral systems and markets. Sixthly, I am grateful for the support and helpful suggestions of the *African Issues* series co-editors, Alex de Waal and Stephen Ellis, and Douglas Johnson of James Currey Publishers. Finally, the book benefited from comments and different inputs from several other individuals, including Abdi Umar, Tag Dement, Layne Coppock, Chris Barrett, Abdillahi Aboud, Alex Dickey, Michael M. Horowitz, Andrea Layne, Curt Grimm, Gerald Karaska, Stefano Tempia, Lee Cassanelli, Vittoria Cagnaloti, Ricardo Costagli, Karl Lohr, Friedrich Mahler, Mohamed Hussein, Chip Stem, Christine Cornelius, Leif Manger, Tim Leyland, Milena Hileman, Dennis O'Brien, Chris Ackello-Oguto, Joel Pett, Sven Torfinn, Salim Shaabani, Giorgio Sartori, Joyce Turk, Deborah Rubin, Zelleke Sza Sza, Vincent Lelei, Abdi Aden Ali, Eric Silver and Andre Lesage. If I have overlooked anybody, I apologize in advance. None of the above individuals and institutions, of course, are accountable for the contents of the book.

My wife, Ellen, and children, Nelly, Katey, and Peter D., have been supportive as usual and have provided a wonderful escape to the drudgery of finishing a book. I also am grateful to the numerous Somali herders and traders who so generously shared their vast knowledge with an outsider and who have so adeptly learned to 'get on with life' under difficult circumstances.

PREFACE

Thinking and writing about Somalia, a territory without a state in the Horn of Africa, has been as paradoxical for me as the country itself. Since the collapse of any vestiges of a central government in 1991, it has been difficult to match the descriptions of chaos, hunger, and anarchy that frequently appear in the Western media with my own accounts of Somali social and economic life. There is a glaring disconnect. However, to assess a situation that has been so badly misrepresented – while not looking to condone it – is equally problematic. Depending on one's perspective, Somalia can invoke both elements of economic optimism – a free-wheeling, stateless capitalism – and political pessimism. On the global landscape it embodies the 'never, never' land of non-states and failed diplomacy and represents the longest period of any nation in modern history without a government despite recent efforts to re-establish one.

During the past 12 years, Somalis have endured a stateless environment and innovated a range of creative institutional and behavioral responses to adapt to it. For some individuals the lack of a government has provided opportunities to accumulate wealth, but for the majority it has been a matter of survival. With inconsistent and minimal international assistance, there were few options but to develop a 'second economy' based on cross-border trade and smuggling, informal finances, and a global system of remittances that has allowed the territory to maintain a level of economic welfare comparable to some of its neighbors. No doubt Somali resiliency has been enhanced by its strong dependence on nomadic pastoralism, a livelihood well adapted to stateless circumstances but brutally defensive when threatened, and by a wide-ranging kinship system that facilitates personal contacts and strategic relationships. The Somali case holds important lessons for large parts of Africa and the rest of the world, including central Asia, where stateless or near stateless conditions prevail. Like in so many of these regions, local communities have had to resort to their own devices while defending themselves against brutal warlords, global opportunists, and other extremists.

This book has been a very long time in the making. I left Somalia in March 1988 after nine months of field research on pastoralism and trade during a two-year period. A central government headed by the late Siad

Barre still existed but strong fissures were growing, especially in northern Somalia (Somaliland) where an all-out civil war had effectively begun. By early 1988 commercial aircraft in the country, commandeered and converted for military purposes, could frequently be seen in Mogadishu loading up troops and supplies for the north. What I did not know at this time is that the composition of my own research sample, in terms of clans, occupations, and locations, was to encompass the major political fissions in the south that erupted so violently in the 1990s. Indeed, the focus of my work, cattle trade, reflected deep-seated conflicts in the southern Somali borderlands that later became the basis for destructive political factions. It included the Mohamed Zubeyr sub-clan of the Ogadeen, who were in the interior and focused heavily on cattle pastoralism, and the Harti, who were concentrated in Kismayo town and its environs and emphasized trade and pastoralism. Later on the Mohamed Zubeyr became the backbone of the Somalia Patriotic Movement (SPM) and the Harti traders of Kismayo were to throw their support behind General Mohamed Said Hersi Morgan's Somali National Front (SNF), and both played a role in the overthrow of Siad Barre. The two factions strongly defined political events in the region and engaged in fierce military battles throughout the 1990s and, in Morgan's case, until 2002. As of now it is clear that much of the ongoing hostilities in the region – and elsewhere in Somalia – is for control of lucrative urban centers like Mogadishu and Kismayo, where much of the foreign aid and investment was concentrated during the 1980s.

Upon my return to the US in 1988 I completed the required data analysis and write-up to accommodate grant and project requirements. After producing a series of unpublished research reports, I left the Somalia materials for most of 1989 and 1990 while I completed a manuscript about Kenya. In fact, other than co-authoring a report on the project and a few minor publications and conference papers, I really did not get back to the Somalia data until after the violent removal of Siad Barre in 1991. For those of us working in Somalia, the coup was not a surprise since Barre's regime had been without much legitimacy or influence in its waning years. The phrase, 'Mayor of Mogadishu,' was commonly used to describe his rule in those final years, a reminder of his limited control of the country. In the case of the Lower Jubba Region and its borderlands, his authority had effectively ceased in 1989 when local resistance movements took control of parts of the territory. The notion of a central state was always elusive in Somalia, but by the late 1980s its demise was evident.

Thus, my return to the Somalia project roughly coincided with the chaos and war-induced famine that devastated Somalia for much of 1991 and 1992 after the central government's collapse. An area that I had resided in, the Kismayo region, and its impoverished inhabitants could be seen almost weekly in Western newspapers and on television. Somehow plans for writing up materials for scholarly publication seemed misplaced – even morally questionable. I retreated into some fund-raising activities for the Somali predicament and other research activities, and I left the write-up of the Somali data for another time. Through conferences, journalist accounts, and the media I stayed on top of what was generally happening (at least what was reported to be occurring). On occasions when I was in Nairobi, Kenya I spoke with Somali refugees, NGO personnel, and others involved with relief work in Somalia.

After the US and United Nations (UN) fiascos in the early 1990s, so graphically depicted in the recent Hollywood film production of *Black Hawk Down*, and with the persistence of misperceptions about the country and its people, I returned to writing about Somalia. The fact that Somalia had proved to be less of a social and economic 'basket case' than popular and 'expert' accounts portrayed it was a strong motivating factor. For those of us who have worked with Somali pastoralists and traders, their perseverance in the face of excruciating challenges is not surprising. Indeed, rather than a collapse following the departure of the UN in mid-1995, the economy actually seemed to improve. Even the Somali currency, without a government to support it, stabilized after an initial devaluation. Clearly, social and political conditions remained poor, but claims of anarchy and economic 'crisis' in Somalia had been overstated. A dilemma of representation, however, persisted.

In 1996 I initiated a study on the effects of the Somali war on livestock traders and cross-border trade between Somalia and Kenya – the most important and dynamic commerce in the region. I based myself out of Garissa, Kenya, the main market for trade with southern Somalia, and began a series of interviews with Somali traders and herders. I followed this work up with shorter stints of research in the Garissa and Nairobi markets during the summers of 1998 and 2001. What the research showed is that rather than in decline, the Somalia trans-border trade with Kenya was booming, and other indicators showed that the pastoral sector of southern Somalia was doing surprisingly well. In fact, in 1996 I was able to find information on about 80 percent of the traders whom I had interviewed in 1987–8, and many were still in the livestock business. The story was becoming more interesting. Somalia was without a state, a ministry of finance, or a central bank but trade was flourishing. Ragged, time-worn Somali notes remained in circulation and an elaborate network of money changers and informal finance houses had emerged to support the economy. Security in many areas had moderately improved and market transaction costs actually were not much higher than during the pre-war period. How could this occur without a central government maintaining security, regulating and supporting currency exchanges, and providing services to its citizens?

By 1999 the need to write a book went well beyond concerns with stereotypes: the Somali case challenges many social science notions about economy, governance, and institutions and has relevance well beyond its borders. Adequate treatment of the Somalia story, with its

complex social and historical contexts, required a book-length manuscript. Even then it is not possible to portray all the intricacies and
complexities of the Somalia case, an account that is still unfolding. The
recent international attention on this stateless region as a possible harbor
of global terrorism following the tragedy of September 11, 2001 only adds
to the story's complexity and the urgency to finish the book. If this work
can counter popular notions of Somali chaos, anarchy, and 'tribalism' and
provide some understanding of what it is like for the majority to live in a
stateless economy, then it will have achieved an important objective. If it
can actually contribute in a small way to a more compassionate and realistic acknowledgement of Somalis and their struggles as a foundation for
a peaceful re-entry into the international community, then the exercise of
the past six years will have been well worth it.

1
Introduction ▎ to a Stateless Economy

The efforts of the United Nations to end the human suffering in Somalia, foster reconciliation among the warring factions and promote national reconstruction led to one of the most challenging, arduous undertakings in the Organization's 50-year history (Boutros-Ghali 1996: 3).

The merely incredible gives way daily – in the flow of world events – to the astonishing and the unbelievable (Crawford Young, cited in Villalon 1998: 3).

This book is about the persistence of a society and economy that has endured instabilities along all fronts – political, social, and environmental. What is happening today in Somalia, a stateless part of the world that was of marginal international concern until the recent events of September 11,[1] holds relevance to other volatile parts of Africa and the globe. Its story sharply challenges conventional ideas about economy, politics, and social order and confronts the very premises under which Western diplomacy and development agencies operate. These include assumptions about the role of states in maintaining order and services, as well as ideas about official trade and economic planning. These phenomena need to be carefully scrutinized in large parts of Africa and especially in Somalia, a nation that has been without a central government since 1991. In the words of one writer, 'becoming another Somalia' is the fate to be avoided by every African state (Luling 1997: 287).

An assessment of Somalia in the twenty-first century requires an understanding of the different influences that global forces and institutions have played. The Somali community increasingly is 'globalized', perhaps as much today as any African society, and depends heavily on a wide-ranging

[1] The 'events of September 11', of course, refer to the devastating terrorist attacks in the US on that day in 2001. As will be discussed later in the book, the aftermath of these tragic incidents has had important impacts on Somalia and its people.

diaspora and laissez-faire, trade-based economy. Yet, the policies and actions of the United Nations (UN) and other global actors have played their part in Somalia during the past decade, with particularly ironic and occasionally tragic twists. For example, international bodies, such as the UN and World Bank, need governments to operate, accept their loans and aid, and impose their policies in the same way that colonialism often required 'traditional' authorities and bounded polities to operate. In the colonial period if there were no chiefs, they invented them (see Hobsbawm and Ranger 1983); in the absence of a government in Somalia during the 1990s, the UN and the US tried unsuccessfully to create one in a situation where, as Menkhaus (1998b) points out, all politics are local. Indeed, the failure of US policy in Somalia, so evident in the Mogadishu tragedy of October 1993 that killed hundreds of Somalis and left 18 young American soldiers dead on the city's streets,[2] had far-reaching implications for American foreign policy throughout Africa and the world. Recall the 'wait and see' stance of the US toward the horrific Rwandan genocide about one year later, a direct result of the lingering nightmare of Mogadishu. President Clinton's aides recently referred to the Somali quagmire as one of the low points of his administration (Perlez 2000).

Thus, the Somalia dilemma is two-dimensional: (1) the problem of the West's (especially the US's) inability to comprehend the Somali situation, and (2) the internal conflicts in Somalia itself, which traverse common language, religion, and social structures. The ultimate paradox, it will be shown in this book, is that some sectors of Somali economy and society are doing quite fine – as well, if not better than during the pre-war (pre-1991) years.

Beyond the images of chaos and warfare that still shape outside perceptions of Somalia, hundreds of thousands of herders and traders effectively produce and trade Somalia's most valuable commodity, livestock. The Somalia based on arms and urban warlords is markedly different than the Somalia based on livestock and skilled herders and traders. The gap could hardly be wider. As an activity, livestock-based commerce is at the heart of Somali livelihoods and social relationships. It has the potential to unite as well as divide, and provides a convenient lens into the causes of conflict and the ways that the majority of the population has survived since 1991. The current Somalia situation is rooted in deep-seated struggles over material resources, and most scholars have focused on contestations over land and foreign aid as causes of the initial conflict (de Waal 1997;

---

[2] This unfortunate episode refers to the US's unsuccessful attempt to capture key 'lieutenants' of the Mogadishu warlord, General Mohamed Farah Aideed, at his headquarters in the former capital city (see Bowden 1999). The impact of this event on American foreign policy and the general public was chilling, as graphic videos of dead American soldiers being dragged through the streets of Mogadishu were shown on virtually all the major news networks. It represented a rather poignant contrast to the optimistic media extravaganza of December 1992 when leading American journalists Dan Rather, Tom Brokaw, and Ted Koppel were on the beaches of Mogadishu welcoming US troops and the start of the humanitarian effort called Operation Restore Hope.

Menkaus and Prendergast 1997; Besteman and Cassanelli 1996). With few exceptions (Abdi Samatar 1992, 1994), livestock trade, the most significant commercial activity in pre-1991 Somalia, and its relationship to contemporary problems have received scant attention.[3]

Like Somali society itself, the heterogeneity of trade needs to be acknowledged and blanket generalizations avoided, even within the same geographic area. This book mainly focuses on one region of the country, the Somali borderlands that are adjacent to (and include parts of) neighboring Kenya, but it offers comparisons to other parts of the country. While treatment of the so-called Somali tragedy often suffers from overgeneralization where local differences are discounted, this study largely is situated in a single geographic and ethnographic context and makes comparisons from this optic. The borderlands as defined here comprise parts of the Lower Jubba Region of southern Somalia (primary) and neighboring Garissa District, Kenya and define a vibrant trade region. As will be shown in later chapters, important generalizations from the area are applicable to other parts of Somalia and to sub-Saharan Africa generally. Why trade figures so prominently in recent events of Somalia relates to the fact that (1) its economy has always been external and market-oriented (Cassanelli 1982; Dalleo 1975), and (2) the current statelessness promotes an excessively open and unrestricted economy.[4] Since at least the sixteenth century, Somali pastoralists have traded animal products and other goods to Middle Eastern markets (Cassanelli 1982).

Two terms, resilience and border, are used throughout the book and encompass much that is both challenging and significant about the Somali case. The first concept, resilience, is fairly straightforward and implies the capacity of a society to withstand incredible hardships and challenges without collapse. Flexibility and persistence are also words that embody similar attributes and capture what has happened in Somali and other communities of rural Africa that have survived daunting challenges during the 1990s. Wars, famines, collapsed governments, and epidemics are among the catastrophes that Africans have confronted in the past decade. Their struggles for basic amenities and livelihoods make the problems of most other parts of the world pale in comparison.

---

[3] There is a substantial body of literature on the Horn and other regions of Africa that generally views political conflict as the result of 'competition for resources in conditions of great scarcity' (Markakis 1994: 217; also see Deng and Zartman 1991; Doornbos et al. 1992; Hjort af Ornas and Salih 1989). With few exceptions, however, this corpus of material lacks the analytical precision and local data to move the debate much beyond general assessments often conducted at the country and multi-country (regional) levels.

[4] Qat or Khat (*Catha edulis* spp.), the mildly narcotic stimulant that many Somalis consume, is also a significant trade item in the region. Unlike cattle, however, it is mainly produced in neighboring Kenya and Ethiopia and air-shipped to the largest towns in Somalia, such as Mogadishu and Kismayo. Information on this trade is extremely difficult to gather and little data on the topic were collected in my field research (for a recent account of the trade but with little actual data, see Green 1999).

'Border,' on the other hand, is used in multiple ways in the book. Primarily it describes a geographic or political feature, the territory ('borderlands') that straddles two countries – in this case Kenya and Somalia. As applied to Africa, this notion captures the porous nature of political boundaries on the continent and the informal economic opportunities they afford (see Nugent and Asiwaju 1996). However, border has other meanings. The term can signify an arbitrary edge or divide between two parts that can entail considerable ambiguity – a kind of 'between and betwixt' condition, to use the late Victor Turner's phrase (1969: 95). Where does the border between two phenomena exist? Where does one condition begin and one end?

As the term is used in the book, the borders between many social phenomena are fuzzy in the Somali case, including distinctions between formal and informal, conflict and peace, government and non-government, and so on. Blurred borders usually make standard classifications and terminology difficult to apply (see Kopytoff 1987).[5] For instance, Somalia often is coined as a war-torn area but, as Helander (1997: 1) shows, it really is in a state of 'not war—not peace' since large-scale hostilities have ceased but real peace has not ensued. This dubious condition has widespread implications for how the country is treated both regionally and globally. For instance, Somalia was defined during the 1990s as a conflict-ridden, non-state by the UN and Western countries, but neighboring states, such as Djibouti and Kenya, have foreign policy initiatives for Somalia that assumed some type of governance existed. Bi-lateral negotiations and agreements between nearby Ethiopia and the breakaway state of Somaliland have existed since the late 1990s (see Chapter 7).

In the economic arena, boundary issues are even more complicated because borders between official and unofficial economic activity have always been problematic, even prior to the government's collapse. Yet, the Somali economy is not formally acknowledged by global bodies like the World Bank and International Monetary Fund (IMF), although it 'officially' exports bananas and livestock products and had (has) foreign investment and trade with legitimate ('official') international firms, such as Dole Fruit Inc and a subsidiary of General Motors (Luling 1997; Nduru 1996; African News Service 2000). Even without a state treasury and official economy, Somalia has forged economic agreements with neighboring countries and with specific trans-national firms. Thus, the Somalia economy in some respects can be classified roughly as 'not official/not unofficial,' a reality that increasingly is found in other African countries

---

[5] Border or frontier communities themselves are fascinating subjects for anthropological and social science research generally. They often are dynamic arenas, where cultural and economic creativity proliferate, and where normal social norms are ill-defined (see Kopytoff 1987). One need only visit vibrant Africa towns like Taveta, or Namanga, which straddle the Kenya and Tanzania border, or Kassala, Sudan, to witness the kinds of innovativeness and dynamism displayed by border communities.

where the informal (shadow) or unofficial economy drives most economic activities. As the book will suggest, these ambiguous 'half-statuses' may be the best that Somalia and other parts of Africa can garner at present and may represent more than just transitory states. In essence they are what allow rural and urban populations to survive dismal formal economic and political circumstances. Both scholars and policy makers need to confront the implications of this unsettling reality and acknowledge that they are unlikely to disappear with a few policy or diplomatic tweaks.

It is important, however, not to equate the relative success of certain segments of Somali economy and society with an overly rosy picture that 'all is well in Somalia'. It simply is not the case as large segments of society continue to endure terrible deprivations; public institutions in health and education remain largely destroyed; the political situation in the south of the country is still extremely volatile; and brutal faction heads (warlords) remain with too much influence and military clout. In addition, large numbers of Somalis remain outside of their homeland, many in refugee camps in neighboring countries where conditions often are deplorable. Indeed, the large number of Somali refugees and the rapid growth in the Somali diaspora are telling indicators that all is not well at home. The Somalia paradox has had some 'winners', but it also has had many, many 'losers', including women and children and Somali minority groups. By highlighting segments of the population, traders and herders, and an activity, trans-border trade, that have attained some successes in the 1990s, the book does not propose that a government-less Somalia has been good for society as a whole or represents a basis for a political solution.

Finally, this book does not promise general policy prescriptions for Somalia, including its breakaway states in the north (Somaliland) and northeast (Puntland).[6] Indeed, it would be presumptuous of me to indicate so. Nor does this work seek to fully theorize or account for the frequent changes in social and political outcomes in southern Somalia, a place where political assessments quickly become *yesterday's news*. The renewed US and international interest in Somalia after September 11, 2001 is an informative example of this. Instead, by looking at one region's most important economic activity, cross-border livestock trade, and the social groups and actors associated with it, this work tries to capture the realities of a stateless economy. Unlike other publications focused on the collapse of the Somali state and the tough period from 1991 to 1993 (see Adam 1995; Hashim 1997; Omar 1992), this book mainly examines what happened during 1993 to 2000. Recently Somalis themselves have acted to forge their own political destinies, although mainly on a regional basis. In the northern parts of the former country an independent government, Somaliland, and a regionally autonomous state, Puntland, have operated

---

[6] In the book the use of the terms Somaliland and Puntland should not be interpreted as an endorsement of their political legitimacy.

on minimal resources for more than six years; while in the south a newly
created government based in Mogadishu (2001) holds some hope for re-
establishing a central administration there and perhaps uniting the
different regions of the country. These initiatives are not without very major
challenges and inherent fragilities, but do point to some of the valid
political efforts that are underway (see Chapter 7).

Theorizing the current situation

It is a contention of this book that comparative studies and theory are
helpful in understanding the Somalia situation, a phenomenon that in
many ways is unprecedented in contemporary history. The country may
represent an extreme case but it still has strong parallels to other parts of
the world where conventional political and economic idioms also are
vigorously challenged. This includes so-called rogue states like Sierra
Leone, Afghanistan, and the Democratic Republic of Congo (DRC)
(formerly Zaire). A comparative treatment of contemporary Somalia challenges perceptions of it as a 'peculiar society' (*The Economist* 1996: 38),
as well as essentialist ('tribalist') arguments about what is happening in
the country. Based on an anthropological perspective that emphasizes the
local and regional on the one hand, and cultural resiliency on the other, it
is possible to incorporate ideas about (1) the 'informal' economy, (2) trust
and social relations, and (3) the state and social order, in order to understand the Somali case.

A totally 'informal' economy?
There are at least two ways that the informal economy[7] can be observed in
Africa, including Somalia. The first is in terms of internal or domestic
economic practice and the other is in regard to external trade ('smuggling'). This twofold distinction is important, although most of the social
science literature focuses on the domestic rather than external side of the
unofficial economy (for important exceptions, see Ellis 1999b; Ellis and
MacGaffey 1997; MacGaffey and Bazenguissa-Ganga 2000; Humphrey
1999). It will be argued here that the later aspect, especially as reflected in
unofficial cross-border trade, assumes considerable importance for
Somalia and the Horn of Africa[8] generally. However, relevant empirical
studies to draw on are sparse, although we know from often anecdotal
data that cross-border trade is absolutely critical to the economies of
Mozambique, Sierra Leone, Djibouti, Liberia, DRC, Benin, and several
other African states (see Ellis 1999a; Nugent and Asiwaju 1996; and Reno
1995). The information gap is particularly glaring, since unofficial trade

---

[7] Various terms are used to explain this phenomenon, including black market or underground
economy, shadow or parallel economy, and second or unofficial economy.
[8] This region normally includes the countries of the Sudan, Ethiopia, Eritrea, Djibouti, Somalia
(including Somaliland and Puntland), and the northeastern part of Kenya.

also is critical to understanding many political regimes worldwide, from Saddam Hussein's Iraq to General Shwe's Myanmar (Burma), which continue to function commercially despite strong barriers from the global community. Indeed, political boundaries and informal trade are difficult to monitor as the UN has learned in the case of Iraq, and the US in the case of Mexico, and hard to study as well. With its obelisk-shaped geography accounting for one of Africa's largest coastlines and with vast international borders, Somalia poses particular problems for those who might wish to control its trade, either in livestock or contraband goods.

Even prior to its collapse, Somalia on the domestic front operated more as an unofficial or 'unconventional' economy rather than an economy of wage earners, formal institutions, and legal contracts (Jamal 1988a). At the time it was similar to Zaire (currently the DRC), Sierra Leone, and other countries where economic activity was mainly 'off the books;' and in recent years (1990s) with large parts of the former USSR and Eastern Europe (see Burawoy and Verdery 1999; Humphrey 1999). Even in the 1980s unofficial trade (including illegal exports of ivory), unrecorded pastoral production and exchange, and remittances from Somalis working abroad accounted for the bulk of domestic economic value. Remittances alone are said to have brought in annually about $200 million in imports and cash and subsidized a vast amount of local consumption and investment, especially in urban real estate (Jamal 1988a). As is currently the case, remittances entered the country at the time either as hard currency or as goods, which could be resold or given directly to family members. The difference between the official and 'street' exchange rates for the Somali shilling was as much as 275 percent during the 1980s (see Mubarak 1996; Abdurahman 1998). The economy as recorded in official government and World Bank reports probably reflected no more than 30 percent of the real economy of Somalia in the 1980s. And that is an important reason why unlike other African countries, where World Bank/IMF reform programs have been associated with horrific social costs, they were simply too inconsequential to have done much harm in Somalia.

Although there are clear continuities between the pre- and post-1991 economies, there are important differences that need to be acknowledged. The Somali state controlled the only bank in the country in the 1980s, the Somali Commercial Bank, and imposed border controls and duty agents that did restrict some unofficial imports and exports. The government created an environment where formal commercial transactions were difficult even when they were pursued. Its banking facilities were few and concentrated in a handful of large cities; port and transport infrastructure were poor; communication and postal facilities were limited and inefficient; and bureaucratic approvals for trade and currency transactions were painfully slow and concentrated in Mogadishu. Often the state was paralyzed in providing even these minimal services, which hampered both formal and informal trade. For the merchant today, there are still fees to be paid to greedy faction leaders and militia at ports and roadblocks, but levels of taxation and trade restrictions are considerably below what they were pre-1991.

If defined in relation to a state and its formal economy, then the economy of southern Somalia – both its domestic and external dimensions – is entirely unofficial. There are no government laws or regulations to determine the differences between official and unofficial, nor are there official requirements for currency transactions. Other African countries, such as Sierra Leone and Liberia, which are effectively stateless or have been for large parts of the past decade, fall into a similar category to Somalia: the official/unofficial dichotomy is increasingly meaningless. Each of these countries also engages in particular circuits of international and regional trade, in some cases involving high-value commodities, such as diamonds and iron ore, and attracts investment from legitimate transnational corporations (see Ellis 1999a; Ellis and MacGaffey 1997; Richards 1996). The effective collapse of national monetary systems and financial and regulatory institutions in other African countries like the DRC and Angola also means that most of the domestic economy is unofficial and regional, and trans-border trade is mediated through private entrepreneurs not government bodies. In strict terms this practice is considered to be smuggling, but the term is increasingly meaningless in large parts of Africa where what is officially legal and illegal are increasingly blurred (Hibou 1999). On a less spectacular scale the domestic economies of Ghana (Clark 1989; Ninsim 1991), Mozambique (Little and Lundin 1992), and Tanzania (Tripp 1997) have also witnessed partial collapses during recent periods, when their official economies captured very little of the real economy.

Even in highly legalistic, capitalist countries the lines between legal and illegal trade can be confounded. How and where a particular good is sold often assumes more importance than its origin and means of procurement, both of which may be mired in criminal activity. At the retail end the provenance of items can be easily disguised. Recent reports out of Europe shocked Western governments and consumers by revealing that a sizable percentage of diamonds sold annually at legally licensed establishments in Belgium have been smuggled out of war-torn African countries like Angola and Sierra Leone (Brackenbury 2001). These so-called 'blood gems' are extracted from conflict-ridden regions through a series of middlemen and brokers, purchased at sanctioned auctions in Europe, and then sold legitimately in some of North America's and Europe's most fashionable outlets.[9]

Even without a government, it may be more accurate to view the Somalia economy as an extreme entry along a continuum of formal-to-informal (or legal-to-illegal) commerce rather than as a distinct case. It is a

---

[9] The global uproar over this shady trade has instigated a revamping of diamond certification practices and new assurances by major mining companies and auction houses that smuggled diamonds will be kept out of legitimate markets.

question of degree not difference. For example, Somali livestock that are imported 'illegally' into Kenya but openly traded, discussed, and inscribed in daily practice assume official status in the border regions and can even appear in trade statistics. Some Kenyan officials with whom I spoke did not think cattle were contraband commodities, nor the trade illegal when in fact on paper it really is. Other smuggled imports, such as drugs or weapons, are secretively traded but treated as *more illegal* in status than animals. If discovered by Kenyan border officials, they likely will be confiscated. In the same fashion, electronic goods and clothes, some of them imported 'duty free' from Dubai through Somalia's ports and smuggled into Kenya, also are more prone than cattle to be confiscated by authorities if discovered (This assumes, of course, that the Kenyan border officials are not bribable, an increasingly dubious assumption these days.) However, when these same goods reach a licensed retail store in Nairobi and are resold, a common practice in Kenya, legal recourse usually is not taken. Parallel examples are gems sold at up-scale stores in Europe (discussed above), or pirated lobsters obtained through questionable means and marketed through franchised restaurants in the US (see Nietschmann 1997). Thus, what represents legal or illegal (official and unofficial) trade is negotiable and contingent.

What does it mean for economic agents, like traders and middlemen, to work in a context of collapsed economic and political institutions? Based on the Somalia example, the impacts are not as significant as one might envision. For the economic agent port fees to import and transport goods safely must still be paid, but instead of going to representatives of a central state the revenue is going to warlords, clan militias, or local administrations. It varies by region and town. The entrepreneur still has little access to formal financial institutions, as was the case when a government existed. However, small traders now can utilize one of the numerous informal facilities that recently have opened and, therefore, their access to banking services actually may have improved during the past decade. For example, the electronic wire transfers initiated in the mid-1990s have proven to be an efficient means of facilitating trade and moving large sums of money securely between distant locations (see Chapter 6). Moreover, the merchant is probably no less likely to see visible benefits of current fees and tax payments than in the pre-war years when most services were absent outside a few large cities (see Chapters 2 and 3). In short, from the trader and herder's perspectives, the differences between the earlier era of central government, especially after 1978,[10] and the present (2002) are not as major as popular accounts would imply. With formal economic institutions and financial systems exceeding fragile in the 1980s, their subsequent collapse in Somalia meant little for most of the population.

[10] It is clearly important to acknowledge differences between the various political regimes and eras after Somalia's independence in 1960. The 'democratic' regimes of the 1960s and the early period (1969–1978) of Siad Barre's reign delivered considerably more development services for rural populations than Barre's later years (1979–1990).

Trust in a risky environment
Whether it is state-sanctioned (legal) or not, trade requires some level of mutual trust and norms to function. To trust somebody assumes that agreed outcomes, behaviors, and prices are followed and that parties do not have to carefully monitor each other (see Gambetta 1988). Trust and fair practice especially are critical in the current Somali economy where legal enforcement is minimal, but they also are important to the functioning of Western capitalist economies. As Alan Greenspan, US Federal Reserve Chairman, remarks, 'without mutual trust and market participants abiding by a rule of law, no economy can prosper' (*Lexington Herald-Leader*, 13 September 1999, p.10). Much of what goes on in Western industrialized economies is surprisingly vulnerable to deception and unscrupulous behavior, of which only a fraction is detected. The different dealings of financial markets and the occasional sanctioning of high-profile violators, such as the Enron Corporation in the US,[11] are cases in point. Violations of trust by corporate officers, financiers, and regulators in modern capitalist economies can result in heart-wrenching human suffering on the part of the unsuspecting public, just as can happen elsewhere in the world.

In countries like the US, the kinds of deception ('untrustworthiness') and market risk described above are countered by the use of formal contracts and regulatory bodies, such as a Securities and Exchange Commission. Economic contracts usually specify the responsibilities and rights of the different parties, agreed prices and volumes, and sanctions for failure to comply. In economistic terms contracts are said to reduce risks for parties, lower transaction costs, and aid economic planning. Where contracts are used in Africa, however, most firms indicate trust and goodwill are as critical for insuring fair practice as a legal document (see Little 1994). Even when buyers and sellers have few social or moral ties to each other, non-economic (trust) factors can still play a role in contract compliance.

Market actors, both in the West and in Africa, seek to enhance trust by building on existing social relations or what political scientists and economists like to call social capital. This can include relatives, friends, and other acquaintances, as well as local organizations and associations. These types of social relations can facilitate economic transactions, as well as reduce fraud. The complex web of client-based suppliers and retailers among Japanese firms is a good example of this (Dore 1983; Landa 1994), as are friendship-based sub-contracting activities in France (Lorenz 1988). In America investments in social relations have become central elements of corporate culture as well. A trusting

---

[11] The bankruptcy of the Enron Corporation in 2002, once the eighth largest corporation in the USA, resulted in the loss of massive retirement savings for thousands of Enron employees and stock holders who *trusted* the corporation's financial reports, auditors, and managers. Right up until its collapse in January 2002 stock holders and employees were misled by accountants and unethical corporate officers who issued misleading financial reports.

business deal there often is sealed with an elegant dinner or game of golf. These practices reaffirm the reliance on the social even in highly advanced economies.

Elements of both formal (contractual) and personal relationships, therefore, are inscribed in 'modern,' as well as less developed economies. Moreover, in both settings trust relationship(s) can be better indicators of business practice than formal rules and legal stipulations, which often can be renegotiated and contested anyway (see Little 1994). This reality is an important reason why transnational agribusiness firms in Africa often sub-contract with members of the local community, who then are responsible for contracting with local farmers and traders and enforcing market rules. Unlike the outside firm, the member of the community can bring multiple relationships and social pressures to bear on the arrangement, which will enhance contract compliance. Prior to the coup some Somali enterprises pursued this strategy: (1) the state-owned Kismayo Meat Factory in southern Somalia depended on contracts with local traders for its animal supplies; and (2) livestock exporters who had large orders from Saudi Arabian importers also utilized contracts with local traders and herders. These agreements were rarely backed by tightly worded documents but, nonetheless, sanctions could be invoked to prevent deception, including the threat of permanent banishment from the trade and social rebuke from the local community.

Legal contracts in the border areas of Somalia are currently meaningless, as they are in other stateless or near-stateless regions of Africa. Instead, other means are in place to facilitate transactions, minimize risks, and enhance trust. For example, traders in the border region have always invoked social relations – especially those based on kinship and ethnicity – to gain access to markets, whether during periods of prosperity or decline. The instability of the region during the past century has shown that investing in social affairs and loyal clients is a prudent strategy (cf. Berry 1989; Clark 1988). The livestock business of the border region also has social institutions and practices to encourage fair trade in the absence of formal contracts and controls. One of these is the *dilaal*, a market agent (broker) that insures the validity of market transactions and guards against sales of stolen animals and products (see discussion in Chapter 5). It is a common institution throughout the Middle East and Islamic regions of West and East Africa (see Cohen 1969). The notion of trust is inherent to the institution of *dilaal* and relevant to understanding 'unofficial' economies like Somalia's. Trust implies a strong faith in the outcome of an agreed market arrangement between market actors, even 'with inconclusive evidence or proof' (Hart 1988: 187).

In the Somali case trust has been strongly challenged by recent acts of seemingly random violence, but it also was compromised earlier by the brutalities of the previous government and its representatives. In some cases recent events have reinforced the importance of trust within certain social groups, such as clans, while unfortunately heightening conflict and distrust between groups.[12] In the words of Anna Simmons (1998: 70): 'Now more than ever, knowing genealogy does chart who can and who cannot be trusted.' The segmentary kinship principle of political alliances and trust has always been present in Somali politics (see Chapters 3 and 6), but has assumed more significance recently as faction leaders have deliberately used clanism ('genealogy') as a political weapon and have brutally insured that other forms of identity do not occupy political space. Clans and their territories, in turn, have become forcibly isolated from each other and interactions restricted by armed factions. This forced isolationism accelerates hostilities and mistrust between groups, since social interaction and communication are important for facilitating trust-based relationships (see Giddens 1990).

In southern Somalia horrible atrocities, such as rape and the killing of women and children, which have been committed since 1991 have also intensified distrust between social groups. A horrendous occurrence was the purposeful butchering of nine elders, traders, and an 11-year-old child in Gobwein, a village located about 12 km north of Kismayo, by a militia of a prominent warlord in the area (All Africa News Agency, 22 February 1999). This tragedy took place in 1999 and was meant as a warning to surrounding villages that loyalty to General Morgan, the warlord who controlled Kismayo until 1999, would not be tolerated. Clanism, a topic that has engaged considerable scholarly debate (Lewis 1994, 1998; Abdi Samatar 1992; Besteman 1996), is an unfortunate reality in Somalia today where it is strongly shaped by the viscous politics of misguided opportunists.

For trading practices, trust within clans and lineages has become more prominent under these conditions and seemingly has reduced risks and transaction costs between economic agents. It has facilitated unofficial trade between southern Somalia and northeastern Kenya, since both sides are dominated by the same clan (Ogadeen) (see Chapter 5). The costs of enforcement and market information are minimized in this case, as is the risk of default by related persons. What has happened, however, is that trust between members of different clans and sub-clans has deteriorated to the point that there is almost no trading links between certain parts of Somalia.

In these volatile, risky environments, Somali traders rely on their extensive kinship ties and on members of their own groups. These social strategies are very common in contemporary Somalia, but also increasingly

---

[12] Oxymoronic as this may sound, there is some support for the position that 'statelessness' actually enhances trust-based relations between social groups. Drawing on his experiences with nomadic groups in northern Africa, the late Ernest Gellner suggests that 'anarchy engenders trust and government destroys it; or, put in a more conventional way, that anarchy engenders cohesion' (1988: 143). For him, the absence of a central government may create greater social cohesion and trust among herders because they are compelled to rely on traditional alliances based on trust, rather than on outside mediation.

characterize informal trade elsewhere in Africa and between the continent and other parts of the world. For example, Bayart (1999: 39) shows how patrilineal-based networks of buyers and transporters among the Ibo of Nigeria facilitate the growth of global trade in a range of commodities, including illicit drugs. MacGaffey and Bazenguissa-Ganga (2000), in turn, show how kinship (and religious) relations are important to a specific recent trade circuit, the Congo-to-Paris, France market, that is important for the DRC. Earlier ethnographic studies of trade in Africa also highlight the critical role of kinship and social relations generally in rural markets and trade networks (Bohannan and Dalton 1962).

As might be expected, regional commerce in Somalia reflects politics and clan divisions that can disrupt trade between rural areas and towns, as well as shift the activity toward markets in Kenya. These kinds of divisions were present during the pre-stateless period (pre-1991), but not to the extent that they are currently found. The sporadic checkpoints and prohibitions that militia leaders have placed on movements have only heightened the distrust between clans and broken down important inter-clan trading relations, especially in the livestock business. In the past the interaction of different clan members in daily business practice helped to increase familiarity, reduce suspicion, and to establish trust. As will be discussed later in the book (Chapter 5), the 'booming' trade-based economy of southern Somalia has been shaped by these relationships, which have isolated certain groups but enriched others.

The ultimate test of public trust in southern Somalia may be the continued faith that traders and consumers have displayed in the Somali shilling (SoSh). There is sufficient confidence that the currency remains the standard medium of exchange even in the absence of a central treasury or bank to guarantee its value (see Chapter 6). Considerable debate in economics and, to a lesser extent, economic anthropology centers on whether the state's role in monetary systems is critical (Crump 1981; Simmel 1978), and stateless Somalia represents a wonderful test case (see Chapter 6). For Frankel, an economist, the emergence of money as a medium of exchange depends more on trust and morality than on the dictates of government: 'without trust the monetary system would break down' (1977: 38). Hart, an economic anthropologist, takes this argument in a slightly different direction by showing how the state and civil society often both are symbolically represented on a coin or currency note, but it is the civil dimension – rather than government – that determines a currency's sustainability (1986: 638–9). In Somalia there is sufficient public demand and trust that the SoSh remains redeemable in the country.

Stateless order

If a state were a required component, then the Somali economy could not exist, and nor could those of several other African countries, where the formal government has virtually collapsed (see Villalon and Huxtable 1998; Zartman 1995; Chabal and Daloz 1999). The Somali example raises some particularly interesting theoretical questions about (1) whether the Somali state ever 'captured' its rural pastoral inhabitants, either politically or economically, and (2) how much of what we are observing today in Somalia is a renaissance of the indigenous political system (see Brons 2001). Regarding the latter, the pre-colonial political system was a classic stateless system where a segmentary kinship system traced to a founding ancestor (real or fictive) through males (patrilineality) defined political alliances and opponents. Political and social order were maintained through different aggregations of clans, sub-clans, and lineages in the absence of the types of institutionalized leadership and political hierarchy that were found in other regions of Africa (see Chapter 3). Indeed, early anthropological studies of stateless societies often were based on pastoral societies like Somali, where political hierarchy was minimal, at least among males (Lewis 1961; also see Fortes and Evans-Pritchard 1940; Spencer 1965; Schneider 1979). Among pastoral Somali it was noted that every man was a potential power broker, a true individualist: 'men are divided amongst political units without any administrative hierarchy of officials and with no instituted positions of leadership to direct their affairs' (Lewis 1961: 1). A centralized state, both colonial and post-colonial, obviously was incompatible with this level of decentralization and essentially was 'suspended above a society which would never have produced and did not demand it' (Luling 1997: 289). Thus, the current radical political decentralization and statelessness in Somalia has at least some foundation in earlier principles of the segmentary lineage system.

To assess relations between the former state and its rural populations – especially the pastoralists – it is necessary to discuss what the state in post-colonial Somalia really was. While it is common today to hear of the collapsed African state, invoking images of political girders and structures falling into an abyss, the applicability of the phrase to Somalia since at least 1979 can be questioned. This is even more so in the context of the country's borderlands where official controls always have been weak. For instance, can we really speak of a failed state, if it is questionable whether a meaningful state ever existed? Let's take the perspective of rural inhabitants, which still comprise the overwhelming bulk of Africa's population. For most Somali herders and farmers, services and infrastructure were minimal, reliance on judicial means of dispute settlement was nominal, and support for the established leadership was almost non-existent. In critically addressing these issues in the context of Mobuto's Zairian (DRC) 'state', Ellis captures some of the essence of political life that has relevance to pre-1991 Somalia:

> It is a pyramid, in which power and prestige flow from the top downwards, while wealth is simultaneously sucked from the bottom upwards; wealth or opportunities for advancement are redistributed within clientelist systems by the provision of gifts, commercial opportunities, and so on, to the supporters of political

patrons. The donor community refers to such systems as a government or a state, and the head of the network is called a President... . Why should we call a certain large building in Kinshasa the Central Bank of Zaire when it has no money and fulfills none of the functions of a central bank? ... Why, for that matter, should we refer to a self-serving clique which survives by racketeering and manipulation, as a government? (1996: 9)

While Somalia's corruption and abuses under Siad Barre never reached Zaire's levels, Ellis's quote does challenge the use of terms like state to describe such political systems, including pre-1991 Somalia. As Ellis points out, 'diplomatic convention and international law require us to use the vocabulary of statehood in regard to every member-state of the United Nations' (ibid: 9). It does not mean, however, that we have to assume these states have the capacity or will to govern, nor the support of more than a small political clique that feeds regularly on political patronage. In southern Somalia, such resources never reached the rural areas (see Chapter 2), nor did herders ever assume the state was a reliable partner for mediating conflicts or administering justice.

The Somali regime of Siad Barre was decidedly exploitive and, in some cases, brutally forceful like other authoritarian regimes in Africa. But outside of Kismayo and other key towns its presence in the border zone was minimal until the late 1970s when it began to take notice of the region's resources. At that time the state indirectly intervened in the area's pastoral sector by encouraging exports and constructing export routes, water points, and quarantine grounds for overseas livestock trade (see Chapter 2). However, even in these areas its interventions were inconsistent and the government never returned a fraction of earned revenues to the region. Roads were never constructed, health clinics never built, and schools never established in the pastoral areas. Instead, they were concentrated in the urban areas and in a few of the agricultural areas near Mogadishu.

Thus, as indicated earlier indigenous Somali society and polity is a particularly poor match for the hierarchy of a modern state. This awkward fit was especially true during the colonial period in Italian-ruled southern Somalia. Here pastoral resistance was strong and the colonial state's presence haphazard, especially after Italy's defeat in World War II when Britain took over the territory under a UN trusteeship. Additionally, the fact that most of the population was nomadic for parts of the year made effective administration difficult, even impossible at times. Administrative experiences in north Africa, central Asia (including Afghanistan), and the Middle East further validate the difficulties and strong resistance that mobile herding populations can have to externally imposed political structures, either colonial-based or other (Barfield 1993; Gellner 1988). In the past 20 years alone numerous political resistance movements in Africa (e.g. Algeria, Ethiopia, Kenya,

Mali, Somalia, Sudan, and Uganda) and elsewhere (e.g. Afghanistan, China, Iraq, Israel, Pakistan, Turkey, and Yemen) have emerged in pastoral areas that have been economically and politically discriminated against, as well as forcefully subjugated to foreign political structures and at times compulsory settlement.

In the Somali borderlands administrators were concentrated in a few large towns like Kismayo, and what limited Italian settlement took place was restricted to the Jubba Valley. Not surprisingly, local systems of governance took precedence over arbitrary and incomplete foreign rule. When political independence was achieved in 1961, there was a slight increase in administrative presence in the rural areas, but large parts of the border region remained with few government administrators, and communities continued to rely on themselves. The state was an entity that extracted some local resources and was punitive at times, but could not be counted on to govern daily affairs.

As Lewis (1961) and Ahmed Samatar (1994a) have noted, local institutions flourished in the absence of a strong administrative presence. These included the so-called *diya* system, a lineage-based 'blood payment' group of up to several hundred families and an individual's immediate recourse during conflicts and times of need. *Diya* payments served as an important sanction against conflict and violence, since up to 100 camel had to be paid between *diya* groups if one killed a member of the other (Marchal 1998). Other customary institutions included the *xeer*, a type of social contract that binds members of a *diya* unit and 'delineated directives that guided conduct in intra- and inter-kin relations' (Ahmed Samatar 1994a: 109); and the *nabadoon,* a local political position that helps to mediate conflicts and works with clan elders to resolve and avoid conflicts. The latter position was reinforced by the Barre administration to serve to represent the state and to help resolve local disputes (Lewis 1993: 49). At times these institutions, particularly the *diya*, conflicted with formal administrative positions and on some occasions were forcefully suppressed by the state. However, they remained important in the daily affairs of local social and political life and assumed more importance in rural areas once the administration began to unravel in the late 1980s. In the border region when the state actively engaged residents, either with force or ill-conceived development projects (see Chapter 2), herders had little more than contempt for it and its representatives. The government was perceived as little more than a personal patronage machine that benefited certain clans and urban centers, while distributing few resources to the local population.[13] As will be shown in subsequent chapters, efforts to rebuild a state in Somalia are marred by brutal opportunists and memories of a government that had little relevance and few benefits for most residents.

[13] The chilling prospect for international organizations like the United Nations is the potential for 'other Somalias' across the continent, where impoverished, alienated populations have little confidence in their own governments and receive few benefits (see Chapter 7).

A note on data and methods

The materials presented in this book derive from several different sources and stints of field research dating back to 1987. Most information was collected over a 15-month period during 1987 and 1988, and during the summers of 1996, 1998, and 2001. In 1987–8 data on marketing were gathered from seasonal surveys of herder households in Afmadow and Kismayo Districts, Lower Jubba Region; structured and unstructured interviews with a sample of livestock traders in the region; weekly monitoring of livestock sales in four market centers; and collection of secondary data, including government statistics, reports, and archival materials. During 1996 to 2001 information also was collected from traders, butchers, and secondary sources at the three key Kenyan markets for Somali cattle, Garissa, Mombasa, and Nairobi. The sample of traders in the recent work was biased to cover merchants who worked the transborder commerce between Somalia and Kenya. Where possible, the subsequent chapters highlight those changes that have occurred since the earlier period of research.

The trader samples in both stints of fieldwork, 1987–8 and 1996–8, were remarkably similar with respect to one variable: the type of animals sold. In both cases the samples emphasized cattle trade, which as noted earlier is the main focus of the cross-border trade, and they captured a range of different types and scale of cattle merchants. In addition to trader interviews, discussions were held with key development and non-governmental (NGO) personnel who are involved with relief and development work in the border region. Information was gathered on food aid deliveries, perceptions of risks and changes during the 1990s, and observations on social, political, and economic conditions in the border region.

Archival and secondary sources were also heavily utilized, especially during 1998 and 2000–1. In particular the project had good access to weekly market data collected during 1995 to 2000 by a network of NGOs working in southern Somalia. This database was computerized and managed by the Famine Early Warning Systems (FEWS) (now called FEWS-Net) project of the United States Agency for International Development (USAID)/Somalia Office, on behalf of a multi-agency unit called the Food Security Assessment Unit (FSAU) for Somalia. The Food and Agriculture Organization (FAO) of the UN coordinates the work of FSAU and publishes monthly bulletins that summarize price information and market trends.

The United Nations Development Office for Somalia (UNDOS) also maintains a valuable documentation center and library at its headquarters in Nairobi, and their sources were particularly helpful to understanding political events and the period of UN occupation in the 1990s. Another archival source of considerable value was the Somali collections at the Rhodes House Library, Oxford University and at the Public Records Office, London, England. These historical materials contained detailed accounts by colonial officers posted in Jubaland, southern Somalia during the period of British occupation and provide good evidence of early trade patterns and conflicts. Finally, Kenyan government reports and statistics, both in Garissa and Nairobi, were also used and of considerable value to the study.

About the book

This chapter has presented the Somalia case in the context of wider debates about statelessness and informal economies. In subsequent chapters the book will return to many of these themes, particularly as they relate to other African cases. In the next chapter (2), the topics of ecology and economy are explored as necessary backdrops to later discussions about trader and herder livelihood strategies and stateless economies generally. With abundant livestock and relatively easy access to international markets, it will be argued that southern Somalia has a special comparative advantage in commerce.

Chapter 3 complements the ecological and economic discussions by providing a regional overview of history and social structure, and by examining the key role of rural–urban dynamics in the pre-1991 period. The themes of urbanism and clanism are treated in the context of a vibrant livestock trade, an activity that later contributed to explosive strains between town and country and between different clans.

Chapter 4 shifts the discussion to how Somali herders make decisions under widespread economic, political, and environmental risks. What has allowed herders to weather this increasingly volatile situation? The chapter suggests that the answer lies in their capacity to maintain mobility, so that seasonal patterns of population and animal movements have changed little with the collapse of the government. The persistence of pastoral mobility strategies, as well as herders' continued access to rich pastures largely explain why pastoralism remains a viable enterprise in the region. It will be shown that these special characteristics also inform why Somali herders have been spared some of the hardship that farmers in Somalia and other volatile countries, such as Liberia and Sierra Leone, have endured.

In Chapter 5 key livestock markets and the traders and brokers that operate them are examined. By addressing these processes, the chapter points to the ways that a booming unofficial export trade to Kenya has partially compensated for the loss of overseas markets in the 1990s. In fact cattle exports to Kenya more than doubled after the state's demise. Chapter 5 also documents how critical political alliances and factions in the southern Somali borderlands draw support from the same clans that dominate business in the region.

Chapter 6, in turn, treats the theme of 'life goes on', both from the perspective of Somali merchants and herders. It demonstrates how some degree of stability returned to the area during 1993 to 1999, especially among the region's herders.

In the concluding chapter (7), the book returns to some of the theoretical and development issues raised in earlier chapters. What does the persistence of a non-state society in Somalia tell us about political order and economy in Africa? Will the Somali economy eventually wither without a state and a peaceful re-entry into the international community?

2
A Land of Livestock

Many of Somalia's productive sectors, already weak before the civil war, have been damaged in the course of the country's ten years of armed conflict and state collapse.... . Factories that sustained a fledgling industrial base have been dismantled and sold for scrap metal.... . Agricultural yields have declined sharply from pre-war levels, due to deteriorating canal and flood control systems, lack of agricultural inputs, and poor security. The livestock sector, historically the most productive part of the Somali economy, has survived reasonably well, due in part to its relative autonomy from government services (United Nations Development Programme [UNDP] 1998: 3).[1]

A young Somali herder holds up the framed skin of a calf that has recently died. He is brushing it alongside of a cow, the mother of the dead animal. While staying behind the extended calfskin and making gentle, click-like sounds, the young pastoralist hopes the diversion will encourage the cow to produce milk. An elderly woman holds a wooden container below the cow waiting to milk the animal. In another nearby scenario three local herders line up a herd of more than 100 thirsty cattle at a water point. In the midst of the dry season the anxious animals have not been watered for almost two days, but the herders amazingly keep them in an orderly line, three-by-three, while they wait their turn to drink. Such examples of skilled husbandry witnessed by the author have allowed large segments of rural Somalia to survive the past decade without a government and with little international assistance. Somali pastoralists of the borderlands know their livestock and possess a complex knowledge system to manage and care for their herds.

---

[1] Although this report is under a general United Nations Development Programme (UNDP) authorship, there is little doubt that Somalia experts Ken Menkhaus and Roland Marchal played key roles in its drafting. The preface to the report states that Michael Hopkins and Jawahir Yusuf Adam helped with the report, but 'that Ken Menkhaus and Roland Marchal served as joint leaders of the final draft' (UNDP 1998: 1).

Local herders and their animals thrive in a well-endowed but uneven environment. Some of the zones in southern Somalia include only arid and unproductive shrublands, while others support lush perennial grasslands. The best pastures of the area are replenished annually by the flooding of the Jubba River and seasonal streams and define some of the finest livestock-producing areas in the entire Horn of Africa. These blessed locations are home to literally hundreds of thousands of cattle and boast some of the wealthiest livestock owners on the continent (Hendy 1985; Little 1996). The so-called heart of this 'land of livestock' is Afmadow, a pastoral bonanza of ancient water wells and perennial grasses that is located about 70 km west of the Jubba River and 130 km east of the Kenya border. The name itself, *afmadow*, signifies an area of black soils and good pastures that for any herder traveling across the barren lands to its west must have seemed like 'the promised land' (see Schlee 1989; Chevenix-Trench 1907).[2] It is little wonder, therefore, that recent conflicts in the region stem in part from struggles over these lands and over the valuable commodities they produce.

This chapter highlights the critical ecological, geographic, and historical features of the southern Somali borderlands, a necessary start for understanding the area's social and political dynamics. It lays the basis for understanding how local communities coped and even prospered in a stateless environment. In this story livestock are the basis of the economy, the source of cohesion as well as conflict, and the commodity group that underlies social and political relations. They dictate a simple fact of daily life: livestock require pastures and water to be sustained. This basic ecological mandate means that herds must be moved to areas where fodder and water are available. Like other semi-arid rangelands of Africa, however, the availability of these resources varies spatially and seasonally, which poses a serious constraint to production and trade during dry seasons. The ongoing conflict in southern Somalia has affected the pastoral areas, but not to the extent that they have devastated the region's sedentary agricultural and urban settlements. What follows in this chapter is a regional overview of the border area and the resources that make this region and Somalia itself a land both of livestock and contestation.

The region

An international boundary – the border between Kenya and what once was the Democratic Republic of Somalia – traverses the region of study. While it has never really constrained population movements, the border

---

[2] In discussing the oral histories of Cushitic-speaking groups (including Somali and proto-Somali clans) of the area, Schlee points to the ecological richness and mystical qualities accorded the Afmadow area: 'Af Madou [Black Mouth] was a virgin, a beautiful girl, she had never been married, a girl with a black mouth, like soot [or charcoal]. A girl beautiful like this had never been heard of. Whenever one got near her it was [like] daybreak' (a Sakuye tale recorded in Schlee 1989: 108). In 1891 it was estimated that the Afmadow settlement alone had more than 110 wells (Chevenix-Trench 1907).

has been problematic since early in the colonial period and, most dramatically, after Kenya's independence in 1963.[3] With the collapse of the Somali state in January 1991, the boundaries between the two countries and between different administrative units on the Somalia side became even more ambiguous than before. Herders and traders still talk about this or that 'district' of Somalia as if they are government units, and, surprisingly, some degree of local civil administration exists in the absence of a formal government. However, in 2001 administrative and even international boundaries assume secondary roles to the 'real' demarcations enforced by different militia and clan-based factions. These divisions curtail population movements between different militia-controlled areas, generate transit taxes from merchants and others, and in the case of the area's largest city – Kismayo – cut it off from the rest of the region.[4]

As noted in the previous chapter, the main study region for this book includes primarily the Lower Jubba Region, Somalia, and secondarily the border district of Garissa, Kenya. The Kenyan side mainly assumes significance for trade and serves as the main market outlet, while the Somali part is important both for livestock production and marketing. As a unit, the border area shares common social, ecological, economic, and historical features, and forms an important marketing unit for the growing trans-border trade. It will be shown later that it has strong similarities to other trans-border trade zones, such as the one to the north circumscribed by the Somaliland, eastern Ethiopia, and southern Djibouti frontiers. The core of the southern Somali borderlands is the Lower Jubba Region, a former administrative unit that straddles the Kenya border and is bounded on the east by the Jubba River and on the south by the Indian Ocean (Fig. 2.1). The Lower Jubba comprises 35,114 square km of remarkably flat land, more than 90 percent of it classified as rangeland (Resource Management and Research 1984: 40), and it encompasses five administrative districts.

Garissa District, Kenya, in turn, lies adjacent to the Lower Jubba Region and covers 43,931 square km of similar terrain, with the Tana River forming its western border. The two rivers, the Jubba and the Tana, flow parallel to each other in a southerly direction and roughly shape the external limits of this region. The distance from east to west between the two waterways is an estimated 360 km. Prior to the government's collapse the Lower Jubba was headed by a regional governor based in Kismayo town and comprised four districts – Afmadow, Badhaade, Jamaame, and Kismayo – each headed by a District Commissioner. Since the collapse of a central state, a fifth district (Hagar) was established in 1994 from the northern half of Afmadow District, bringing the total to five. The addition of a new district, a joint effort of local clan elders and the occupying UN force at the time, illustrates

---

[3] The so-called *shifta* wars of the 1960s represented an attempt by the Somali state to annex that part of northeastern Kenya mainly inhabited by Somali.

[4] To simplify discussion and the use of maps, I generally employ the administrative units that existed prior to the collapse of a central government in 1991.

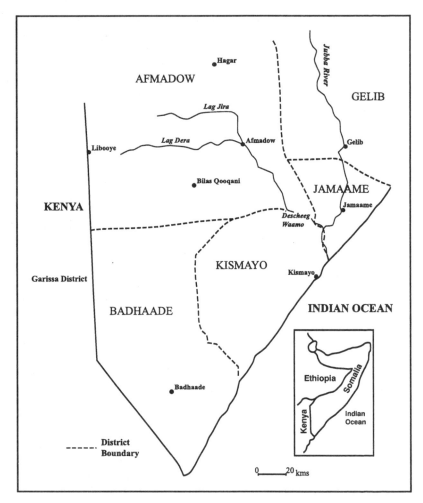

Fig 2.1 Lower Jubba Region: southern Somali borderlands

just how much local politics are alive and well in southern Somalia even in the absence of a state.

Most cultivation in the region is carried out in Jamaame and Kismayo Districts on the Somalia side and along the western portion of Garissa District, Kenya. It is concentrated in the alluvial areas near the Jubba and Tana rivers, relatively lush zones amid semi-arid plains, and along the coastal plain to the south of Kismayo town. While cultivation takes place in other, more pastoral areas, it is usually a 'hit or miss' activity that results in low or no yields in at least two out of five years. The large-scale irrigation schemes, managed by government, no longer exist in most of the Jubba Valley (discussed later in the chapter). The majority were pillaged shortly after the government's collapse or, in a few cases, have been taken over by militia heads and their followers (see Menkhaus 1991; FAO 1994; and Menkhaus and Craven 1996).

History

Originally the Lower Jubba Region was a part of the British Empire and administered as a separate province, Jubaland, of the Colony and Protectorate of Kenya. British control over most of the region, however, was minimal and on more than one occasion local herders violently resisted their presence. Prior to colonialism the coastal zone – especially the towns of Jumbo, Gobweiyn, and Kismayo – were under the general control of the Sultan of Zanzibar. In the 1880s a Zanzabari garrison was located at Gobweiyn near the mouth of the Jubba River and about 20 km from Kismayo town (Menkhaus 1989: 91). In 1895 the British formally took control of Jubaland, which roughly included what is today the Lower and Middle Jubba Regions and the Gedo Region, and administered the area until the 1920s. Jubaland was transferred to the Italian colony of Somalia in 1924 'at a solemn ceremony at Kismayu', in exchange for Italian assistance in World War I and for agreeing to withdraw further claims to territories in northern Somalia (Hess 1966: 158). Although the Sultan of Zanzibar laid claim to large parts of Jubaland at the time, he was never consulted during these negotiations, a strong indication of his political decline in the region (ibid: 159).

During its occupation the British presence was relatively weak and, as indicated above, they encountered strong opposition by herders in the area. On different occasions British officials were engaged in skirmishes with Ogadeen (primarily) and Marehan Somalis (secondarily), both groups that also were to create havoc for the UN and other agencies in the 1990s. According to Turton, the early phase of resistance to colonial rule 'was characterized by the armed resistance of Somali pastoralists, and also by their migration away from areas under firm government control, by non-compliance with government orders and by a generally negative attitude towards the expanding administration' (1972: 120). One of the most note-worthy incidents of opposition was the slaying in 1900 of Arthur Jenner, the British Sub-Commissioner of Jubaland. The event involved Jenner and about 31 police escorts of the Harti clan. They were ambushed at the Kenya/Somalia border town of Libooye by a contingent of 300 Ogadeen from the Mohamed Zubeyr sub-clan. After the skirmish the British retaliated with vengeful force and effectively pacified the area until 1916, when another pastoral Somali uprising resulted in the killing of a second colonial officer, F. Elliot (Menkhaus 1989: 199; also see Besteman 1991). In this case the resistance came from another sub-clan of the Ogadeen, the Aulihan, and once again the British responded with imperial vigor. Losses of Somali lives were in the hundreds and literally thousands of livestock were either confiscated or destroyed. Notwithstanding their superior military prowess,

British administration in the area, even in Kismayo town where its presence was relatively strong, was generally ineffective: 'British police patrols could not enter the native quarter of Kismayu, not even to intervene in case of murder' (Hess 1966: 159). As Menkhaus points out, 'Even during the height of the "pacification campaigns", there were only seventeen British citizens in the region' (1989: 203).

Although relatively weak by any measure, both the British and Italian colonial experiences in the region sharpened existing ethnic and clan tensions that remain today. They capitalized on and exaggerated clan rivalries by paying off certain clans to insure safe passage of trade goods and merchants, while purposely provoking others. Colonial administrators usually sought alliances with clan groups that could help to control the feared Ogadeen, who had the power to disrupt caravan commerce in the area and make life generally difficult for the British. As Dalleo (1975: 82–3) points out, Ogadeen sub-clans were mainly focused on production rather than commerce, but they exerted an early influence on regional trade patterns by controlling caravan movements in and out of Kismayo town. They could harass merchants who attempted to traverse their territory en route to important markets of the upper Jubba River Valley in what is today the Gedo Region. Livestock and livestock products assumed some significance in the caravan commerce, but the most important commodity was ivory.

If anything, the British favored the Harti clan group, who had migrated to the Kismayo area from the north during the nineteenth century. They were known to the British in the north because of their extensive trade relations with Arabia, Yemen, and other areas of strategic interest. The Harti, in turn, were looking for an ally in the area to counter the dominance of the larger, militarily superior Ogadeen. The British rewarded the Harti with employment and paid off their leaders with stipends, while at the same time they recruited them for armed campaigns against the Ogadeen. Because of the difficulties with the Ogadeen, the Harti gained 'a virtual monopoly of government jobs... They were trained as askaris [policemen] and, for a time, they monopolized the Kismayu police force' (Turton 1972: 122). As noted, they even were recruited as soldiers in campaigns against other Somali groups in the region. This favoritism on the part of the British strained existing clan relations between the Harti and the nearby Ogadeen, who were frequently in conflict over the caravan trade and grazing resources. While the Harti were concerned about their status when the Italians took over the province in 1924, their fears were unwarranted as the Italians also strongly supported them (Hess 1966).

In assessing the region's turbulent history, one is struck by the parallels between the contemporary era and the situation during the colonial period. For instance, while the US- and UN-led interventions of the 1990s were instigated under humanitarian auspices after reports of thousands of famine-related deaths (Hirsch and Oakley 1995; Clarke and Herbst 1997), they had striking similarities to earlier European occupations. The US-led

'Operation Restore Hope' campaign and the multi-nation UN Operation in Somalia (UNOSOM) started out mainly to deliver food and secure distribution channels, but soon realized that political and military actions were necessary to accomplish these objectives. In attempting to resolve political conflicts between the Harti and the Ogadeen in 1993–4, the UN seemed to mimic earlier Italian-brokered peace settlements of the 1920s that tried the same tactic of playing one clan off against the other, and with equally disastrous results, even when it was unintentional (see Hess 1966: 159). Moreover, earlier Ogadeen concerns about Harti favoritism and their role in regional commerce in the early 1900s echo similar complaints against recent humanitarian efforts, including UNOSOM.[5] In each instance, Ogadeen (Mohamed Zubeyr) reaction was the same: to forcefully restrict Harti trade activities and settlements in the region and to isolate Harti-controlled Kismayo town from lucrative interior markets (see Chapter 3). Is history repeating itself but under different global conditions and actors? As these examples reveal, there is little doubt of the historical depth to current clan conflicts in the area and outside efforts to resolve them (see Fig. 2.2).

The histories of other non-Somali groups often are overshadowed by discussions of the region's dominant clans (see Besteman 1999a; Menkhaus 1989). What needs to be remembered is that neither the Ogadeen nor Harti resided permanently in the region until the nineteenth century, although the Ogadeen had been there centuries earlier and then migrated north (Turton 1975). In fact it is argued that the Ogadeen's migration across the Jubba region in the 1800s 'represented a reconquering of territory that had been lost to the Oromo pastoralists centuries before' (Menkhaus 1989: 80). While the Mohamed Zubeyr moved into the region for a second time in the late 1840s, large numbers did not arrive until the 1870s and 1880s when they were forcefully expelled from what is today western Ethiopia (Dalleo 1975: 37). They moved out in response to the expanding Ethiopian empire and to a series of inter-clan conflicts among the Somali themselves. The Mohamed Zubeyr were only one of several Ogadeen sub-clans that migrated out of the Ogadeen region of western Ethiopia; other Ogadeen groups that moved during this period are the Aulihan and the Abdwak (see Turton 1975). By the 1870s the Ogadeen had taken control of the lower Jubba hinterland, forcing Oromo herders, small groups of hunter/gatherers, and Bantu ex-slave farmers to abandon the area or to be absorbed as clients.[6] Besteman's (1991; 1999a) recent work among settled farmers in the Jubba River valley documents the important Oromo and Bantu elements that characterized the area in the latter half of the nineteenth century.

---

[5] For instance, some Ogadeen-based groups in the Lower Jubba felt that the UN initially favored General Morgan and his Harti-based faction, which allowed them to obtain a foothold in Kismayo and maintain it during much of the 1990s (author's field notes).

[6] For purposes of brevity, this is a gross oversimplification of population movements in the region. For more detail on the history of different groups in the Jubba area, see Dalleo (1975), Menkhaus (1989), and Turton (1972, 1975).

Fig 2.2 Editorial cartoon by Joel Pett (Lexington Herald-Leader) 5 March 1995
(© Joel Pett)

As noted earlier, the Harti moved to the area from their northern home-lands in the nineteenth century, in order to take advantage of expanding commercial activities around Kismayo. The Harti were experienced traders who had been involved for several centuries with northern Somalia's trade with the Arabian peninsula. In the Kismayo/Jubba area they recognized early on that they would be in competition over resources and markets with other groups and, thus, required additional support. Menkhaus shows how the Harti traders 'were accompanied by clansmen who relocated in the region with their herds, in part to offset competition for control of local land and trade from the Maxamed Zubeyr sub-clan of the Ogadeen clan' (1989: 81). Their immigration to the area also was encouraged by British colonialism, which already employed Harti in their Somaliland colony in the north. The Harti adapted well to a settled lifestyle, and by the latter part of the nineteenth century they had become 'the dominant group of petty traders along the coast between the Jubba and Tana Rivers' (Cassanelli 1982: 181).

The Oromo, in turn, inhabited much of the territory between the Jubba and Tana Rivers prior to the occupation by the Ogadeen.[7] Remnant groups of them reside in parts of Tana River District, Kenya (see Ensminger 1992),

---

[7] A Cushitic-speaking hunting group, the Boni, inhabited large parts of this territory, especially near the coast, but are not treated here since their numbers are very small and they figure little in trade or current political issues.

the Middle Jubba Region, Somalia, and other parts of southern Somalia. In conquering the border region, the Somali groups subordinated the Oromo into lower-status clients and at times incorporated them into their own communities. Besteman (1991), who has done the most thorough research among Oromo populations in the Jubba Valley, describes how this happened: 'The Darood [Somali] insurgency was so strong that most of the surviving Orma fled beyond the Tana River, leaving the Jubba–Tana area in Somali hands' (Lewis 1988: 30, cited in Besteman 1991: 89). The Orma [Oromo] conquered by the Somali in some cases remained as clients and in others as slaves' (1991: 89). Besteman goes on to suggest that: 'Somali pastoralists in southern Somalia (including the Jubba–Tana area) clearly had control over substantial numbers of pastoral slaves and serfs by the turn of the century. These slaves were primarily, if not entirely, of Boran and Oromo (Warday) origin' (ibid: 92). Many Oromo descendants currently reside as settled agriculturalists or tenant farmers of wealthy Somali in parts of the Jubba Valley, and are held in low esteem. They suffered badly from recent violence, famine, and pillage and not surprisingly comprise a relatively large number of the region's displaced populations in Kenyan-based refugee camps (CARE 1994: 5–14).

Another minority group in the region are the so-called Gosha peoples, the Bantu descendants of former slaves and indigenous agriculturalists who reside in large parts of the Jubba Valley. The majority of Bantu descendants in the Lower Jubba Region are former slaves from Tanzania and Mozambique who were brought to the region by the Zanzibar regime as laborers for coastal plantations. As a collective, they comprise more than one dozen different ethnic groups (Menkhaus 1989: 96). Their servitude in the region is said to have persisted well into this century, often at the hands of Somali pastoralists, and later on they suffered terrible discrimination and loss of land during the Barre regime (Menkhaus 1989). In fact large chunks of their rich agricultural lands were converted into state irrigation schemes during the 1970s and 1980s without any compensation, while powerful Somali politicians also randomly expropriated their farms for private purposes, either evicting the Gosha families or turning them into tenants on their own land (Menkhaus and Craven 1996).

The plight of the Gosha people worsened with the government's collapse in 1991. Almost immediately different militias pillaged their farms and possessions and violently brutalized them. Thousands perished from famine and vicious attack, while others sought refugee status outside the country or in the numerous camps of Kismayo town (see CARE 1994). Their history and recent brutal treatment are documented in the works of Besteman (1999a), Menkhaus (1996), and de Waal (1997) and their plight rightfully has received some international coverage.

As would be expected, not only has the war resulted in the proliferation of refugee camps, but it also has altered population distribution in other ways. While exact figures are not available, the important regional towns of Jamaame, Gelib, and Bulla Xaaji towns all have been sites of major conflicts and large numbers of residents are said to have fled from them (see Detouillon 1993). Jamaame and Gelib are located in the heavily contested Jubba Valley, while Bulla Xaaji is located south of Kismayo town near the disputed boundary between Harti and Ogadeen clansmen. The movement of refugees from the Jubba Valley and nearby areas, in turn, has swelled Kismayo's population. Its residents in the 1990s were estimated at about 100,000 to 120,000 (Vigneau 1993), an approximate 100 percent increase over 1988. Most of that growth was accounted by internally displaced refugees who fled to camps in and around Kismayo.

Climate and seasonality
History and population patterns in the area are greatly affected by climatic factors. While little meteorological data have been collected since the state's collapse, there is good satellite coverage for the 1990s and good rainfall data for the pre-war period. These sources reveal an average annual rainfall of approximately 560 mm for the borderlands, ranging from 750+ mm in the Jubba River Valley to less than 350 mm near the Kenya border (Hubl 1986: 56). The area's variable climate and ecology makes the cattle trade between Kenya and Somalia highly seasonal. Animals are trekked to Kenyan markets from southern Somalia, passing through arid areas where water and pastures are available only seasonally. During long dry periods – January to March and August to September – the business slows or stops all together. In the pre-war period, the cattle trade was reoriented toward regional (Kismayo) and national (Mogadishu) markets during dry periods. These outlets filled a void when the Kenyan market slowed, so astute traders vigorously pursued them. However, these markets now are very risky, prone to violence, and avoided in most cases.

Too little rainfall
Drought is the main climatic risk and a *normal* occurrence in the region, as it is throughout the Horn of Africa. Localized droughts are very common in the borderlands, forcing herders to adjust grazing patterns every three to four years regardless of political conditions. A localized drought means that at least some parts of the region experience a marked rainfall decline or delay in the onset of the *gu* season. Full-blown regional and/or national droughts have occurred in the area about every eight years during the past three decades. A regional drought means that the short (*deyr*) and long rains (*gu*) have failed in the entire region, while a national drought signifies a complete failure of both rainy seasons throughout the country. The most devastating recent national droughts, ones which also affected neighboring countries, occurred in 1991–2 and 2000–1.

Although not nearly as serious as national (and multi-country) droughts, a localized drought was experienced in 1996 when many parts of Garissa District, Kenya received less than 30 percent of expected rainfall amounts and the long rains arrived three months late. Fortunately, the early rains (April–May) were good in southern Somalia, as well as in the southern portion of Garissa District. However, both of these options for local herders had problems: the south Garissa grazing zone is in the tsetse fly belt,[8] while southern Somalia had pockets of armed conflict at the time. Despite considerable risks, several Kenyan Somali herders moved their cattle near the Kismayo coast of southern Somalia, a distance of about 225 km. Rainfall there had been good but armed conflict also was widespread. It is a disputed zone between the region's two major clan-based factions but herders moved their animals there nonetheless. The strategy was pursued only after a verbal agreement was reached with local elders stipulating that the migrant herders could not carry armaments with them. The move took place without incident and is indicative both of the flexibility of grazing strategies and of the willingness of competing pastoral groups to recognize drought-induced problems even during times of hostility. Reciprocal grazing rights are a way that herders, even those in areas of conflict, adjust to climatic volatility.

The political chaos of 1991 and 1992 tragically correlated with a terrible drought and famine in southern Somalia that left communities very vulnerable and resulted in at least 50,000 deaths in the borderlands alone, particularly in the Jubba Valley, and as many as 300,000 throughout Somalia (Prendergast 1997). As noted earlier, this event provoked an international response of historic proportions, but only after much of the suffering had taken place. Distinguishing the deleterious effects of this drought from the general anarchy and violence at the time is problematic. Both contributed to loss of life and widespread human misery, but the resulting famine mainly was man-made as fighting disrupted trade, production, and food deliveries. While Garissa District, Kenya did not confront similar levels of violence and famine, drought was widespread and rainfall amounts there were only 50 to 61 percent of normal levels in 1991–2 (Kenya 1993a: 7; 1993b: 19). In short, precipitation was desperately inadequate and, consequently, cattle mortality rates were as high as 60 percent in parts of Garissa District.

On the Somalia side, needed grain supplies and aid were unable to reach starving communities because of factional fighting. The drought drastically reduced milk and meat yields and left pastoralists, particularly the poorer segments, in a desperate state. Even worse off, however, were settled agriculturalists in the Jubba Valley, who were wantonly looted, terrorized, and left with few resources to cultivate. Their depressing plight and that of agropastoralists in neighboring Bay Region played key roles in motivating the US and UN responses mentioned earlier. For sedentary communities war was probably more of a cause of

---

[8] Tsetse flies cause a deadly disease in cattle called trypanosomiasis. The tsetse fly belt in the region is concentrated along the Jubba River and along the coastal zones south of Kismayo and including the northern Kenyan coast. Herders try to avoid these fly zones during the rainy season when infestation is especially strong.

famine in 1991 and 1992, while for pastoralists it was a combination of armed conflict and drought.

The harsh period from the beginning of 1991 to the end of 1992 was the time when grazing patterns of the border region were most affected, and the term 'chaos' probably best captured local realities. In subsequent years conditions vastly improved and herders occasionally did alter migration patterns, but nothing on the scale of 1991 and 1992. During these two years of frequent clashes and hardships, many Somali herders moved their animals either to Kenya or to Ethiopia. There is even evidence that certain grazing areas of the Upper Jubba Valley area were planted with deadly mines by the fleeing forces of the deposed dictator, Siad Barre (see de Waal 1993; 1997). This brutal tactic was taken to disrupt the movements of rival herders and militias.

However, since 1993 seasonal herd movements have been affected more by climatic factors than by war. For instance, during 1995 and 1996 herders of the Lower Jubba migrated with their cattle to their normal seasonal pastures and a similar pattern was followed in 1998 and 1999. In short, the pastoral sector has fared surprisingly well following the turmoil of 1991 and 1992, despite the absence of a central government.

Too much rainfall
In the border region excessive rainfall and floods are far less prevalent than drought, but when they occur can be cataclysmic. During 1996 to 1999 floods were particularly destructive, with the most serious occurring in 1997–8 as a result of an El Nino event (see Little, Mahmoud et al. 2001). Along the Jubba River there are no longer effective flood control canals and dykes, since they mainly were built during the colonial period and were not maintained in recent years. Their lack of maintenance is a casualty of the stateless era. On the Kenyan side the Tana River also has experienced volatile river flows, mainly in response to dam construction upstream. Rains in the catchment areas of both rivers have few release areas and often flood low-lying depressions nearby, as happened so catastrophically in late 1997. This El Nino-induced event turned areas between the Jubba River and Kenya border into shallow lakes with widths up to a kilometer or more in certain cases. In some places rainfall at the end of 1997 was estimated to be as much as 20 times above monthly averages (IRIN 1997: 1; Cathy Clark 1998: 2). These floods reached the key wet-season grazing zones well away from the Jubba River, inundating more than 1,000 square km of prime rangelands and creating a continuous sheet of water across large expanses of pasture.

On the Kenya side the El Nino event was equally destructive. The Tana River dramatically exploded its river banks and turned parts of Garissa District into virtual lakes, as well as destroying most of the district's existing irrigation works (IRIN 1997). The floods covered much of the key agricultural and pastoral zones of Garissa District, devastating most of the area's small ruminant herds and killing an estimated 25,000 cattle. Unlike goats and sheep massive losses of cattle were avoided because they were moved north and northwest to drier patches of land. It is estimated that by early 1998 some 120,000 herders and farmers had been displaced by floods in Garissa and Mandera Districts, Kenya (IRIN 1997). What were the other El Nino losses and destruction in the Somali borderlands? Most serious were human losses due to epidemic-level outbreaks of malaria and, later, the dreaded Rift Valley Fever (RVF), a disease spread by mosquitoes that causes hemorrhaging and certain death if left untreated. Actual human deaths due to the flood and associated outbreaks of disease numbered more than 2,000. Nutritional and food security problems also were aggravated by the widespread flooding of cultivated zones. In excess of 60,000 hectares of crop lands and the bulk of the agricultural crop of 1997 were lost in the Lower Jubba Region. Similar losses were reported on the Kenyan side (FSAU 1997; FEWS 1998a). Because the floods destroyed transport links, local shortages could not be supplemented by normal imports or food aid. For the low-income consumer this resulted in grain shortages and steep monthly price increases, in some cases in excess of 500 percent in key markets like Afmadow (FSAU 1997).

Informal trade activities also were hard hit by the floods. Because of road destruction and the imposition of market quarantines in Kenya due to the outbreak of RVF, livestock markets virtually closed between November 1997 and February 1998. More dramatic, however, was the imposition by Saudi Arabia of a livestock ban on all live animal imports from the Horn of Africa. This action particularly hurt Somaliland to the north, which exported about 2.2 million animals to Saudi Arabia in 1997, but it also caused a general decline in sales and prices in southern Somalia as well (FEWS 2000c: 2–3). In Somaliland it is estimated that the ban reduced incomes of pastoralists and traders by about $10 million and state revenues by about 45 percent from March to October 1998 (Steffen et al. 1998; UNDP 1998: 17). While the ban was lifted in April 1999, it was reimposed in June 2000 after more than 20 consumers in Saudi Arabia contacted RVF. The effects of these market quarantines on regional welfare are addressed further in Chapters 5 and 6.

Wells, dams, and ponds
Surface water points are critical to the Somali economy, but have been susceptible to destructive action in the stateless era. More than a few motorized boreholes and wells were destroyed during 1991 and 1992. Prior to this wealthy herders and traders made private claims to pastures in southern Somalia by constructing and controlling access to a water point. An individual could control nearby grazing by constructing a pond or well and restricting water rights to the individual's herd (for a parallel case from southern Africa, see Peters 1994). Without the means to water their livestock, a herder or trader could not use the surrounding range area, allowing the water point owner a virtual monopoly over nearby

pastures. However, some owners did allow herders to use the water in exchange either for cash payment or labor for the maintenance of the water point. Those large traders who did not allow local herders to use their water were the source of strong hostilities in the area. They had benefited from the government's ambitious (and corrupt) water development program in the 1970s and 1980s and had built private water points with state subsidies (see discussion later in the chapter).

Prior to the war there were 10 functioning motorized boreholes on the Somalia side of the border. As of 1999, approximately seven were operating at least part of the year, with some of these rehabilitated with funds from an NGO or UN agency. In the government era, boreholes were expected to be managed and maintained by a state agency, but in principle this did not occur because of insufficient funds. At the time herders were charged ridiculously cheap subsidized rates that did not allow the government to meet its costs. In 1988 official charges for watering animals were equivalent to about US$0.01 per head of cattle. Currently communities manage and maintain boreholes and charge rates based on use and actual operating costs, a practice that they were forced to initiate even before the government's collapse.

The boreholes were initially developed along stock routes leading to Kismayo port in the hopes of encouraging overseas exports. Optimistically – but unrealistically – the state anticipated that livestock from Kenya and even southern Ethiopia also would use the infrastructure en route to the Kismayo market. As will be shown later, the trade actually ended up moving in the opposite direction, from the Kismayo export trade to informal markets in Kenya. Although the overseas trade only benefited a small minority, the government viewed it as a potential source of scarce foreign exchange and encouraged its growth. The boreholes and stock routes were to facilitate this and were financed in the 1970s under a World Bank project called the Trans-Juba Livestock Project (TJLP). This venture allocated millions of US dollars to export market infrastructure in order to encourage commercialization and overseas exports. The expensive 'experiment' actually had very little effect on livestock trade in the region. As of 1999, it was those boreholes financed by TJLP and closest to Kismayo town that were inoperable, an ironic ending to an unfortunate story.

Key environmental resources

The Kenya/Somalia border area is a classic example of a 'patchy environment' (see Scoones 1989). Key natural resources, like grazing and water, are concentrated in patches around seasonal flood plains, swamps, and depressions. Access to them often determines whether or not herders survive harsh years without massive livestock losses. Yet, these vital pockets are threatened by civil unrest, and on the Kenya side by dam construction and irrigation schemes. Local conflicts among different clans and ethnic groups are often about control of these key resources.

Three important environmental features ('patches') characterize the Lower Jubba Region. First is the presence of the Jubba River, Somalia's only true perennial river.[9] Its annual flood is vital to the regeneration of local pastures, ponds, and wells in the eastern part of the region. The Jubba River originates in the Ethiopian highlands and is formed from three tributaries there. As Evans et al. note, 'there is a high degree of variability in annual river flow' (1988: 12). Based on more than 20 years of data, monthly discharge of water in the river varies from only 4 to 991 cubic meters/second; and average annual volume of river flow varies from 71 million cubic meters in February to 1,224 million cubic meters in October (AHT 1987). The latter month represents the tail end of the rainy season in the Ethiopian highlands.

The wetlands of the Jubba River Valley are more likely than other areas to have good stands of perennial grass during dry seasons. As a result, the concentration of cattle in the floodplains is the highest of any region in the country and among the highest anywhere in eastern Africa (see Watson 1987). In some parts of the river valley they support cattle densities of more than 150 per square km during the long dry season (*jilaal*) (ibid). At that time of the year herders of Afmadow and Kismayo Districts migrate to the riparian pastures, a pattern that continues and has persisted since at least the end of the nineteenth century (Chevenix-Trench 1907). Grasses in the seasonally flooded zones 'form tall dense swards' with annual fodder production in excess of 10 metric tons per hectare (Deshmukh 1989: A-38).

A second important ecological feature is the Lag Dera basin (including the Jira plains), consisting of a series of meandering seasonal rivers and associated grasslands in central Afmadow District (see Fig. 2.1). This basin defines an excellent grazing resource for cattle and, along with Afmadow itself, figures strongly in the region's oral histories and early population movements. It covers several hundred square km and is fed by seasonal rivers and streams that at times originate in Kenya. Its annual flood often empties into the Descheeg Waamo, a flooded depression of rich wetlands in the Jubba Valley. According to an ecological survey of the area, 'The Lac Dera is reputed to flow for 2–3 months [of the year] mostly in the gu' [rainy season] collecting local runoff, principally from lands downstream of Afmadow where the annual rainfall exceeds 500 mm' (Hendy 1985: 37). Yet, the construction of hundreds of water ponds (*waro*) during the 1980s has allowed herders to use these pastures during dry seasons, when they should be migrating out of the area. Lag Dera is relatively free of tsetse fly, but does not sustain the high stocking levels found in parts of the Jubba Valley.

---

[9] The Shebelle River of southern Somalia is often classified as a perennial river, but the lower parts of the river actually dry up during the dry season. Unlike the Jubba, the Shebelle does not exit to the Indian Ocean but, instead, disappears into swamps east of the Jubba River about 30 km from the coast.

The third significant environmental characteristic of the border region is its approximate 150-kilometer coastline in the southeast, which links the region to global markets. The Kismayo port area, in particular, served as a major livestock export facility and the third largest port in Somalia before 1991. As discussed earlier, it has been an important trade center since the nineteenth century.[10] The location of the Lower Jubba, with its sea links to the outside, brings nomadic herders and local traders into close contact with global livestock markets. This proximity to international markets is atypical of most pastoral regions of sub-Saharan Africa.

As noted earlier, conflicts between different clans and ethnic groups often involve these key environmental resources. Prior to the changes of 1991 the Barre regime awarded certain client groups preferential access to arable land and water, an ill-advised practice that will be discussed later in the chapter. Indeed, the Somalia case is a good example of ethnic (and clan) favoritism where private land-grabbing in the Jubba and Shebelle Valleys favored the late president's clan, the Marehan, while alienating other groups (for example, the Gosha communities) (Menkhaus and Craven 1996; Besteman 1999a). It heightened already existing social tensions between pastoralists and settled farmers who both depended on the valley.

Livestock resources

The environmental characteristics discussed above help to explain the significance of the livestock sector to the region's economy. While the camel clearly is the prestige animal in Somali culture, many parts of the Lower Jubba area are best suited for cattle pastoralism and local identity is more closely associated with it.[11] In the words of one range management specialist, it is 'cattle country' (Box 1968: 390). Indeed, prior to the war the region contained approximately 25 percent of the national cattle herd or an estimated 900,000 animals, but only 4 percent (214,000 camels) of the national camel herd. In terms of small stock, the region also contained about 229,000 goats or 1 percent of the national flock, and 57,000 sheep or

[10] Archaeological evidence suggests that Kismayo may have been an important trading center in the fifteenth and sixteenth centuries, participating in East Africa's trade with the Middle East and Asia. Its status seemed to have been short-lived, however (Menkhaus 1989). Kismayo was a relatively insignificant actor in East African commerce until the latter half of the nineteenth century. The ports of Brava, Merca, and Mogadishu were far more important in pre-1850 trade (see Cassanelli 1982).

[11] The following Somali saying reflects the priority given to camels and the lack of status for cattle herders: 'A camel man is a man, a goat man is half a man, and a cattle man is no man at all' (Abdullahi 1990: 72). This phrase, of course, reflects the views of camel and goat herders and is based on research among camel pastoralists in central Somalia. Nonetheless, it points to larger issues in Somali ethnography that often go unacknowledged. These include that: (1) significant cultural diversity exists among Somali-speakers, a point that Besteman (1999a) and Menkhaus (1989) have demonstrated so well; and (2) the so-called 'camel complex' is most typical of central and northern Somali groups and not all of Somalia.

0.5 percent of the country's total (Janzen 1988; Hubl 1986). The dominant cattle type kept in the Lower Jubba, particularly around Afmadow, is the white Boran-mixed specie, referred to locally as *lo caddey*. On the other side of the porous border, there were an estimated 422,400 cattle, 240,000 goats and sheep, and 60,000 camels in Garissa District, Kenya in the late 1990s (Hendy and Morton 1999: 58; Kenya 1993a: 35).

Recent reports and surveys of the area – as well as my own interviews with livestock traders and herders – indicate that the livestock herds of southern Somalia have not suffered nearly as much as elsewhere in the country (Lohr 1995; Stefano Tempia, personal communication). Even the civil strife of the early 1990s apparently did not have a major impact on the region's livestock population, at least in areas away from the main towns (see Lohr 1995; Stockton and Chema 1995).[12] In 1992 and 1993 staff of the International Committee of the Red Cross (ICRC) vaccinated and/or treated 197,640 cattle in only one part of the Jubba region, implying that cattle numbers were relatively robust at that time (ICRC 1992/1993: 1). Just one year later another source notes that in southern Somalia 'some interpretations of satellite scanning hold that there is not much difference in current animal populations nor in their spread and range resources as compared with the situation in the late Eighties' (FAO 1994: 4). A more recent (2000) estimate based on aerial surveys and ground observations estimates that livestock herds are at or even a little higher than in the pre-war period (see FEWS-Net 2001a).

Household-level data also confirm the rich livestock resources of the region. Families keep cattle herds that are well above the country's average and considerably higher than most other East African pastoralists. Although herd ownership varies substantially, the average cattle herd per household in Afmadow was approximately 75 or 8.33 per capita (author's field data).[13] This figure places them at a wealth level above other cattle-rich pastoralists of East Africa, such as the Borana of Ethiopia (Coppock 1994) and the Maasai of Kenya and Tanzania (Zaal 1998; Little, Smith et al. 2001).

The national picture

Before the coup of 1991 Somalia derived more than 80 percent of its export earnings from the livestock sector. The economy was (and still is) very dependent on livestock production and trade, although remittances are probably more important today (see Chapter 6). These pastoral-based activities are not trivial. Somalia (including Somaliland) remains a major player in livestock trade on a regional and global scale, accounting for more than 60 percent of all livestock exports from East Africa during the 1990s (see Zaal and Polderman 2000). In what is now

[12] One local NGO, the United Somali Sahil Professionals' Association (UNISOPA), estimated that the Lower Jubba area lost about two-thirds of its cattle as a result of drought, war, and disease (UNISOPA 1993: 2). I would strongly question these figures, as would others (see Lohr 1995).

[13] Ownership of both camels and cattle in the region is highly skewed (see also Chapter 3).

sometimes called Somaliland and Puntland (formerly northeastern Somalia), production and annual exports of small ruminants from the ports of Berbera and Bossaso actually exceeded pre-war levels and showed no signs of slowing down until the recent import bans by Saudi Arabia. When the ban was lifted in April 1999 exports recovered quickly, reaching a record level of 2.9 million animals during that year (see FEWS 2000c: 2–3).

In the border region overseas exports of live animals have been virtually non-existent since 1990, and in Mogadishu they have been equally poor. However, in the mid-1980s the Lower Jubba Region accounted for 35 to 40 percent of the country's exports of cattle and about 20 percent of its camel exports (the latter figure includes camels from Kenya). More important for the border region in recent years has been the 'unofficial' export of cattle to Kenya, which has boomed since 1991. The Lower Jubba Region alone exports to Kenya about 70,000 cattle per year, which is more than twice as many as during the pre-war years (see Chapter 5).[14] Even during 1987 and 1988, when the state and Western development agencies strongly encouraged overseas exports, unofficial sales to Kenya exceeded official exports from Kismayo port by a factor of about five (Little 1992a).

A second livestock-based activity that contributed to the national economy was meat processing. Its significance, however, had declined precipitously even before 1991. During 1984 to 1988 the government-owned Kismayo Meat Factory (KMF) was open an average of only three months per year. From 1977 to 1987 annual earnings from the export of the factory's canned meat dropped by more than 85 percent, and in the 1980s the number of cattle slaughtered at the KMF declined from 16,237 (1980) to less than 2,000 (1988) (Little 1989a). During most of the 1970s, the era of 'scientific socialism' and Soviet dependency, Somalia received preferential access to Russian and East European markets (see Ahmed Samatar 1988). At this time sales of canned meat were an important component of regional and national exports. Thus, in the mid-1970s the export of processed meat from Kismayo accounted for about 6 percent of the country's total export earnings, while by 1988 it contributed less than one percent. The KMF has not operated at all since 1990, an inconsequential event for most herders.

The export of hides and skins was a third regional activity that contributed to national income, but like the meat industry it was in serious decline even before the war. The former Hides and Skins Agency, the main purchasing arm for state-owned tanneries, offered prices to herders that were less than one-half of those paid on the open market in neighboring

---

[14] It is obviously very difficult to estimate the annual volume of unofficial trade to Kenya. Cassam (1987) conducted research in both Kenya and Somalia in 1987 and estimated that about 30,000 cattle from southern Somalia were exported annually to Kenya. I have used data from trader interviews and market statistics at Garissa to arrive at my estimates (discussed in more detail in Chapter 5).

Kenya. While the tannery in Kismayo had an annual processing capacity of 125,000 cattle hides and 375,000 goats and sheep skins, it processed only 22,000 cattle hides and no skins in 1988 (Little 1989a). The industry relied heavily on supplies of hides from the KMF, and because the latter enterprise seldom operated the tannery had few raw materials to process. As Verdery has described for state-owned corporations in Eastern Europe, incentives to effectively manage inventories and to control costs were noticeably absent (Verdery 1996). Managers were more concerned with meeting their quotas than seeking alternative sources of supply and profit, and pursued silly strategies, like transporting low-value hides more than 400 km just so the factory had supplies to process. Key personnel often were absent from KMF, usually engaged in private business and other activities. In more than 10 trips to the massive plant during 1987–8, I found key personnel on the job only twice and was usually told the same line: 'you just missed them.' With the collapse of the state, there have been some private exports of hides and skins from Kismayo, but the levels are extremely low (Stockton and Chema 1995).

The 'development' dimension
By 1988 the bankrupt Somali state was effectively comatose in providing services to the livestock sector of the Lower Jubba Region. For example, the massive region was allocated only $120 per year for fuel and maintenance of the veterinary department's vehicles. The situation on the Kenya side was not much better, and in fact public water sources were more reliable in southern Somalia than in Kenya, mainly because communities themselves took over their operation and maintenance. Historically the Kenyan government has invested very little in the livestock sector of northeastern Kenya. As a result, Somali herders from Kenya often use pastures and water points in southern Somalia, a practice that helped them to survive the long drought of 2000–1 (author's field notes). Prior to the war the Water Development Agency (WDA) of Somalia, another government-owned and operated enterprise, was supposed to manage and maintain boreholes and dams but rarely did so. In 1998 communities themselves organized maintenance and operation activities, and users were charged the cost of fuel, maintenance, and a fee toward the salary of the operator.

The livestock development potential of the border region attracted the interest of international development agencies as early as the 1960s. With funds from the US International Cooperation Administration, the predecessor to the US Agency for International Development (USAID), the area was surveyed in 1960 and the report indicated several million hectares of grazing land for potential development (Konczacki 1978: 73; Abercrombie 1961: 149–53). The US government followed this up with a range management scheme in the border region, with a focus on Afmadow District, and sent a number of livestock 'experts' to introduce 'modern' range management techniques, as well as providing more than

US$4 million in funds (see Box 1968; Konczacki 1978; Iannelli 1984). At the time the 'science' of range management was just being established in the USA and the dry rangelands of southern Somalia afforded both an exotic laboratory and 'a development challenge for US technical expertise' (Rawson 1994: 159). Early attempts at rotational grazing, bush clearing, and other questionable interventions were implemented in the area, and none of them were successful either on economic or social grounds. In particular, local herders were resistant and outright hostile to imposed management techniques that restricted their mobility, the main means of coping with volatile weather conditions. As Konczacki points out, 'these experiments proved unsuccessful because local populations did not agree to limitations in the use of range required by its *rational management*' (my emphasis) (1978: 85). Their lack of cooperation and protests led to the closure of the project within a few years. When I visited the project area in 1987 its remnants were hardly visible – a few firebreaks and old fences – nor fondly remembered by local communities.

With World Bank financing of about US$10 million another ill-fated attempt at livestock development, the Trans-Juba Livestock Project (TJLP), was instigated in the region. As highlighted earlier, its lofty goals were to improve livestock infrastructure, increase animal exports from the region, and bring economic benefits to herders. The project was expected to absorb almost 50 percent of available government funds for the livestock sector during 1974–8 (ibid: 96). By almost any criteria of measurement, this project was a non-starter from the outset and a dismal disaster in the end (see World Bank 1983). The aspect of the project that had the most enduring but negative impact was the project's massive water development program. By 1988 there were an estimated 1,500+ small water ponds in Afmadow District alone, of which more than 500 had been established by the project between 1975 and 1980 and another estimated 800 or so were built with project-financed equipment after the World Bank withdrew. Following the World Bank's decision to pull out in 1983 after a series of extremely negative evaluations, local Somali officials aggressively leased out the equipment to herders and private traders, so they could construct their own water points and the employees could earn a handsome return. There apparently was little supervision and oversight of the loan by World Bank or central ministry staff, even during the early years of the project. The Bank's own evaluation reports described it as a flawed project with negligible benefits for herders 'that must be regarded as a failure in almost all its aspects' (World Bank 1983: iv). On more than one occasion its staff recommended that the project be closed and funding withdrawn.

The project continued, however, even after the World Bank halted additional financing, since the equipment was there as well as some remaining credit from the initial loan. On equity grounds there was much to criticize, since most of the water facilities benefited wealthy export-oriented herders and traders, who monopolized the services and machinery. These elites were charged only nominal fees, and it was widely speculated that certain project officials were reaping considerable revenues from 'renting' out this equipment. The TJLP charged wealthy traders and herders a modest fee of about US$800 to construct a pond of approximately 30 × 30 meters. They used bulldozers and other earth-moving machines to complete the activity within 3–4 days. It was a classic example of the 'privatization' of a public good that resulted in considerable local resentment, as well as serious environmental problems. In 1988 a conscientious civil servant based in Afmadow actually mapped out for me the extent of water point development and explained how it negatively affected pasture use and herd movements.

The 'private' water development, ironically financed by a development project to benefit local herders, provoked enough local and regional dissent for action to be taken. As early as 1984, Ogadeen herders protested about the number of water points in the area, which was inviting excessive immigration by outside herders and overgrazing. They were disturbed by the influx of non-local herders, the uncontrolled construction of water points by outside traders, and the deterioration in range conditions. They even took their case to the regional governor to demand that the lease program of the TJLP be halted. They eventually succeeded and it was closed in 1987, but not before hundreds of ponds had been dug. During the 1980s the construction of water ponds allowed herders and traders to overuse pastures during dry seasons when they normally would have migrated out of the area. These new resources, as well as the pull of being closer to Kismayo town, attracted herders from the Upper Jubba area (Gedo Region). As will be discussed later in the chapter, the tension surrounding the immigration of these herders, who were mainly members of the President's Marehan clan, was to contribute to the violent eruption of conflict in the region.

It should come as no surprise that the Somali state had virtually no effective policies regulating land and water use in the border region. The National Range Agency was charged with maintaining certain controlled grazing areas for holding export animals in the region, but in principle there was no regulation or enforcement. Local resource use was mainly regulated by herders and groups of local elders. However, when the land and water rights of herders conflicted with the state's agricultural interests in the Jubba Valley, the pastoralists usually lost ground. The state's policies on irrigation affected resource use by cutting off herder access to certain water and grazing points near the river. Obvious examples were the state-sponsored Mogambo Irrigation Scheme (cotton), the Fanoole Irrigation Scheme (rice), and the Juba Sugar Project, as well as the numerous private and state banana plantations in the valley. The total area of the three large irrigation projects was 16,327 hectares and included 'some of the best land in the region' (Menkhaus 1996: 147).

With the exception of a few of the banana farms that were taken over by local faction leaders, the large state irrigation schemes were destroyed during the war, including most irrigation and flood control devices. Local herders had a strong negative attitude toward these schemes, but it was actually the small groups of minority (Gosha) farmers along the river who were most negatively affected by them (see earlier discussion). The obliteration of these schemes seems to have done little to ameliorate the plight of the settled farmers, but it has clearly opened up productive pastures for regional herders. It was noted that after the destruction of one state scheme, Fanoole, 'the abandoned project serves as an excellent pasture for local herds' (Menkhaus 1991: 12). While a wasteful and destructive means of doing so, these expensive projects did little for the local population until the war destroyed them and reopened them for grazing.

The Somali state's role in livestock marketing also was minimal, except in the overseas export trade.[15] Through the Ministry of Livestock, Forestry, and Range the government was responsible for operating holding grounds and quarantine stations near Kismayo, where export animals were required to be held for a period of up to 14 days prior to shipment. These services were provided for traders and the marketing department had very little contact with herders. At a time when the government began to unravel, infrastructure for the export trade was being improved under an expensive development program that received US support. In Kismayo the sad reality was that following the project's installation of high-priced, modern infrastructure for the export business, marketed animals had better access to safe drinking water than did the local human population. At the time (1988) the entire Lower Jubba Region, including Kismayo town, had no safe potable water systems, leading locals to make sarcastic reference that the government 'treated export-quality animals better than Somalis' (author's field notes). This infrastructure and that at the Mogadishu Port were heavily damaged during the fighting of 1991–2.

Struggles over resources

The discontent among herders in southern Somalia took on new dimensions when the state began to directly and indirectly deal with two prized and valued resources: water and pasture. As was noted earlier, Ogadeen herders of Afmadow District were confronted with aggressive encroachments on their water and pasture resources from the President's own clan, the Marehan. Many Marehan camel herders from the Gedo Region of the upper Jubba Valley migrated to take advantage of (1) the improved water availability financed under the TJLP and (2) pastures

---

[15] The most significant regulation of the export trade was the requirement that traders exchange at least 50 percent of their foreign exchange earnings at the 'official' exchange rate. In March 1988 the official exchange rate was SoSh 99 = US $1, while the real market rate was SoSh 220 = US $1 and losing value at about 8 percent per month. As would be expected, there was considerable underreporting of profits and use of offshore financial institutions to avoid this requirement.

seasonally vacated by cattle herders. When the Ogadeen cattle pastoralists abandoned their seasonal grazing areas each year, camel herders would move in and occupy them. After a period of about four years some Marehan herders decided to remain in the area for most of the year, in effect becoming permanent residents.

The process accelerated in late 1988 when Marehan herders began to spontaneously 'privatize' water points and surrounding pastures by demarcating them with thorn fences. Some individuals went so far as to have their water points registered with district officials in Afmadow town. As was noted earlier, this pattern of encroachment was facilitated by the expansion not only of water points but also of other market infrastructure built with World Bank funding. Aided by the confidence that any disputes with other groups of herders would be resolved in their favor, the Marehan took advantage of the situation. After all, they were members of President Barre's clan and could invoke strong political support if needed. In one case in 1988 I observed an Ogadeen herder verbally abusing a water department official for allowing outside camel herders to utilize a local borehole. The civil servant confided to me that the local pastoralist was correct in complaining, but that there was little he could do because of the government.[16] Cattle owners of Afmadow also claimed that the large presence of camels was turning their excellent grasslands into shrub land. Because camels mainly consume browse and bush species, they were said to promulgate bush encroachment by passing seeds of woody species through their dung, thereby turning cattle pastures into unproductive land.

The increased presence of camel herders resulted in several conflicts between Marehan and Ogadeen herders, especially those of the Mohamed Zubeyr sub-clan. By the summer of 1988 it was common to hear of armed skirmishes between Marehan and local Ogadeen herders at water points in the region. When Colonel Omar Jess, a member of the Mohamed Zubeyr sub-clan of the Ogadeen but not from the Lower Jubba Region, helped to mobilize the area's armed resistance to the Barre regime in the late 1980s, these tensions erupted in large-scale fighting, and the Somali army was called in to punish the 'rebels' and to protect the Marehan migrants. One rebel leader's account of the clashes in 1989 points to the conflicts caused by the movement of outside herders into the area:

> 'We of the Lower Juba Province particularly protested against the increased infiltration by people from the neighbouring Gedo region, who were in turn crossing into Kenya to partake in poaching activities in the Kenya national parks and highway banditry,' Major Barre [no relation to President Barre] explained.
> ... But the Absame [Ogadeen] tribesmen who predominantly inhabit the Lower Juba Province were soon accused of oppressively

---

[16] Recall that mention of clan in the presence of foreigners was illegal at the time, so the official merely referred to the Marehan herders as 'those camel herders'.

flushing out Siad Barre's own Marehan community and that was the beginning of the whole in-fighting episode (*Kenya Standard*, 16 August, 1989, p. 10).

The Kenyan newspaper account goes on to discuss how Siad Barre's Somali army unleashed a battalion of armored vehicles and tanks, under the command of Major-General Hussein Abdullahi, a Marehan, to brutalize civilians and destroy towns in the area, including Afmadow. This was the beginning of large-scale conflict in the region. It did not slow down until the government was toppled in 1991. Although the Ogadeen and Marehan clans are from the same large clan family (the Darood) and were allies at times during Barre's tenure, they have opposed each other since the late 1980s. The local armed resistance movement in the area, called the Somali Patriotic Movement (SPM), was under way by 1989, bent on revenge against the Barre regime and against those groups, like the Marehan, who reaped benefits from their alliance with the state. The SPM, initially comprising Ogadeen clansmen (especially those of the Mohamed Zubeyr and Aulihan sections), did not start as early nor receive the kind of publicity accorded other Somali resistance movements operating at the time, but for all practical purposes many parts of the Lower Jubba never again came under state control.[17] When the time came in 1991, they temporarily forged an alliance with non-Ogadeen-based factions, such as the United Somali Congress (USC) and marched toward Mogadishu where they were on the city's outskirts when Barre and his Mogadishu clique were overthrown.

[17] During the 1990s this armed faction acquired considerable notoriety in the international media when they temporarily took control of Kismayo city where US troops later were to be stationed. The SPM eventually splintered into competing groups, one of which was closely allied to General Aideed's party (Somali National Alliance) and the other with Morgan's own group (which latter took on the name of SPM). Kismayo and the different factions of the SPM were the focus of substantial international attention during 1993 and 1994, when several attempts were made by the US and the United Nations to bring peace to the Lower Jubba Region.

3

The Destruction of ▐ Rural–Urban relations

> There have always been well-established links between nomads and the towns. Most nomadic clans had allies within the towns who acted as hosts or emporia in centuries past when the towns were mainly trading emporia... The Somali of today has one foot planted in the countryside and one in the town (Hashim 1997: 42–3).

As the opening comment implies, Somalia was once a country of strong, symbiotic relations between town and countryside. Nomads and townsfolk moved fluidly between rural and urban sectors, and urbanites maintained livestock herds with rural clansmen. The boundaries between the two sectors were blurred and complementary, 'and goods and information passed readily across the cultural divide between town and country' (Cassanelli 1982: 27). While this may have been the case in the recent past, it clearly does not reflect the reality of contemporary Somalia where cities have become isolated pockets of violence and decline. Why has the Somalia of the 1990s been so different, a decade of raging rural–urban hostilities and clanism?[1] What has isolated the cities of southern Somalia from their hinterlands to such an extent that population movement is markedly restricted and long-standing linkages violently severed?

Answers to these questions require an in-depth assessment of the different aspects of rural and urban relationships, especially as they relate to politics and trade. This chapter lays out those relationships and urban-based activities that underlie current realities in the Somali borderlands. It shows why clan and rural–urban relations became so contentious in the 1990s and how they have come to influence current political and economic processes.

---

[1] For general background on the Somali conflict, see Ahmed Samatar (1994b), Hashim (1997), and Adam (1995).

Clans and communities

The notion of clan is to outside perceptions of Somali life what 'tribe' is to recent, post-September 11 stereotypes of Afghan politics. These customary units are said to overwhelm all other forms of identity and to symbolize a primitive, uncompromising commitment to ethnic loyalties and an inherent resistance to rational politics and modern governance. An understanding of the social divisions and struggles embedded in the Somalia crisis, however, must move beyond sterile debates about clanism and its role in the current conflict (for sharply contrasting views on the importance of clan loyalties, see Lewis 1993, 1994; Abdi Samatar 1992, 1994). That current hostilities and political discourses are expressed in terms of clans and ethnicities sheds little light on the reasons for rural- and urban-based violence and for the frequent reshaping of identities in response to changing external situations. For example, why have particular identities based on clans or sub-clans (invented or real) emerged only in the past decade and why has most of the conflict centered on urban centers and their control?

One can turn for help in addressing these issues to the exemplary work of Roseberry and O'Brien (1991) and Wolf (1982) who treat ethnicity as historically constituted and subject to interpretation, manipulation, and negotiation. As Wolf (1982: 6–7) points out, Western models of social structure that rely on 'internally homogenous and externally distinctive and bounded objects' may allow the social world to be neatly sorted into categories like clan and tribes, but they create false depictions of reality. Thus, rather than treat clans as rigid (natural) units of social and political organization, they should be viewed as products of 'changing ... social and political processes' (Roseberry and O'Brien 1991: 10). In these terms, the starting point for analyzing clan differentiation in Somalia must be the larger political and historical contexts in which it is located. These reflect a peculiar history of rural and urban relations that at times takes on identities of classism and clanism, but derive from relationships traced to the early colonial period.

By pursuing identity questions along the theoretical contours outlined above, it is possible to make sense of the contradictions in Somali clan politics, as well as the emergence of clan and sub-clan identities that have been dormant for decades. Instead of searching within 'traditional' social structure for explanations each time a new (or old) clan identity or alliance is expressed, one needs to examine the external power relations and the material benefits associated with such changes. And these have been exceptionally dynamic in the past decade. The clan system is amazingly adaptable to the changing demands of the international community, as well as to the challenges of statelessness and pastoralism. In fact there is little doubt that the proliferation, fragmentation, and – in some cases – consolidation of clan identities were strongly influenced by the presence of outside, resource-rich groups, such as the United Nations and Western development agencies. They held static, traditionalist definitions of what a clan is and the necessary resources to reinforce these stereotypes.

Is it surprising then that Somali clans began to fracture and/or consolidate along sub-clan and lineage lines when external agencies worked within a clan idiom themselves, often insisting on proposals from clan 'elders' even when some of these were disguised militia heads (see United Nations Operation in Somalia [UNOSOM] 1993)? The number of acknowledged clans quickly multiplied in response to such requests and opportunities, and some of these clan leaders were concealed warlords who claimed to have clan support.[2] Approximately 20 separate clan and sub-clan affiliations were represented in one UN-financed peace conference held in Kismayo town during May to June 1994 (UNOSOM 1994a), an astounding number for a limited area. The number of identities is especially impressive given that very few rival Ogadeen or Absame members were represented at the Lower Jubba meeting. Because they perceived of the Kismayo gathering as a Harti/Marehan affair, the Absame (including the Ogadeen) held their own competing meeting in a nearby border town, where 11 sub-clans and 500 representatives attended (United Nations 1996: 423). Overall more than 28 separate clan and sub-clan identities had emerged in an area where only seven years earlier I had identified fewer than 10 of any significance. While clans could be united on one front – for example, vis-à-vis external threats by other clans and outsiders – they easily segmented when it came to negotiating representation and benefits along clan lines. This pattern of consolidation and fragmentation, which is the core principle of a segmentary kinship system, was exactly what happened in response to the US armed attack on Mogadishu in 1993 and its aftermath (see note 1, Chapter 1). At that time a divided Somali population unified in opposition to what was perceived as an external threat. The situational and flexible nature of Somali social structure continues to elude outside mediators, as well as social scientists who seek rigid classifications.

At the same time that outside parties like the UN were trying to reconcile clan differences in the country, they also were contributing to the country's urbanism by concentrating their resources and hired clients in the large cities (see Prendergast 1997; Eikenberg 1995). The urban bias in Somalia was at the heart of some of the country and border region's early political tensions. One estimate is that more than 60 percent of the country's foreign aid in the 1980s ended up in Mogadishu and that by 1990 'up to 95 percent of the country's negotiable assets [were] controlled by residents of Mogadishu' (UNICEF 1992: 23; also see Rawson et al. 1993; Mubarak 1996). Recent actions in the name of humanitarian aid only amplify existing problems. A few large cities, including Kismayo, continue to possess the bulk of the country's economic resources, infrastructure, and flows of development aid.

[2] The same proliferation also took place in the number of registered Somali non-governmental organizations (NGOs). In 1995 more than 320 were registered with the United Nations office in Mogadishu, often in response to funding opportunities (see Eikenberg 1995). When I worked in Somalia in the late 1980s there were no more than 15 local NGOs in the country. Not surprisingly, 'in times of low donor activity in Somalia, many of the local NGOs seem to wither away' (Helander 1997: 1).

Clan distribution
The distribution of clans and settlements in the border region reflects several historical and politico-economic processes that contribute to the strained, often violent ties between Kismayo town and its hinterland. These historical forces were discussed in some detail in the previous chapter but will be elaborated here. To begin, in no way does the geographic distribution of clans and sub-clans correlate with neatly defined territorial boundaries, as current factional politics imply. The patchy environment and contingencies like drought and migration blur the relationship between clan and space. They increasingly make problematic local assertions by certain groups regarding an indigenous 'homeland'. The latter claim was at the source of considerable debate between clans and UN peace-keeping forces during 1992 to 1995 and there was considerable heated argument about who was indigenous to what area. Efforts centered on defining 'traditional' homelands of different Harti and Ogadeen groups, as well as other clans in the area, in an effort to claim and ethnically 'cleanse' certain lands. For instance, in a meeting of clan elders in 1993 a written request was made to the UN, with copies to the US embassy in Nairobi, defining which clans were indigenous to the border areas and asking that non-indigenous clans and their leaders be resettled outside of the Lower Jubba Region. Old ethnographic maps from the early twentieth century, which showed what clans supposedly occupied what territories at the time, were attached to support the elders' claims (see UNOSOM 1994b). Terms like 'indigenous', 'clan', and 'traditional' were used frequently in the written statement and in other similar pieces (ibid), since this was a discourse that seemed to play very well with the UN and Western governments. While apparently no action was taken by the UN, the local clan elders had clearly devised a political strategy in response to what they perceived as UN priorities for territorial claims and assertions on development resources.

Despite the recent migrations of the Marehan clan described in the previous chapter and the presence of other clans (e.g. the Shekaal and the Bimaal), the two most important clan groupings in the border region are the Ogadeen and the Harti (especially its Majerteyn clan).[3] Their significance is reflected in demographic, economic, and political terms. The Ogadeen, especially its Mohamed Zubeyr sub-clan but also including the Aulihan and Abdwak, are the majority group and greatly outnumber the Harti in the region (see Fig. 3.1). Because of their large size and

---

[3] The so-called MOD (Marehan, Ogadeen, and Dulbahante) coalition of Darood clans was considered to be the backbone of the Barre regime during the 1970s and the early part of the 1980s. In the 1970s the Ogadeen groups were particularly strong allies of Barre and were grateful for his attempt to capture Ethiopia's Ogadeen territories during the so-called Ogadeen War. In practice, however, political patronage and benefits were not evenly distributed among the three clans: 'the lion's share going to the Marehan, the leopard's share to the Ogaden, and the hyena's share to the Dulbahante' (Saed Samatar, cited in Markakis 1994: 252–3). The Dulbahante are part of the larger Harti group. What is important to note here is that at least some Ogadeen sections fought against their fellow Darood clans and allies, sometimes drawing support from non-Darood groups.

genealogical depth, Ogadeen identity and clan organization is exceedingly complex in the area. A prominent Ogadeen sub-clan, for example, can easily be larger than one of the region's smaller clans, and it is not uncommon for a Mohamed Zubeyr Ogadeen to identify his/her lineage affiliation when asked about clan affiliation. The Rer Abdille is a well-known Mohamed Zubeyr lineage that is especially prominent in cross-border trade activities in the area.

The Harti group, in turn, is largely represented in the area by its Majerteyn (primarily), Dulbahante, and Warsengeli clans. As mentioned in Chapter 2, they moved to the area from northern Somalia around the 1870s and have traditionally controlled parts of the Kismayo area since then. As a minority clan group in the area, their collective members referred to themselves in the 1980s simply as Harti, rather than use specific clan names (see Fig. 3.1). The Harti label also is how others referred to them. This is clearly no longer the case. With the increased fragmentation of clans and the competition between different sub-clans, the labels of Majerteyn and Dulbahante are commonly used now instead of Harti, and in some cases certain sub-clans of the Harti have opposed each other in local political battles.

The very terminology associated with kinship and clans in Somali culture is ambiguous, and I have found several Somali colleagues who are equally baffled by the terms and levels of clan organization. They do not easily sort themselves into discrete, mutually exclusive categories and even local respondents would contradict themselves when queried about kinship links. Part of the problem is that the different units are inherently unstable, combining and breaking apart as they respond to different political and economic conditions. One key, however, is that in a segmentary kinship system like Somali society, each unit is genealogically connected via male lines (patrilineal) to one founding ancestor. As Lewis points out, 'Genealogies tracing descent (*tol*) from common ancestors are the basis for the division of the population into clan and sub-clan' (1993: 47). In a segmentary kinship system like Somali society the overall structure provides the individual and groups with a guide to social relationships and location, but the smallest units of social organization, the family and lineage, are of most immediate relevance. Only under extreme circumstances, such as during times of conflict, do these smaller units aggregate into larger clan groupings for meaningful action.

If we use Lewis's (1955, 1961) clan schema, it is possible to place some descriptors on different levels of clan aggregation in the border region. At the highest level and in descending order of aggregation in Fig. 3.1 is Darood, one of the six main clan families in Somali society.[4] It encompasses and unites at a high level of aggregation the three main clan groups in the study region. Below this level but genealogically connected

---

[4] This is a very simplistic treatment of clan structures in Somalia and is limited to clans of the border region, particularly the Ogadeen and Harti. There are many good sources on Somali clan structures, including Lewis (1961; 1994) and Mansur (1995).

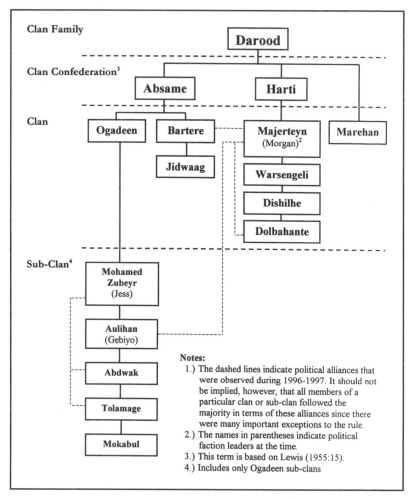

Fig 3.1   Darood clan groupings and political alliances in 1996–7, Somali borderlands[1]

nonetheless are what Lewis (1955) calls clan confederations, which in the border area are the Harti and Absame. These represent collections of individual clans, such as the Majerteyn, Dulbahante, and Ogadeen, which are the next level of aggregation in Fig. 3.1. The clan itself then can be divided into sub-clans, followed by lineages or primary lineages and families. The latter category serves as important identities only for the larger clans in the region, such as the Ogadeen (see Fig. 3.1). While a sub-clan can trace its origins back 15+ generations in some cases, a family may be limited to three or so generations depending on the circumstances. Within every primary lineage are *diya*-paying ('blood payment') groups of about four to six generations that are the main politico-jural units of customary political culture, and define the rights and responsibilities of members vis-à-vis other *diya* groups.[5] As Farah and Lewis point out, the Somali kinship system 'has the capacity to place each and every citizen in a corporate dia-paying lineage, where his basic rights are guaranteed and obligations clearly defined' (Farah and Lewis 1993: 12).

Negotiated identities
The failed 1994 Lower Jubba Peace and Reconciliation Conference cited earlier shows just how fluid and negotiable clan identities are, as well as how much they can be shaped by external forces. At the time Absame was an identity that was being invoked to try to unite a range of Ogadeen sub-clans and non-Ogadeen clans, such as the Bartere and Jidwaag (see Fig. 3.1). It was emphasized by Ogadeen elders and militia leaders, Colonel Omar Jess and General Nur Gebiyo[6], to counter a perceived alliance between the Harti and Marehan who both were wary of Ogadeen dominance. With its larger size, the Absame label allowed them to assume more of a national role for their movement, especially vis-à-vis other sizable political movements in Somalia (for example, the late Mohamed Farah Aideed's Hawiye-dominated United Somali Congress [USC]). Absame is an identity that was never mentioned at any time during my stay in the late 1980s, but seems to be the equivalent of a 'clan confederation' (like the Harti) using Lewis's terminology. As an Ogadeen Somali residing in Nairobi explained to me: 'It is a vague level of organization that is somehow genealogically above the Mohammed Zubeyr and Ogadeen' (Interview, 15 May 1996). When questioned further, he emphasized that it is a principle of clan organization that was not commonly heard in the area until the recent conflict and peace negotiations. When pushed on the point, he said 'it could be a clan, in some contexts being the equivalent of Ogadeen'. In the end the elusive Absame identity never became a political force in the area and some of the Absame clans, like the Bartere, eventually moved to Morgan's Harti-based faction.

Ambiguity over clan identity and political allegiance is increasingly the norm, rather than the exception in Somalia. Rarely is there a complete consensus among sub-clan and clan members regarding political affiliation. There always are members who cross clan and sub-clan lines. Even in the case of the Lower Jubba conference discussed earlier, at least six of the 80 participants were Ogadeen who shunned their own Absame meeting for a gathering dominated by non-Ogadeen (UNOSOM 1994a). It

---

[5] According to Lewis (1994: 20), the 'dia-paying group is essentially a corporate agnatic [patrilineal] group whose members are united in joint responsibility toward outsiders. The most important aspect of their unity is the collective payment of blood-compensation.'

[6] Gebiyo, a former Minister of Defense in the Barre government who eventually was jailed by the regime, emerged as leader of a militia faction with a strong Aulihan representation (Ahmed and Green 1999: 119).

is likely, however, that they were Kismayo-based Ogadeen who were involved in urban businesses. When one examines recent changes in political alliances, the pattern is especially confused if one looks only at clan affiliations. For example, within General Hersi Morgan's faction, a major political group in the region also called the Somali Patriotic Movement (SPM), important clan-based contradictions are revealed. Morgan himself is a Majerteyn, but there is a political rift between his and other Harti clans, while at the same time some Absame clans have joined his movement. Some of the client groups within the Majerteyn – such as the Gaaljaal – also have broken off and have clamored for their own recognition as a clan. By 1996 they were opposed to Morgan's Harti-based SPM and had allied themselves with other clans and sub-clans.

Among the Ogadeen clan relations and political alliances are equally baffling. For example, there was a major split among the Ogadeen between Omar Jess's Mohamed Zubeyr and General Gebiyo's Aulihan factions. This occurred in the mid-1990s and Gebiyo's group actually ended up joining with Morgan's forces. More recently (2001) Gebiyo's group has been part of the alliance headed by different warlords (including Hussein Aideed [the son of the late Mohamed Farah Aideed] and Morgan) that are opposed to the recently formed Transitional National Government (TNG) (see BBC Monitoring Service 2001). The Mohamed Zubeyr sub-clan, in turn, seem to have increasingly removed themselves from factional politics in the Lower Jubba, in part because of the failed leadership of Jess and others. This isolation has allowed them to concentrate more on pastoralism and commerce and, according to one elder, has enhanced their role in cross-border trade (interview, 20 June 2001). An additional outcome of this withdrawal seems to be a breakdown in the Marehan and Harti alliance. By 1998 the major conflicts in Kismayo town were between the Marehan and the Harti who have increasingly lost political control, and not between the Ogadeen and the Harti.

Not only do these endless clan scenarios impede political predictions, the fact that certain sub-clans and clans have special contractual and marriage relationships with other groups further complicates the matter. The Somali have a concept of a social contract (*xeer*) that crosses clan and sub-clan lines and is based on a number of different principles, the most important being that contracted parties are morally bound to assist each other (see Lewis 1994; Ahmed Samatar 1994a). Social groups united on the basis of *xeer* might reciprocate in terms of grazing and watering rights, commerce, and/or political affairs. When I would query an elder about why one particular sub-clan joined a particular political faction, even when it meant violating the segmentary kinship principle, there always was a cultural rationale for the action: 'they have always had a special arrangement with each other and have helped each other during hard times' (author's field notes). Marriage also is a common means used to justify inter-clan alliances: 'we have frequently married their daughters and they help us because of this' (ibid).

This process of clan construction (invention?) is not limited to the border area. Writing about another region of southern Somalia, the Bay Region, Helander et al. point out that 'some groups [the Asheraf] that in the past were regarded as "religious groups" not requiring a secular leadership on their own are now organized as the other clans ... the Asheraf have moved towards establishing themselves as an "ordinary" clan' (Helander et al. 1995: 6). Thus, to return again to the chapter's earlier discussions about identity construction, it is possible to make sense of these processes in the Lower Jubba when one pursues 'the historical construction of cultural differences [identities] within unequal fields of power' (Roseberry and O'Brien 1991: 9). In short, shifts in power relations are reflected in the region's changing configuration of clan and sub-clan identities, which in turn are shaped by the political context, not primordial, rigid allegiances.

The economic dimension

Politics notwithstanding, there also is a material basis to some of the clan and other social differences revealed in the region. For example, the Ogadeen Mohamed Zubeyr and the Harti generally vary in their economic pursuits, which in turn reflect important rural and urban differences. The Mohamed Zubeyr, who inhabit much of rural Afmadow District and a territory extending more than 100 km inside northeastern Kenya, are closely associated with cattle pastoralism and rural life. They are the primary reason why the region enjoys such large cattle herds. By contrast, the Harti pay considerably more attention to camel pastoralism than do the Mohamed Zubeyr, and reside mainly in Kismayo District. Until recently they comprised the majority group in Kismayo town. Many Harti are deeply engaged in commerce (including livestock trade) and control a number of the businesses in Kismayo town. While merchants from the late President's clan, the Marehan, made strong inroads into the cattle export trade during the 1980s, Harti remained central to this activity. The Ogadeen, in turn, are more exclusively pastoral; their commercial activities are limited to small retail trade and more recently the cross-border commerce. In short, the Ogadeen of the region are associated with cattle production and oriented toward Kenyan markets and towns, while the Harti are involved with cattle and camel trade and focused on Kismayo town.

Urbanism and clanism are not the only factors determining regional economic relations and patterns. There was clearly a class of businessmen and civil servants in Kismayo that traversed clan lines and rallied to support certain government policies that favored them. There also was a strong urban-based underclass of youth, who begged on the streets, shined shoes, engaged in petty theft, and later on served as armed thugs for different warlords. For some scholars, most conflicts were based on these inherent inequalities as evidenced in a widening gap between rural and urban: 'Many nomads had been called by their clan elders to

Mogadishu to help in the civil war and, once there, grew bitter at the stark contrast between rural and urban environments' (McGown 1999: 8). And so these pastoral migrants joined with the urban and unemployed youth, adding to an already volatile situation in Somalia's main cities. In explaining the roots of the Somali conflict, Abdi Samatar (1992) and Ahmed (1995a) probably come closest to arguing that urban-based class structures and glaring tensions between rural and urban (especially Mogadishu) populations are at the heart of the nation's predicament, not primordial clan hostilities. As Ahmed astutely points out, one of the most revealing outcomes of the civil war was that it 'revealed the "hidden" class character of urban areas like Mogadishu' (1995a: ix). Nonetheless, these class relations are increasingly articulated through an idiom of clans and sub-clans.

As described in Chapter 2, the influx of Harti clansmen brought them into direct confrontation with the Ogadeen over control of the Lower Jubba. The Harti in the 1880s 'were engaged in a struggle for political supremacy and control of local commerce with elements of the neigh-boring Maxamed Zubeer clan' (Cassanelli 1982: 181), and raids between the two groups were not uncommon. A few of the early Harti migrants eventually moved out of Kismayo into the surrounding range-lands and settled in areas as far south along the coast as Nilagaduud,[7] about 75 km south of Kismayo city. They also moved to smaller, Ogadeen-dominated centers like Afmadow, in order to establish market alliances with the Ogadeen nomads and to be closer to sources of live-stock supply. A small number of Harti merchants married Mohamed Zubeyr women. The town-based Harti merchants and large middlemen often extended credit to Ogadeen herders and small middlemen whom they depended on for trade, developing a network of market alliances in the area that crossed clan lines and extended into what is today northeastern Kenya (see Dalleo 1975: 142). When the cattle trade in the colonial period was centered on Kenyan rather than Somali markets, the Ogadeen nomads and middlemen reaped a substantial share of the commerce. When market conditions changed to favor the Kismayo port in southern Somalia, which often happened with surprising rapidity, the status of Harti traders was enhanced while that of Ogadeen declined. Despite the civil war, market networks of this type continue today and are crucial to understanding how traders have responded to recent political crises.

The majority of overseas export traders, most of whom were Harti or Marehan, were based in Mogadishu rather than Kismayo and, thus, approximately three-quarters of their net income left the region (see discussion in Chapter 5). What trader profits remained in the area were concentrated in Kismayo city itself, with virtually none of these

---

[7] The real name of this town has been changed to protect its identity. Nilagaduud is a fictitious name.

revenues accruing to traders in smaller centers, like Afmadow. Thus, the overseas commerce essentially benefited urban-based merchants and large cities, both of whom eventually became targets of armed conflict in the region. As recently as January 1999, a group of about 30 Harti residents from Kismayo were slaughtered by an armed faction in the region (*Daily Nation*, 7 January 1999) and other such incidents occurred in the 1990s (Reuters 1998). In contrast to the overseas trade, a large percentage of traders involved in the cross-border trade to Kenya reside in the region or across the border in Kenya, and most of the revenues from this commerce remain in the region. On the Kenya side, the vast majority is Ogadeen and is based in Garissa, where they comprise about 84 percent of the population (Kenya 1994: 6–24). While little of the net revenues from the overseas trade accrued to traders in smaller market centers, the distribution was very different for the cross-border trade. Fifty percent of trader profits from the Kenya trade remained in the Lower Jubba Region, with about 35 percent accruing to traders based in small Ogadeen towns.

In the pre-1991 period most of the middlemen who served as full-time agents for the export trade were from large towns of Kismayo District. While there are important exceptions, many of those who were tied into the overseas export trade were Harti. Agents also were frequently from the same clan as the exporters, but this was not always the case. Clan relationships did not eliminate the possibility of domination and exploitation by export traders. The manipulation of clan ideologies by larger, urban-based traders disguised to some extent what were markedly class-based relations.

Thus, regardless of clan allegiance traders often competed with each other and with local herders over markets and prices. As noted above, some of the clan divisions found in the region stem from the early colonial period, when British administrators found it expeditious to favor outsiders, like the Harti, and to encourage their migration to Kismayo town and its environs. The late Siad Barre's clan-based policy of 'divide and rule' and his favoritism for his own Marehan clan only deepened existing ethnic and rural–urban divisions and reinforced clan identities. The state's policies and control of force simply restricted the necessary political space for other types of identity to form. Like the rest of Somalia, mafia-type warlords in the area were able to capitalize on existing rural-urban and clan tensions after the overthrow of Siad Barre, through the recruitment of followers along clan and class lines

Clan affiliation also does little to mask the distinct wealth differences among herders and town-based merchants and among herders themselves. Since the 1980s the literature has documented the extent to which economic differentiation exists within pastoral communities, some of whom have been represented as relatively egalitarian (see Little 1992b). The border region is no exception. Among a sample of 88 herders the richest 12.5 percent of herders own nearly 70 percent of the camels in the region, while 12.5 percent own 39 percent of total cattle. The bottom 50 percent of pastoralists, in turn, control only 15 percent of total cattle. In terms of understanding rural–urban relations in the region, the significance of this is that wealthy herders[8] tend to have: (1) access to larger traders and more lucrative markets; (2) some involvement in non-farm (town-based) economic activities; and (3) consumption and expenditure patterns that are different from other pastoralists. Those herders with more livestock were likely in the pre-war period to have non-pastoral investments in towns and marketing relations with large-scale traders.

The dismantling of rural–urban ties

The towns of the border region assumed important social and economic roles in the regional economy prior to 1991. They played important roles as marketing, service, and consumption centers for surrounding herders and were focal points for the delivery of veterinary inputs, fodder, and, in some cases, water. For surrounding herders veterinary drugs were the major urban-based inputs that they purchased in the 1980s. As was noted in the previous chapter, the presence of trypanosomiasis in the region posed (and still poses) a major problem for pastoralists, and helps to explain the relatively large amounts of cash herders expend on veterinary drugs. In addition, smaller settlements within 60 km of Kismayo city served as critical watering points for herders, providing a critical input for herds during dry seasons. Prior to the war, the repair and maintenance of these boreholes depended on parts and skilled technicians from Kismayo or Mogadishu.

From an urban perspective, many town households maintained beneficial linkages to the pastoral sector that aided them immensely. Complex patterns of animal loaning and investment were maintained, whereby rural kinsmen and hired herders managed the livestock of urban residents. Urban-based livestock loaning and herding arrangements were widespread and linked the different sectors. In small pastoral towns, such as Afmadow, virtually all settled households kept livestock in the vicinity of the center, while in Kismayo town approximately 50 percent of households maintained herds in surrounding areas (Evans et al. 1988). In the case of Kismayo, these types of livestock exchanges are not nearly as extensive now (2002) as they were in the 1980s.

The regional market for goods and services still exists, but herders increasingly avoid the Kismayo market because of danger and political insecurity. By the mid-1990s Kismayo was virtually cut off from its live-stock-producing hinterland and from large parts of the agriculturally rich

---

[8] The term wealthy is used in a relative sense and is not meant to imply that herders are rich in absolute terms or in comparison to other social groups, including wealthy urban residents.

Jubba Valley, and traders from the main cattle-producing areas around Afmadow avoided the city's markets. Even earlier observations of the 1990s indicate that the town is 'cut off from its economic hinterland and most people in Kismayo fall into two categories, the hungry or the very hungry' (UNOSOM 1994b: 3). Part of the reason for the break with Kismayo market is the glaring tensions between the Harti-based faction and the surrounding Ogadeen-based militia, hostilities that erupted during 1991 and 1992 and in subsequent years as well (see discussion later in the chapter).[9] As this chapter has shown, the strains between the groups reflect long-standing differences that were 'silent' for most of the 1970s and 1980s but had existed since the early colonial period. Just as the colonial powers before them had done, outsiders (warlords) such as Jess and Morgan manipulated and aggravated these rivalries.

These tensions result in market segmentation and strong price and supply distortions in the region. For example, retail prices for such locally produced foods as maize, sorghum, and milk, are as much as two-to-three times higher in Kismayo than in surrounding markets (FEWS 1999a; WFP/FSAU 1995; also see Chapter 5). In addition, widespread shortages of food items in Kismayo result from its poor ties with surrounding areas. These patterns clearly were not evident in the pre-1991 era when regional market prices were fairly well integrated and price usually varied by local supply and transport costs (Evans et al. 1988: 78–9).

What is equally noteworthy is the absence of Kismayo and its merchants from the cross-border commerce with Kenya. Because they have to traverse Ogadeen lands, Kismayo cattle and products are rarely transported to lucrative Kenyan markets despite the obvious economic benefits of doing so (here again the caravan conflicts of the nineteenth century come to mind, see Chapter 2). Less than 2 percent of cattle sold during March to November 2000 at the largest border market – Garissa, Kenya – were from Kismayo (personal correspondence, Stefano Tempia) and virtually no Harti traders were found at the market. In short, hostilities have created extreme market and price distortions in and around Kismayo town, at one time the major market for the entire Jubba Valley.

Seasonal market settlements

The use of small market centers in the border region has replaced the reliance on large towns, but it varies according to the seasonal movements of herds and people. During the dry season purchases are made at small, seasonal settlements and at seasonal ('flying')[10] market centers

---

[9] For example, several references in the UNOSOM files and correspondence are made to skirmishes between the Ogadeen and Harti around Kismayo and south of the city during 1994. Outnumbered in the rural areas, Harti elders frequently sought UNOSOM's help in resolving their widespread conflicts with the Ogadeen (UNOSOM 1994b).

[10] The expression, 'flying' market centers, comes from a colleague and friend, Michael Cullen, who also worked in the area during 1987–8. He noted that seasonal markets packed up and moved so quickly that they seemed to be 'flying'.

established near dry-season water points. Whole market centers, ranging from a few to close to a hundred businesses, quite literally move as the herds migrate seasonally, while others only open during dry periods when herders congregate near water points. This seasonal pattern of markets is still maintained around the large water points and near the Kenya border, but its importance is minimal near conflict-ridden Kismayo and its suburbs. The fact that merchants have to 'chase' herders to sell products and buy animals rather than vice versa, shows the extent to which the seasonality of pastoralism influences the market. Herders mainly sell at times of the year when herd productivity is low and they need cash to buy food.

The seasonal marketplaces are composed of temporary structures that are hurriedly constructed to sell retail goods and a range of services. In the words of one shop owner with a retail business in the Lower Jubba Region: 'we move our small business to the watering points during the dry season; we know the herders will be there and will need to buy goods' (author's field notes). These temporary settlements assume considerably less importance during wet months, when herders and livestock disperse over a wide territory and the demand for consumption goods and the need to sell animals declines.

Prior to the war Kismayo, Afmadow, Jamaame, and other sizable centers were the most reliable sources of veterinary supplies. However, even then their importance in the veterinary trade also varied according to the seasonal movements of people and animals. For example, the importance of Kismayo town declined in the dry season when cattle herds congregated near the Jubba River and at the area's smaller, seasonal watering points. In the herder survey of 1987–8 Kismayo town only accounted for 30 percent of veterinary sales to herders in dry seasons, while it accounted for 76 percent in wet seasons when some herds moved toward coastal pastures. Yet, with the heightened tension between Kismayo and its hinterlands, few Ogadeen herders of Afmadow currently rely on the town to purchase veterinary supplies, or to sell livestock. Instead, they buy their inputs from itinerant traders who reside outside of Kismayo and who move with the nomads to different seasonal water and grazing sites.

Diversification and income distribution

In terms of income patterns the vast majority of pastoral household income, not surprisingly, is derived from animal sales (more than 75 percent of total). Milk sales and non-farm activities, in turn, account for only 7 and 13 percent of income, respectively. As will be discussed later, milk trade is a highly gendered activity that is dominated by women. The most common form of non-farm investments in the region was urban real estate and retail business and these mainly involved the wealthiest families. The majority of herders who had investments in Kismayo town were Harti and, to a lesser extent, Marehan, and this

Photo 3.1   Seasonal market settlement, Lower Jubba Region, Somalia (Peter D. Little)

pattern generally remained the same throughout the 1990s, with the exception of an increased Marehan involvement. For Kismayo herders, patterns of non-pastoral activities have been strongly disrupted in almost every year since 1991, while income patterns for Afmadow herders have changed little since 1991. With the destruction of many businesses in regional towns, those few herders with urban-based assets lost many of their investments. During the 1990s several businesses in Garissa, Kenya were started by Somali merchants, who previously owned enterprises in southern Somalia but departed after the state's collapse.

In spite of the overwhelming importance of livestock, many herders of the border region practice some form of cultivation in years of adequate rainfall. While floods, droughts, and warfare reduced the amount of agriculture in the 1990s by 50 percent or more in certain years, herders still pursue cultivation when rainfall is sufficient (Mumin 1995). In a sample of 88 herders in 1987–8, 55 percent of herders practised some form of rainfed agriculture, with an average farm size of 2.17 hectares (author's field notes). A large but undetermined percentage of current residents also pursue cultivation, as well as rely on harvested fodder to feed their herds (see FSAU 1998; FEWS 1997).

Market maidens and dairy trade

The dairy trade, an activity that embraces town and country in interesting ways, provides an informative perspective on rural–urban relations and how they have changed since the 1980s. It is a significant activity in the towns of Somalia and has always been an important livelihood strategy for women. Even prior to the civil war, the country had no 'modern' dairy processing industry, and even the largest cities, such as Mogadishu (population of about one million in 1988), were supplied through a system of petty traders and herders that operated with no government involvement. Dairy trade requires strong rural–urban linkages and market efficiencies, to avoid spoilage and waste, and is closely tied to large urban markets where consumption is concentrated. In the Somali context, pastoral dairy marketing linked together thousands of urban consumers, traders, and herders in a complex delivery system, which – unlike in other African countries – was not burdened by the presence of a large, monopolistic government or private firm.

It is important to understand how the dairy trade operated prior to the events of 1991, which – as will be shown – had important effects on the activity. In terms of rural-to-urban marketing, those herders who supplied milk on a regular basis usually resided within a 50-km radius of a large town. They maintained camels in their herd, because they are more reliable milk producers than cattle in a dry environment. For example, from 1987 to 1988 very few cattle herders in the Kismayo area sold milk, while 46 percent of camel pastoralists had dairy sales. The difference attests to the importance of the camel and town proximity in determining dairy sales.

Three important characteristics of the area's dairy marketing system were: (1) the virtual lack of scale and wholesaling; (2) the competitive nature of the market; and (3) its gendered dimension. Milk marketing was an extremely dispersed activity with thousands of different small-scale women traders involved. Even for the largest markets in Kismayo town, there was a visible absence of any large wholesaling enterprises. Urban-based retailers bought the milk directly from nomads or from traders based in the rural or peri-urban areas. Unlike livestock trade, costs of operation were relatively low for milk traders and, therefore, market barriers were few as long as the trader had retail contacts and suppliers. Because large numbers of women from nomadic settlements would periodically enter the market when cash was needed, competition was high and the market margins of urban-based traders were low.

In geographic terms there is a fundamental contradiction in the market forces shaping regional dairy trade. Traders are compelled to operate near towns because of product perishability and market access, but the bulk of low-cost surplus production is in the distant range areas. To manage this discrepancy, the trader often takes risks by trying to source milk as far away from the town as possible. To ensure that losses are kept to a minimum, Somali traders prefer to trade in 'sour' camel milk, which unlike cow milk can be stored up to three days without significant deterioration. By selling camel milk, they increase the supply catchment area by as much as 30 km and minimize spoilage and transport constraints.

The vast majority of milk sold in the border region was (and is) consumed in the three large regional towns: Kismayo, Gelib, and Jamaame. While milk markets in the large towns remain open throughout the year, they close in the smaller towns if there are no herds nearby to supply milk. Small settlements are directly served by nomadic women who move with their families and herds. By contrast, the large towns are served by peri-urban producers and urban-based milk traders who reside permanently in the location, insuring that the product is available throughout the year.

The normal method of transporting milk to urban markets is by foot or by small pickup trucks. Along the main coastal road south from Kismayo three trucks operated on average five to six days a week in 1987 and 1988. They mainly transported passengers, but they also moved consumer products like milk. In 1998 they operated with less frequency, often traveling only once or twice weekly, and trucks did not travel as far south as Nilagaduud because of factional hostilities. When the system was functioning, the pattern was as follows. The urban-based milk trader (called *abakaar*) sent an empty container(s) out into the rural settlements with a pickup truck every afternoon or early evening. At the other end, the trading partner filled the empty receptacle and delivered it to the truck driver in the morning for transport back to Kismayo. The urban-based trader awaited the filled container on the other end, and would sell the product in the market that day. The system worked remarkably well in the 1980s and there was very little theft. Importantly it helped to stabilize milk prices in Kismayo town, especially when compared to the 1990s.

The pattern of dairy trade changed dramatically after 1991, when Kismayo was effectively cut off from its hinterland and forced to depend on food imports and aid (see Jubaland Relief and Rehabilitation Society 1993). In those few cases in 1998 where transporters still made the coastal milk run, they charged very high fees that were reflected in excessive retail prices in Kismayo town. Transit or security fees also had to be paid, which also contributed to higher retail costs. Rather than being the most reliable milk market as it was in the 1980s, Kismayo soon experienced highly unstable prices and supplies, and became one of the most uncertain markets in the region. Figure 3.2 illustrates how milk prices and their volatility increased considerably in Kismayo during the 1990s relative to nearby Afmadow and surrounding areas. For example, from October 1995 to January 1996 the price of camel milk in Kismayo varied between US$0.33 to 0.67 per liter, which is well above price levels and variability in nearby market towns. While consumers were negatively affected by these changes in the dairy trade, they wreaked far greater havoc on those multitudes of women traders who depended on the activity for their livelihoods. Many Somali women have been forced into other, less remunerative forms of petty trade, such as firewood and charcoal sales.

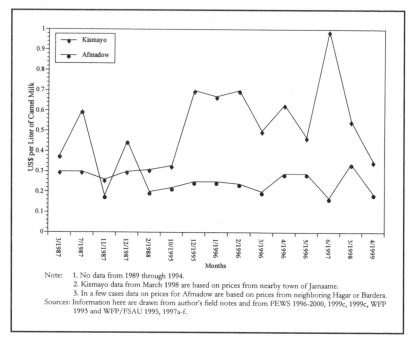

Fig 3.2   Camel milk prices in 1987–8 and 1995–9

Violence and resentment

Earlier discussion in this chapter revealed the differential benefits that urban-based merchants and cities earned from the overseas trade of the 1980s. By the end of that decade the border region was already experiencing a great deal of tension over cattle trade. Many overseas export traders, whose own profits were being squeezed by international competition, were delaying payments to local herders and middlemen; some reneged on payments altogether. Since a number of local Ogadeen pastoralists worked as hired herders for these urban-based Harti merchants, disputes over wages and working conditions also fomented local resentment. Many of the exporters had already aroused the hostility of local herders in the 1980s by constructing their own water points and fencing off areas around them (see Chapter 2). This questionable practice heightened tensions in key cattle zones like Afmadow, where there already were significant conflicts over pastoral resources. By the late 1980s most local herders in the region acknowledged that they had benefited little from the overseas export trade, and that those who had profited lived either in Kismayo city or in Mogadishu.

General Morgan, who entered the regional fray in 1992, was able to recruit members of his Majerteyn (Harti) clan and gain a strong base in the Kismayo area (see note 17, Chapter 2). A son-in-law of Siad Barre and a representative of the late President's faction, the Somalia National Front (SNF), Morgan also drew initially on the Marehan who, as indicated in Chapter 2, were at odds with the Ogadeen. Later the Marehan were to revoke any links with Morgan's group and lead a clan alliance that successfully evicted Morgan and his followers from Kismayo. Morgan depended on his own Harti clansmen who had benefited from the overseas cattle trade and other urban-based businesses. Morgan was a general in the Barre military who was best known for his vicious military campaign in 1988 against Somali opposition groups of Hargeysa in what is now Somaliland (see Ahmed Samatar 1994b). This action earned him the nickname 'Butcher of Hargeysa'. His regional rival in the 1990s, Colonel Omar Jess, recruited followers from the Ogadeen areas of Ethiopia and, at least initially, from the smaller towns of Afmadow District. They were predominantly members of the Mohamed Zubeyr section of the Ogadeen clan.

Some of the alliances, negotiations, and 'flip-flops' in allegiance that have taken place since 1991 are difficult to reconstruct. For example, the SPM split into two factions in 1993, one under the control of Jess and initially allied with the late General Mohamed Aideed's Somali National Alliance (SNA); and the other led by General Nur Gebiyo who was an Aulihan Ogadeen and tentatively linked to Morgan. By 1995 the Jess faction of SPM effectively had ceased to function and the Mohamed Zubeyr elders had begun to reconcile their differences with the Aulihan and Marehan through independent negotiations. Changes in different alliances have become even more complicated and divisions within factions more prominent since the mid-1990s (see Chapter 7). Kismayo remains a town of extreme strife and hardship for the most vulnerable segments of the population, women and children.

Fragile as they have been, the tragic result of the different political alliances was a series of deadly battles between Jess's (and Aideed's) and Morgan's forces during 1991 to 1993. They were mainly focused on Kismayo town and its port and airport. As noted in Chapter 2, the port had been 'modernized' with US government and other Western support just prior to the war and was (is) a prized goal of each faction. The most serious incident, and the one that can be traced most directly to rural–urban trade relationships, was the slaughter in December 1992 of as many as 220 Kismayo civilians by Jess's militia of young fighters (Africa Watch 1993: 7). The victims included prominent Harti clan elders and key Kismayo business, religious, and intellectual leaders. From interviews with Somalis who fled to Kenya and from news accounts, it is clear that most of those killed in Kismayo were Majerteyn/Harti, many of whom were likely to have had some involvement with livestock trade. Despite earlier assurances from UNOSOM and the UN Secretary General himself about regional peace after the signing of the Lower Jubba Reconciliation (Boutros-Ghali 1994), the potential for continued conflict and loss of life remains significant despite recent efforts to re-establish a government.

4
Tough ▮ Choices

> Over the four seasons, the [Somali] nomadic groups travel consid-
> erably, looking for water and for grazing land. Since good grazing is
> often many days of walking from the wells, the nomadic commu-
> nities need to be highly skilled in managing their stock (Laitin
> 1977: 20).

The chapter's opening quotation highlights the critical knowledge that
Somali herders must possess to manage their herds in an unpredictable
environment. These challenges are even greater during droughts when
herds need to be moved quickly over long distances. Despite conditions
of political instability and conflict, herders of the borderlands still must
make tough choices about where and when to move their animals, and
they have done so very effectively. Rainfall and drought, both factors
affecting pastoral decisions, are not affected by the presence of armaments, such as kalashnikovs ('AK-47s'). In terms of location (the 'where'),
pastoralists know well the areas of endemic livestock disease and insecurity, but under stress conditions they often have little choice but to use
them. While the stakes and risks associated with pastoral decision-
making are higher in Somalia than in most countries, insecurity also char-
acterizes large parts of the rangelands in the Horn of Africa, particularly
in the borderlands (see Fukui and Markakis 1994).

The choices governing daily life in the stateless Somali borderlands
generally cluster around the avoidance of three 'evils' of pastoralism:
drought, disease, and insecurity. Common options to overcome these
constraints entail mobility and maintaining favorable access to grazing
and water. Without these alternatives, a herder is extremely limited in
responding to drought and other potential catastrophes. Indeed, a case
can be made that just the single factor of *mobility* explains why certain
herding groups fare relatively well during climatic and other disasters,
while others do not. Mobility not only affects local responses to drought,
but it influences herd productivity and ecology as well (see Cossins 1985;

Western and Finch 1986). As this chapter will show, the maintenance of mobility as a risk management strategy[1] is a key reason why Somalia's livestock sector has not suffered as much as other areas of the economy.

Yet, it is the ability to be mobile, traverse long distances across harsh terrain, and avoid interactions with authorities that have always made nomadic pastoralists threatening to sedentary populations and states. Whether in the historical period of the Moghul empire or in contemporary Africa and Central Asia, pastoral populations often have been able to avoid political domination, as well as disrupt trade patterns and other economic activities when provoked (see Wolf 1982). Terms like militaristic, anarchic, brutal, and untrustworthy are frequently used to describe mobile pastoralists, and these negative labels have been around for several centuries (see Palmer 1977: 297). To quote from the fourteenth-century Islamic scholar, Ibn Khaldun, 'civilization always collapsed in places where the Arabs [nomads] took over and conquered' (1967: 304).

The contemporary examples of the Tuareg of Mali, Oromo of Ethiopia, Berber of Algeria, and Baluch of Pakistan and Iran demonstrate that confrontations between nomadic pastoralists and sedentary states still define important politics in many regions of the world. Their persistence also shows how control of informal trade networks and inhospitable frontier areas (borderlands) can be effective defenses against political and economic domination. The territories of pastoralists are often avoided by governments, because they are perceived as 'ungovernable' or 'insecure' as in the case of the Somali areas of northeastern Kenya. Thus, when formal states collapse, such as happened in Somalia, herders who rely little on government services often survive better than other populations.

The Somali borderlands represent a unique opportunity to address herder decision-making under a range of different risk scenarios. While climatic instability and livestock disease are normal parameters, as they are in most semi-arid areas of Africa, the situation is attenuated in southern Somalia because of widespread insecurity and the lack of a central government. Although there has been considerable attention to herd management strategies under conditions of drought in Africa (see McCabe 1994), few works examine the interplay between disease, drought, and conflict. This gap endures despite the fact that during periods of prolonged low rainfall, disease and insecurity can cause greater losses of livestock than drought itself.

The present chapter addresses each of these risks in the context of local decision-making in the Somali border areas. Ironically, Somali herders of

---

[1] Market access is another critical, risk-mitigating strategy that has allowed Somali herders to survive, and even prosper, since 1991 (see discussion in Chapter 5). At the onset of an unusually low rainfall period a herder might assume the worst (i.e. climatic and livestock conditions will continue to deteriorate) and unload animals on the market, often at severely reduced prices. Since herders are very dependent on grain consumption, they must deal with the market even when conditions are unfavorable. In this sense, distance to livestock and cereal markets can influence herders' decisions and movements, even when conditions are less than optimal.

the region have fared better during recent droughts than their pastoral neighbors in Kenya, who have seen as much as 50 percent of their cattle perish (see Kenya 1993a; FEWS-Net/CARE International 2001: 3–4). While conflict constrains herd movements in some sites, Somali pastoralists generally maintain their strategies of mobility and access. When one gazes beyond the popular images of Somali 'anarchy' and 'chaos' so prevalent in popular media accounts and, instead, fixes on the realities of economic life, the situation is not as depicted. In fact, the pastoral economy is operating relatively well, particularly when compared to herding systems of its 'peaceful' neighbors, Kenya and Ethiopia (see Fratkin 1991; Little 1992b; Anderson and Broch-Due 1999).

The political ecology of herding

To comprehend herding in the borderlands, it is necessary to revisit the area's unique geography and ecology, topics that were covered in Chapter 2. As was pointed out then, herd movements are strongly influenced by several environmental features: (1) the Jubba Valley; (2) the Lag Dera (and Jira) complex; (3) the coastal zone; and (4) the tsetse fly belt. Seasonal migrations are heavily shaped by these different ecological features, which together define distinct dry and wet season grazing zones. Generally the lengthiest herd migrations occur during the long dry and wet seasons and require movements between the coast and the Jubba Valley or between Lag Dera/Jira and the Jubba Valley. In the rainy seasons (April–June and October–December), herders move their cattle to pastures located away from the coast and the Jubba River, where tsetse flies are abundant during these times. The Lag Dera complex, located approximately 50 km northwest of Afmadow town, is home to hundreds of herder families and their livestock during these humid months. In dry periods seasonal pastures in Descheeg Waamo and along the Jubba Valley become very important (see Fig. 4.1). When the long rains fail, as happened in 1987–8, 1996, and 1999–2000, cattle may utilize seasonal pastures for only a few months before being moved to drought refuge areas in the Jubba Valley or outside the region.

Herders also obtain nutrition for their animals from agriculture. After crops have been harvested in the Jubba Valley, it is common for herds to graze on the stubble from the harvested fields. This often takes place at the end of August and September, and farmers usually charge herders as much as US$12 to US$15 for a harvested field of about 2 hectares (see Janzen 1988; Merryman 1996). In some cases, livestock keepers around Afmadow plant sorghum and if the harvest looks to be poor they open the fields to their cattle, abandoning any hope for a crop yield.

The best wet season grazing areas are located in the northern and western parts of the border region, which explains why cattle and people generally migrate from south to north during these months. It is not

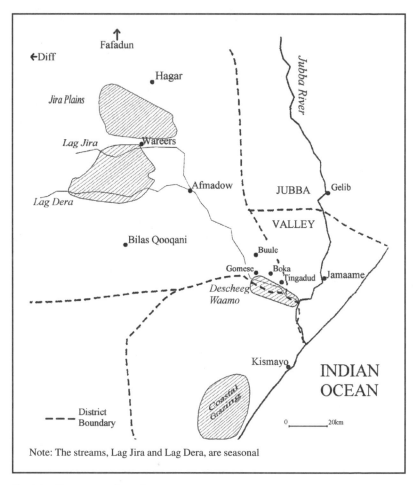

Fig 4.1   Key seasonal grazing areas

uncommon for Somali herders to cross the border and graze their animals in northeastern Kenya during rainy months (similar patterns of border crossing also occur along the Somaliland/Ethiopia frontier, see Samatar 1989). As noted above, the direction of movement is reversed in the long dry season (*jilaal*) and Kenyan herders often cross into Somalia then. The statelessness of the region facilitates these cross-border movements, but they even occurred frequently pre-1991.

The best area for camel and goat production is in the coastal zone of Kismayo District and north of the Jira plains near the border (see Fig. 4.1). Because camels and goats are browsers rather than grazers, they do not directly compete with cattle for feed. However, camels can indirectly affect cattle production by encouraging bush and tree encroachment when they feed. As was noted in Chapter 2, this was a bitter point of contention among cattle herders of Afmadow after their grasslands were encroached by camel herds. Camels usually move in the opposite direction from cattle depending on the availability of labor. During the year, labor-constrained households do not always have the flexibility to move herds optimally, nor to separate animal species into distinct units according to feeding requirements. They also may not have adequate workers to split herds into wet (milking) and dry (non-milking animals) groups, a common feature of pastoral herd management throughout Africa. Camels generally are found near the coast during the long rains, but migrate into the interior during dry seasons. At these times most cattle are trekked in the opposite direction. Camels rarely enter the Jubba Valley area or other potential wetlands, because they are extremely susceptible to water-borne foot infections and to trypanosomiasis.

Sub-clans claim different parts of the rangelands and their customary grazing areas are well known and include both dry and wet season areas. They are generally referred to as *deegaan*, a type of ecological unit encompassing a variety of different landscapes and circumscribing settlement and grazing patterns, but without precise boundaries in most cases (see Barkhadle 1993). More than one sub-clan can utilize a single *deegaan* during the year, as is the case in the border area. Key ecological zones, like the Jubba Valley and Lag Dera, also host multiple claims during the dry season. Except in a drought the sub-clan usually remains within its customary grazing areas, which can cover several thousand square kilometers, and its members carefully defend their prime dry season pastures. Demarcations between different groups and their grazing rights have become rigid in the past decade following increased conflict and competing territorial claims, but some flexibility still remains.

The imposition of boundaries also assumes importance during droughts when good grazing becomes scarce. As the dry season progresses and pastures are increasingly limited, herders may even fence off small parts of a particularly rich zone and restrict use to their calves and milk cows. Once the rains return and the herders move out, the temporary thorn fences are removed and the pastures are again open to communal use or to farming. As was shown earlier, during droughts different clans and subclans make agreements among themselves to allow for movements outside of customary areas and for reciprocal use of grazing and water.

The Mohamed Zubeyr Ogadeen generally control the pastures of Descheeg Waamo and other parts of the Lower Jubba in the dry season. The Aulihan, in turn, hold the middle Jubba Valley areas north of Gelib, while the Harti make use of dry season pastures and water near the coast or in that part of the Jubba Valley nearest Kismayo. The grazing territories of the Aulihan and Mohamed Zubeyr extend across the Kenya border, and the Aulihan, in particular, claim a sizable part of northeastern Garissa

District, Kenya. Because most of these groups are mobile, it is difficult for them to guard against encroachment and, consequently, conflicts are common along the edges of different sub-clans' boundaries.

Natural factors help to regulate the seasonal use of pastures and minimize potential trouble. When surface water dries up in wet season zones, populations gravitate toward areas with perennial water. They are compelled to do so unless they own a water point or can afford to truck in water, which some wealthy traders do. By contrast, when the long rains arrive herders quickly leave dry season pastures, especially those in the Jubba Valley, because of tsetse fly infestation. In short, nature helps to insure some regularity of seasonal grazing patterns, although as will be shown later there are numerous exceptions.

Private and communal rights to water points are better defined than are claims to pastures, which can be particularly fuzzy. Control of water has a major effect on grazing patterns. For instance, the closing of a motorized borehole or group of wells is an especially effective way to insure that herders and herds disperse during the rains. The refusal to allow a group of herders to utilize a private water point is another means of control and sends a similar message. Indeed, decisions about when to open and close a water point, especially a major source like a borehole, have a tremendous impact on seasonal herd movements. With the exception of private wells and ponds, such decisions are made by elders from the community where the borehole is located. Outside herders may petition (and even pay) elders to open up a borehole when water is particularly scarce and in some cases they may succeed. By maintaining some control over access to water, the community is able to regulate grazing in the surrounding areas. As was shown in Chapter 2, local herders are very aware of the environmental damage that can be done by unregulated water use.

Herd management strategies

The prime unit of decision-making for livestock matters is the family home-stead (called *haaz* or *reerka*) consisting of the husband and one or more wives and their children. Under Islamic law a Somali husband can have up to four wives. The main milking animals are kept and herded in this unit and are kept at night in a circular bush enclosure in the center of the home-stead. The *reerka* is a very independent unit with regard to decisions about where and when to move livestock. Its average size in the border region was slightly more than nine members in the late 1980s. Each wife and her children reside in separate one-room dwellings (called *aqal*) within the homestead, as do young married sons and their children. The woven mats and wooden poles that make up an *aqal* are packed up and moved on camels and donkeys when a homestead shifts its base location. Two or three homesteads related through male kinsmen or patrilineal descent may move seasonally together and cooperate in herding and watering activities. These kin-based encampments can include up to 10 related families at times, but rarely are they larger than three or four homesteads in the border areas. They are not stable units and homesteads frequently break off from encampments depending on where they decide to graze and water their animals. During the dry season a settlement consisting of several dozen kin-related and non-kin homesteads may cluster around a vital water point.

During the year the homestead herd is split up and responsibilities for the herding of different livestock species are allocated to specific family members. Young men between the ages of 17 to 26 years are usually out with 'dry' (males and dry cows) herds of cattle for much of the year, especially during dry seasons. Cattle herds under the care of boys and young men are separated from the main homestead at remote camps during the long dry season and part of the long rains. Cattle are often moved to grazing areas that are different from those for camels; mixed herds of cattle and camels only remain in the same area for three to four months of the year. Herd camps are delivered grains and foods from the main domestic homestead. Those domestic units with more camels than cattle tend to be very mobile, since camels are grazed during much of the year at considerable distances from the main family dwelling. Those homesteads that own all four types of animals (cattle, camels, goats, and sheep) usually keep a large proportion of the camels away from the main homestead in separate grazing units (called *geel her*, Lewis 1993: 51) during much of the long dry and wet seasons.

Most homesteads of the border region combine at least some goat and sheep production with cattle and camel raising, although some specialization does occur. Herd diversification, a common strategy throughout Africa's rangelands, is an important risk-hedging tactic because it allows herders to avoid sweeping losses when a single species is affected. Certain advantages, however, also derive from specialization. These include being able to allocate labor more efficiently and adjust seasonal movements and camps according to the grazing requirements of only one animal type. In the border region, herders of Afmadow come closest to pursuing a form of specialized cattle pastoralism.

The main or base homestead usually moves with the female cows and calves and joins up with the other family herds and herders for at least part of the year. When families are on the move between a prime dry and wet season grazing area, a distance of about 80 km in most of the border area, they can move camp every two to three days. They cover daily distances up to 20 km and most of the arduous work of loading and unloading pack animals is done by women. In at least four cases during the 1987–8 drought, homesteads moved their animals by truck to distant grazing locations, in some cases traveling more than 200 km. As noted earlier, small ruminants (goats and sheep) are not usually separated from the main homestead during the year. Consequently they provide an important source of food for families during the dry season, when part of the cattle and camel herds are in grazing camps.

Herding units supplement their own family labor either by hiring herders or by combining their animals with those of other families and then sharing tasks. While only 20 percent of homesteads hire labor – and most of these are involved in livestock trading – a much larger proportion depend on kinsmen and neighbors for assistance. Herders frequently combine herds to facilitate the labor-intensive task of watering animals during dry seasons. Up to five or six pastoralists will cooperate in manually pulling water from a well or wells and pouring it into earthen troughs. At the wells young herdsmen use rubber buckets made from old tire tubes to draw the water, while others toss it into a trough and supervise the watering of livestock. While busily tending to their thirsty animals, herders often joke, socialize, and sing among themselves.

Several important differences in grazing patterns occur in the region. Perhaps the most significant of these relate to mobility and herd movements. Herders of Kismayo District are considerably more sedentary and less dependent on livestock than those of Afmadow District, a pattern that was attenuated during the 1990s. As was noted in Chapter 3, Kismayo District remains generally insecure and as a result population movements are heavily constrained. The differences in mobility between Afmadow and Kismayo pastoralists are especially apparent by the length of seasonal movements. For example, herders of Afmadow migrate their herds and flocks on average about 2.5 times further than Kismayo pastoralists. Afmadow families and their herds move an average of 52 km per season or about 208 km annually, while the corresponding distances for Kismayo homesteads are about 20 km and 80 km, respectively. In addition, 50+ percent of Kismayo herders move their livestock less than 10 km during the long rains (*gu'* season), but only one-third of Afmadow residents move such a short distance. These differences in mobility are even more significant when one considers that Kismayo herders have a higher proportion of camels than Afmadow pastoralists and, therefore, a greater need for mobility.

What are the reasons for these differences in mobility between Afmadow and Kismayo herders? Even before the insecurity of the 1990s at least two processes were at work that might account for the discrepancies. First is the influence of the regional city of Kismayo. The presence of the town encourages a sedentary form of pastoralism, since herders try to remain nearby to trade animal products and purchase cereals and other necessities. Second are differences in tenure and seasonal grazing rights, both of which are strongly influenced by clan and sub-clan membership. These affect mobility as well. Because most Kismayo herders are Harti, their access to Lag Dera and other distant grazing areas is limited. As Chapter 3 pointed out, the Harti originally moved to Kismayo to trade, and herding families who accompanied them settled southeast and northwest of the city up to about 75 km from the town. Beyond those circumscribed areas, their movements are heavily constrained by Ogadeen groups like the Mohamed Zubeyr.

The grazing boundaries for different clans and sub-clans were generally fluid prior to 1991, although even then few Harti herders ventured very far into Ogadeen areas without prior permission. As I have discussed elsewhere, these restrictions have become rigid and the circumscription of Kismayo grazing patterns has only worsened since 1991. There is now a no-man's land (buffer) of about 15 km at the interface between Harti and Ogadeen-controlled areas, where human settlements and livestock rearing face high security risks. The exact location of this buffer area fluctuates according to the fortunes and maneuvers of different regional factions. For example, in 1992 and 1993 the Harti were able to graze their herds as far south as Nilagaduud, a distance of about 75 km from Kismayo town, because of the presence and protection of Morgan's followers in the area. Other political changes in southern Somalia, usually short-term in duration, have affected the movement of buffer zones.

The increased risks of grazing in insecure areas are not purely random, nor have they affected herd movements as much as expected. In discussions with herders and traders in 1996 and 1998, it was clear that insecure areas were well known. Pastoralists had access to sufficient information to decide when security had improved and what grazing conditions were like even in conflictive areas. Recall the example from Chapter 2, when drought-affected families in 1996 successively migrated their animals to unstable areas along the coast south of Kismayo town. Herders of large clans, like the Ogadeen, who control massive chunks of wet and dry season grazing have moved with relative ease throughout their area since 1993.

Seasonality
Regardless of conflicts and politics, pastoralism is strongly affected by seasonality. This is a simple reality of trying to make a living in a dry region where seasonal mobility is the key. In Afmadow District, where the population is considerably more nomadic than in other parts of the border zone, cattle migrations are longest during the long dry and wet seasons. As noted earlier, the pattern of camel movements is different and they often move in the opposite direction from cattle. While the excessive water in the *gu'* season disperses camel herds, it attracts cattle and small stock rather than scatters them. They do not have to move as far then for pastures and water. At other times of the year Afmadow cattle move greater distances than camels, because they are unable to utilize nearby browse species. Regardless of these differences, the data show a general pattern whereby the greatest dispersions are during the long wet and dry seasons and the smallest in the other two seasons (*deyr* and *xaga*) (see Table 4.1). These distances generally exceed the length of seasonal movements on the other side of the border in Kenya, where – as noted earlier – mobility and access to grazing is increasingly restricted.

Despite the infestation of tsetse flies, the Jubba Valley strongly influences regional livestock movements. Its significance explains why

Table 4.1. Distance of grazing migrations of livestock by season: Afmadow herders[1]

Season	Cattle	Movement (km)		
		Camel	Sheep/goats	all
Long dry season	70.22	34.50	61.18	67.32
Long wet season	60.29	135.00	49.89	61.34
Short dry season	44.00	19.00	40.22	42.38
Short wet season	37.64	14.50	29.56	35.40
Average all seasons	53.49	50.75	46.05	52.09

Note:
[1] Based on a sample of 42 homesteads and their livestock holdings.

herders so violently resisted irrigation investments in the valley, often harassing tenants and damaging costly infrastructure. When the opportunity arose following the collapse of the government, these schemes were pillaged and effectively destroyed, which reopened large parcels of riverine grazing. During dry periods the heavy use of grazing areas in the Jubba Valley area highlights the valley's critical role. For instance, in Afmadow alone more than 60 percent of *jilaal* (long dry) season movements are to the Jubba River area, with the figure dropping to 22 percent during rainy months.

The use of the rich ecology of Lag Dera and nearby grazing locations shows equally dramatic seasonal differences. As noted earlier, the main seasonal migrations in the region tend to occur between the Jubba Valley and these upland pastures, covering distances of about 80 to 120 km. If the annual long rains arrive on time, then most herders will move their cattle and small stock toward Jira and Lag Dera where surface water is available. Near the end of the long wet season, herders begin to drift back toward the Jubba Valley unless, of course, there is fighting there. This annual cycle changes if the short and long rains fail to produce sufficient precipitation. Even when armed conflict erupts in the valley, herders know which locations to avoid, or they graze their animals in the northern part of Descheeg Waamo away from the river.

Labor availability and herd size
Why do certain herders remain in the Jubba Valley area for much of the year, despite the presence of tsetse flies and potential conflict, while others do not? By examining differences in herd movements according to a wealth indicator like cattle ownership, we can begin to address this question. Thus, for example, while the average size of mobile cattle herds in Afmadow is about 75 head, it is considerably less for those herders who remain sedentary in the Jubba Valley during most of the year. Most herders who use the Jubba Valley during the long wet season, a period of high disease risk, are poorer on average than other pastoralists (see Table 4.2). They generally own less than 30 cattle, with virtually none controlling more than 50. By contrast, those herders who are mobile and seasonally

Table 4.2. Average cattle owned at different grazing zones, long wet season[1]

Grazing location	Average cattle owned
Afmadow	47.14
Boji	75.00
Boka, JV[2]	6.00
Borsanga	39.00
Buule, JV	41.50
Descheeg Waamo, JV	44.50
Diif	70.00
Fafadun	165.00
Gomese	50.00
Hagar	172.00
Jira	67.20
Bilas Qooqani	95.67
Tingadud, JV	48.50
Tortora	133.50
Wareers	362.00
All	74.74

Notes:
[1] Based on a sample of 42 herder households of Afmadow District.
[2] JV = Jubba Valley.

shift to grazing areas outside the Jubba Valley and its tsetse fly corridor, have relatively large herds. The majority of these households control more than 100 head of cattle and also possess large numbers of other livestock. In short, those herders who are sedentary in the Jubba Valley area where they face additional production and security risks are from the poorest wealth categories, while those who migrate are among the wealthiest.

The important relationship between livestock wealth and labor availability also explains why certain domestic units are less mobile than others. Herders with fewer animals are usually associated with relatively small families and households and, therefore, have less labor for migrating and herding animals. With fewer potential laborers in the household, they are more constrained in management decisions than richer, more labor-abundant units. While the average homestead size in the region is 9.07 members, it is less than 7.5 for units with less than 50 cattle. Among homesteads with relatively small cattle herds there is less polygamy among family heads and fewer dependants (children) to help with herding.

The homestead of Ibrahim is typical of a labor-constrained homestead.[2] With only one young son of about 14 years, and the rest of his children below the age of 10 years, he and his wife do much of their own herding. Homesteads, such as Ibrahim's, which control few cattle and workers, usually do not move great distances during the year. Ibrahim moves his herd of 25 cattle about 20 km between seasons, usually remaining within

[2] Pseudonyms are used for informants throughout the book.

the general proximity of Descheeg Waamo near the Jubba Valley. By doing this, he avoids time-consuming watering tasks and the need for long migrations, but he exposes his herd to additional disease and security risks during the year. In 1987–8, labor-constrained households like Ibrahim's, who migrated less than 100 km during dry seasons, owned an average of about 63 cattle while those who moved more than 100 km had an average of 103 cattle. Clearly, those homesteads with large herds and additional family members have a greater capacity to utilize distant pastures and water points than other herders.

The flexibility to migrate to distant pastures is a key reason why Somali herders are more successful during droughts than their Kenyan counterparts. It also helps to explain why they have been able to avoid many of the war atrocities that settled farmers and agropastoralists have confronted. They simply move when danger strikes. This strategy is dictated by more than herd size and labor availability; it also centers on access to pastures and water. Herders maintained favorable access to many of their customary grazing areas after the government's collapse. Outside of small patches of agriculture along the Jubba Valley and near settlements, there are few impediments on the Somalia side that restrict herd access and mobility. Unlike northern Kenya, there are no large-scale commercial ranches or national parks and wildlife reserves to compromise pastoral movements and, as mentioned earlier, most large-scale irrigation projects in Somalia have been in disuse since 1991. In short, flexible access and mobility place Somali herders at a considerable advantage over their neighbors in Kenya and Ethiopia. In these countries national governments have done much to restrict adaptive strategies and threaten pastoral systems, resulting in herd losses of more than 60 percent during prolonged droughts (see Little 1992b; FEWS-Net/CARE International 2001).

An examination of herd management strategies during the 1987 drought shows the importance of mobility for Somali pastoralists. By July of that year the long rains in the Lower Jubba had consisted of only a few showers, with a combined total of about 20 mm of rainfall or less than 30 percent of normal amounts. Confronted with dim prospects for improvement, several Afmadow herders considered options outside of the Lower Jubba Region. The pastures of the Jubba Valley had been exhausted and movement to Kenya was difficult because of a lack of surface water along the way. However, the long rains had been adequate in the Lower Shebelle Region, a distance of more than 150 km north of the Jubba Valley, and surface water and pastures were plentiful there. Although Afmadow herders have few clan relations in the region, their elders successfully negotiated an agreement with the community to graze there. Despite a certain degree of tension between the different clans, several families were allowed to graze their animals in the Lower Shebelle area where only a few months earlier armed clashes had occurred. Reciprocal grazing rights were respected, in part because earlier in the decade the Lower Shebelle people sought and were granted refuge in the Lower Jubba Region during a previous drought. When I reinterviewed herders who had gone on the long trek in 1987, very few reported high levels of cattle mortality, although there had been virtually no rain for about nine months in the border region.

As was discussed earlier, Somali herders in 1996 were also able to avoid massive drought losses by moving animals more than 150 km to areas along the Indian Ocean coast. They moved to the coast with few incidents and returned to their normal areas when the rains began. While other recent examples of grazing agreements were not recorded, they likely exist based on the relatively good condition of the area's livestock sector in the 1990s. Had mobility and access to grazing been severely constrained and livestock production jeopardized by war, southern Somalia would not have become the major supplier of livestock for Kenyan markets that it has (see Chapter 5).

Confronting risk through 'modern' means

The capacity to utilize key grazing zones that are plagued by tsetse flies is contingent on purchases of veterinary medicines. While Somali herders forcefully resist aspects of modernity that threaten their livelihoods, they embrace modern inputs, such as veterinary medicines, that have proven effective. Chapters 2 and 3 showed how local herders rarely depended on government veterinary services and products, even prior to its collapse. Instead, they relied on unofficial channels to obtain drugs from private traders, a pattern that also was evident during 1996 to 1999. Herders purchase medicines to help mitigate animal disease risks and to graze infected areas, like the Jubba Valley and the coast. It is the reliance on these purchased inputs that further motivates Somali herders to pursue commercial livestock sales, so they will have adequate cash for veterinary expenditures.

Veterinary inputs are just one of the production inputs that pastoralists of the border region purchase. In addition to livestock ('herd capital'), two other purchased inputs are water and fodder. The use of these and other inputs vary considerably by season and cost. For example, both fodder and water costs increase considerably during the dry season, while the use of hired labor declines at that time. In the wet seasons, the presence of trypanosomiasis in the region accounts for the relatively large amount of herder (and trader, see Chapter 5) monthly expenditures on veterinary drugs. Herders usually administer the drugs themselves, which come in capsule or powder form. Almost one-half of homesteads own syringes, utilizing them when injections are required. A very high proportion of herder households – 75 percent of the total – purchase at least some veterinary inputs during the year.

Water also is frequently purchased and affects decisions about livestock movements. Cattle are usually watered daily during most of the year, except at the end of the long dry season when they may be watered on alternate days. Based on their need for water, cattle normally can graze no more than about 30 km from a water source. In rainy periods, herders water their livestock at seasonal ponds, swamps, and other depressions that temporarily hold water. This resource is procured free of charge, as is the use of water from the Jubba River. In dry months, however, local pastoralists rely on water from different sources and often are required to pay for it. For instance, herders are charged fees by owners of water storage tanks (called *barkad*) and at some community-managed boreholes and surface dams. Part of the payment is used to maintain watering points, and in some cases users are asked to provide labor toward maintenance tasks.

Homestead data reveal that a majority of herders (59 percent of the total) purchase water for their cattle during dry seasons. In the border region, the most common source of water in the dry season is motorized boreholes, which at one time were operated by the government but are now under the control of local communities (see Chapter 2). They account for approximately 90 percent of water purchases, with expenditures on water from surface dams and storage tanks accounting for the remainder. Most boreholes are located near market towns, such as Afmadow or Kismayo, or in rural settlements whose population and commercial activities fluctuate greatly depending on whether or not the borehole is open. The boreholes cease to operate in wet seasons, when surface water is available and livestock disperse into wet season grazing zones. During particularly dry years, like 1996 and 1999, herders may be forced to purchase water even during normally wet months.

Thirty-two percent of herders in the region own some kind of a water point. Among those who own water sources, 68 percent have a small surface dam/pond (called *war*, singular; *waro*, pl.), while 29 percent own a well. A large number of the *waro* were built during 1981 to 1987, when the vestiges of the World Bank-financed Trans-Juba Livestock Project operated a water development unit (see Chapter 2). Private wells, in turn, are constructed by hand and many of the current owners inherited them from their fathers. Some have been in the region for more than fifty years. The use of wells generally is restricted to family members and kinsmen, but in practice other herders often utilize them free of charge.

As was mentioned in Chapter 2, the past government charged a fee to use their motorized boreholes, but in reality the fee was determined by the local community and based on the real costs of salary, maintenance, and fuel. With the outbreak of the war in 1991, communities initially depended on NGOs and UNICEF for help in maintenance and spare parts but currently utilize their own resources. A friend and colleague working in the border area remarked how a community approached him in 1999 about finding a particular part for its pump. According to the story, the members of the community showed a remarkable familiarity with the

Photo 4.1   Cattle watering, Afmadow area, Somalia (Peter D. Little)

technology and maintenance requirements, indicating which particular European and American manufacturers were better than others.[3] They were said to know exactly what part they needed and provided information both on the manufacturer and part number. They wanted help in finding a supplier in Nairobi or Europe and volunteered to pay for the part in advance. Such tales further confirm the point that even without a state, Somali herders remain plugged into regional and global circuits of trade and information.

While labor is another important input to livestock production, only 20 percent of homesteads hire labor and, consequently, labor markets have little influence on decisions about herd management and movements. Instead, most labor utilized in livestock production derives from unpaid family contributions or from reciprocal/exchange arrangements. Where labor is hired, the herders usually are paid in animals rather than cash, and the usual payment is a two to three year-old bull plus subsistence food for every six months of work.

The purchase of animals for breeding and herd reconstitution represents the largest cash expenditure for herders. Research on African livestock markets frequently overlooks the fact that herders use them both to sell and, importantly, to restock their own herds (see Bailey et al. 1999). At any given market in the border region up to 10 percent of daily transactions are for purposes of restocking, and access to these markets figure in the daily decisions of herders. Somalis frequently purchase young bulls and cows at these markets to enhance herd reproduction, compensate for animals sold, and/or maintain and fatten for future sale. It is not unusual for a herder to sell and buy animals at the same market on the same day. During drought years, however, very few pastoralists actually purchase breeding stock, but instead they often sell them, effectively jeopardizing future herd growth.

[3] This story comes from Stefano Tempia.

This desperate tactic means that when conditions improve herders usually re-enter markets to purchase animals for rebuilding their herds.

A scenario of tough choices

In the Somali case, three variables largely explain the ability of herders to successfully respond to disasters: *accessibility, mobility,* and *marketability.* Other variables are important, but it is suggested here that they either are not as important or are covered by these three factors. So far, this chapter has shown why accessibility and mobility are vitally paramount for pastoral decision-makers, especially during difficult times, but it has dealt little with the effects of markets. A brief reference to the border region during the drought of 1987–8 illustrates the added significance of what I call marketability. In the Lower Jubba case, where more than 75 percent of cash income for herders derives from the sale of livestock and their products, the terms-of-trade factor ('marketability') strongly influences herder wealth and income (see note 1). When prices for livestock and live-stock products are favorable vis-à-vis the main expenditure item, grain, real incomes for herders rise (also see Chapter 6). In short, marketability influences local wealth and herder incomes, which in turn impact on herding decisions during droughts.

A simplified schema can be constructed that highlights different choices at various points during a climatic disaster: one month, three months, and four months after the start of a drought. The model is derived from field observations during the 1987–8 drought, but is generally applicable to more recent events. Since conflict also existed in the late 1980s and grazing patterns in large parts of the border region remain the same, the model should hold for the late 1990s except in problem areas like Kismayo District. In the 1987–8 drought, an early set of decisions revolved around whether or not to migrate animals and, if so, which stock species and to what locations. The responses to these were to affect other choices later on, particularly regarding livestock sales, veterinary and water purchases, and subsequent herd movements.

In the early stages of this drought, two related questions were especially critical: (1) should herders remain in or migrate animals back to dry season pastures; and/or (2) should they increase sales of livestock in anticipation of a worsening drought situation? Other decisions, such as those related to the slaughtering of animals or seeking wage employment, were not very important during the 1987–8 drought. With the collapse of the state and restrictions on Somali immigration to other countries, the employment alternative is even less important at present. During the drought of 1987–8 the short rains (*deyr*) of 1987 had almost completely failed and the *gu'* rains of 1988 did not arrive until July, four months after they normally begin. In effect, there had been virtually no appreciable rain during a 10-month period of 1987 and 1988.

Herders can be differentiated into two groups based on their initial responses to this 'shock': (1) those who immediately moved out of normal grazing areas (78 percent of the total) at the first sign of a prolonged drought, and (2) those who delayed movement (22 percent). By the end of the long dry season, seasonal pastures are usually exhausted and without any rainfall they cannot sustain herds for very long. This was true in 1987–8. During this period of low rainfall, herders confronted several critical junctures that required important choices. These included decisions regarding the timing of livestock sales; expenditures on veterinary inputs especially for those who stayed in the Jubba Valley; migrations to distant grazing zones; purchases of water for cattle; and expenditures on fodder. Once a herder decides not to move and the situation does not improve, as was the case in this drought, s/he is confronted with a plethora of tough choices. For instance, those herders who opted not to migrate long distances ended up selling more animals (at depressed prices), purchasing more veterinary medicines, and losing a larger percentage of animals than those who moved. As was mentioned earlier, those who remain sedentary in the Jubba Valley for most of the year are generally poorer in livestock than the general population. Their livestock losses, therefore, are especially painful for them.

For both groups – those who moved and those who did not – cattle losses were not particularly high, an estimated 9 and 14 percent, respectively. These declines were minimal compared to normal drought-induced losses in neighboring countries, but nonetheless there was about a 40 percent difference between the two groups. In the Somali case, most herders were generally successful in maintaining their herd capital by migrating and by keeping their animals off a relatively depressed market. Recall from Chapter 2 that during the early months of a drought, the cross-border trade with Kenya virtually stops because of a lack of surface water along market routes. This limits the prospects of a market option during hard times. As will be shown in the next chapter, herders confront a 'Catch-22' situation during droughts, since their main commodity (livestock) drops in price while the costs of their main import item (grain) rises steeply. How herders manage this critical juncture has a major influence on their future welfare, whether in times of conflict or not.

5
Boom Times in a Bust State

In developed countries, the breakdown and subsequent long absence
of economic institutions alone would be devastating to a local
economy.... In Somalia, however, its economy has so far proved to be
resilient. Despite the war, recurrent droughts, famine, and the conse-
quent decline in production capacity, its economy muddles through,
and economic activity stumbles but never stops. Surprisingly, in
some areas the local economy is thriving and is experiencing an
unparalleled economic boom (Mubarak 1997: 2027).

A Western tourist in Nairobi who eats at one of the city's popular 'Nyama
Choma' (barbecued meat) establishments may be unknowingly
consuming meat from conflict-ridden southern Somalia. The likelihood
is high since an estimated 16 percent of the beef consumed in Nairobi
comes from the ungoverned Somali borderlands and its vast rangelands
(see note 13). The animals are trekked on foot for several days to the key
Kenyan border market, Garissa, where they are loaded on lorries and
trucked the final 420 km across a new tarmac road to Nairobi. In Nairobi
they are sold through a mass of middlemen and wholesalers and eventually are slaughtered at one of the town's numerous meat processing
houses. To understand this dynamic commerce, multiple approaches
must be employed and, even then, it is not possible to fully grasp the
significance of this trade, where the final links are to the butcheries and
eating establishments of Kenya's capital city.

   This chapter continues the discussion of social and economic life in the
southern borderlands but with an emphasis on trading, not herding. It
addresses the key activity, cross-border cattle trade, and the social relationships and stories that drive what has been a surprisingly resilient
pastoral economy. Some of these narratives are extraordinary in showing
how individuals, often in unexpected ways, are getting on with their lives
in stateless Somalia. By drawing attention to those social linkages and
strategies that traders invoke, the chapter reveals how merchants endure

prolonged periods of uncertainty. If anything, livestock trade and traders have prospered in many parts of the borderlands and Somalia generally, challenging the popular images of a collapsed Somali economy. The so-called unofficial trade to neighboring countries permits certain groups of Somali traders to weather an environment of extreme economic and political volatility that is exceptional even in the African context.[1]

Historical context of market volatility

The instability of the 1990s was extreme, but elements of volatility and market risk characterized the area for much of the twentieth century. In particular the preceding decade, the 1980s, was a devastating period of decline for Somalia's livestock sector and economic and political conditions generally. It served as a backdrop to a scenario that was to deteriorate even more in the 1990s. During the 1980s the national economy went from bad to worse, as official exports of livestock declined and the value of the Somali shilling plummeted. The value of annual imports in 1989 was about twice the value of Somalia's annual exports, while more than 70 percent of the operating budget of the government at the time was paid out of foreign aid (Mubarak 1996: 101–14). The market value of the Somali shilling declined more than 95 percent between 1983 and 1989, with annual inflation in the late 1980s exceeding 300 percent (ibid; Dool 1998: 215). Even before this crisis, however, Somalia had an economy with 'most of the major symptoms of African underdevelopment, e.g. growing food imports, balance of payment problems, declining agricultural production, malnutrition, and starvation' (Abdi Samatar 1987: 356).

Coupled with this dismal economic outlook was an even worse national political situation in which most of the important regions of the country, including the Lower Jubba, were under the control of different political factions by 1989. Even prior to the overthrow of the Siad Barre regime in January 1991, the southern-based Somali Patriotic Movement (SPM) controlled most of the Lower Jubba region, with the exception of Kismayo town. As Chapter 2 showed, major armed clashes between Barre's forces and the SPM, who initially relied on recruits from the Ogadeen clan, took place as early as August 1989. Weak even during periods of relative stability, the central state had effectively lost sovereignty over most of the Lower Jubba by the end of 1989. Its role in the regional economy was virtually non-existent in 1990.

After more than 15 years of rapid growth in livestock exports, the decade of the 1980s proved especially difficult for the country's most

---

[1] Paradoxically, it was this cross-border trade that the state and development agencies like the World Bank first tried to discourage in the 1970s and then to capture in the 1980s. In fact, the underlying rationale for the development investments in the region's livestock sector was to reorient trade from the border areas to overseas export markets, which could earn the government foreign exchange (see Chapter 2).

important export activity. During the 1970s the dominance of Saudi Arabia as a market for Somali cattle had grown rapidly, and by the early 1980s it accounted for more than 95 percent of the external market for Somali cattle. In volume alone, the expansion of the Saudi market was a dramatic departure from the past, with cattle exports from Kismayo increasing more than threefold from the late 1960s to the late 1970s. The amount of revenue also increased dramatically, as Saudi importers were willing to pay relatively high prices to guarantee meat for their burgeoning domestic market. This growth in Saudi demand correlated with the general oil boom of the 1970s and early 1980s that drove up Arab incomes, and to the growing popularity of the annual Hajj pilgrimage. The seasonal demand for Somali meat correlates strongly with this religious event, which annually attracts more than two million Muslim visitors to Saudi Arabia.

The period from 1983 to 1989, however, saw a reduction in total animal exports to the Arabian Peninsula. Fierce competition from Australia and other countries for the lucrative Saudi Arabian market reduced the volume of goat and sheep exports to that country, but the export of Somali cattle was hurt by other actions. In 1983 Saudi Arabia imposed a ban on cattle imported from Somalia in response to unwarranted fears of rinderpest in southern Somalia. They were to do the same in 1998 and 2000 out of fear of Rift Valley Fever (RVF), a ban that covered all livestock species and the effects of which were strongly felt in northern Somalia (Somaliland) where the post-1991 export sector was booming (see Chapter 2). The immediate effects of the 1983 ban were catastrophic: annual cattle exports declined from 157,000 in 1982 to less than 8,000 in 1984. Although an international team from the Food and Agriculture Organization (FAO) verified early on that the area's cattle were not infected by rinderpest, the ban on cattle exports to Saudi Arabia remained in force up to the government's collapse in 1991. After 1983 some exports of Somali cattle found their way to Saudi Arabia via Yemen, a strategy that circumvented the prohibition. The loss of the Saudi market was particularly disastrous to the economy of the border zone because of its dependence on bovines. From 1982 to 1984, annual cattle exports from Kismayo declined from approximately 51,000 to less than 1,000 and by 1990–1 the export market from Kismayo had virtually stopped (Stockton and Chema 1995: 15).[2] As will be elaborated later in the chapter, this hurt certain merchants more than others and resulted in a redirection of the cattle trade to Kenyan markets.

[2] Civil unrest elsewhere in Somalia had also contributed to the reduction in exports. Activities in the major port of Berbera in what is now Somaliland were greatly slowed during 1988 to 1991 and livestock exports there were reduced by almost one million head in 1988. As a result, the total value of livestock exports from Somalia fell from US$51 million in 1987 to US$22.4 million in 1988 (Woodward and Stockton 1989: 6). By 1992 livestock exports were only about 33 percent of pre-1988 levels, but by 1994 small stock exports actually 'exceeded pre-war levels' (EC–FAO 1995: 9).

How unusual is this sort of political and economic instability? Although the current situation is an extreme case, turbulent conditions characterized the region for much of the past century. The cattle trade, for example, was disrupted by colonial policies of both the British and Italian governments, interventions that included regulation of livestock movements, imposition of quarantines, and restrictions on foreign currencies. Graphic stories are told of Somali merchants who upon arriving at a colonial market learned that their currency had been devalued or was not convertible that week; and of traders who had to move animals at night to avoid punitive and unpredictable blockades and quarantines by colonial administrations (see Dalleo 1975: 128, 171–2).[3] Commerce also was affected by warfare. In the 1890s and early 1900s there were skirmishes between the Ogadeen and the British; in the 1930s between the Italians and Ethiopians; in the 1940s between British and Italian troops; and in the 1960s between Somalis and the Kenyan government. In addition to these constraints, trade has been affected by severe droughts during almost every decade of the past century. Ambiguity and risk, therefore, have surrounded livestock trade in the region for much of the last hundred years.

Several times during the past century reversals in the flow of cattle between Kenya and Somalia occurred, depending on political and market conditions in the two countries. The shift toward Kenyan markets since the 1980s is only the latest in a series of transitions. During the periods of approximately 1890–1910, 1921–40, 1945–50, and 1968–83, the cattle trade went mainly from northeastern Kenya to southern Somalia, especially to Kismayo. By contrast, during 1911–20, 1941–4, 1951–67, and 1984–present, cattle went mainly from Somali to Kenyan markets in the northeast, and to Kenya's commercial ranching areas and large towns (Dalleo 1975). These market trends were not absolute, and during any given year cattle flows could be reversed or go in both directions, depending on seasonal and local market conditions. With this kind of uncertainty, astute merchants have always had to be adaptable and to maintain market relationships on both sides of the border.

Overview of different markets

Cattle markets dominate the domestic and export trade in the border zone. Exchanges of other livestock species reveal neither the complexity nor the volume of the cattle trade, which in 1988 accounted for three and

---

[3] The official rationale for banning the Somali trade was to protect Kenya's commercial herds from deadly animal diseases, but the real reason had more to do with protecting the white settlers' control of the country's livestock sector. Ironically, one of those peculiar 'hidden histories' is that Kenya's European farm sector depended (and still depends) on Somali cattle for breeding and restocking their commercial herds and, therefore, ranchers often violated their own bans when it suited them. It is a well-known fact in Kenya that even today European and African commercial ranchers send buyers to Somali markets, like the one at Isiolo, to purchase immatures and breeding stock for their herds.

fifteen times as many sales as small stock and camels, respectively (Little 1989a). This is not surprising since cattle populations in the region are considerably higher than other livestock types (see Chapter 2). Unlike cattle, very few camels and small stock are exported to Kenya. Camel markets are poorly developed in Kenya and therefore relative demand for the animal is low there, while exports of sheep and goats are uneconomic because of adequate supplies and low prices in northern Kenya. Regional trade in small stock is almost strictly oriented to domestic markets, especially to the larger Somali towns. With the collapse of the overseas cattle trade, merchants who were involved in the local small stock or camel trade were better prepared to confront the market crisis of the 1980s and 1990s than were export traders.

Market channels

Prior to 1991 the cattle trade in the border region was essentially focused on four markets, which accounted for about 90 percent of the region's sales. First was the regional domestic trade that was concentrated in southern Somali towns like Kismayo, Jamaame, and Gelib. This commerce was oriented to local consumption or to the rebuilding of local herds, and involved both low-quality, low-priced cattle and young heifers and bulls (less than four years old). On the consumption side, it was centered on local butcheries in the Lower Jubba Region and accounted for an estimated 40 percent of cattle sales in the area prior to the conflict.[4] The second market was the national domestic one located in Mogadishu, Somalia's largest city, which required cattle treks from the region in excess of 300 km. The Mogadishu market, along with the city's population, was growing rapidly in the late 1980s and cattle prices there tended to be about 20 to 25 percent higher than in the Lower Jubba. Harti merchants were strongly involved with this trade and usually had partners in Mogadishu to market their animals. In 1987–8 the Mogadishu market was the final destination for approximately 16 percent of cattle sold in the region.

The third and fourth market channels in the Lower Jubba involved international exports. In the case of the Kenya trade, animals were sold and moved 'unofficially' across the border to Kenyan markets, particularly to Garissa. This trade accounted for about 25 percent of cattle sales, but up to 45 percent in certain parts of the border region. Very few sales to Kenya took place in Jubba Valley towns, such as Jamaame, both because of distance and control of the trade by Ogadeen traders. Those Harti who participated

---

[4] This figure includes purchases by local herders to replenish their own herds. Because many of these cattle are eventually sold at other markets, the data on regional markets frequently do not capture final sales. The percentages noted here and for other markets discussed in this section are derived from interviews with traders and from a sample of more than 800 cattle sales at four major markets – Afmadow, Kismayo, Bilas Qooqani, and Libooye – during February 1987 to February 1988. For each transaction, the buyer was asked to identify the market destination of the animal. While I conducted the analysis of these data, much of the information at the market centers was gathered by the Livestock Marketing and Health Project, Mogadishu.

usually had some type of alliance with an Ogadeen middleman. As noted earlier, this trade was seasonal: during the long dry season (January to March) few cattle were moved from the Lower Jubba to northeastern Kenya. The cross-border trade with Kenya involves medium- to high-quality animals, which are used for slaughter in urban centers and for restocking and breeding purposes on commercial ranches in the Rift Valley. As will be discussed later in this chapter, this trade has captured the bulk of cattle exports with the collapse of the government and overseas trade.

The fourth market, the overseas export trade, was very different from the other three channels, in that large-scale traders and companies were involved. In 1988 it accounted for fewer than 5 percent of regional cattle sold, although earlier in the decade its contribution was as high as 15 percent. Because it involved high-quality, expensive animals, the overseas trade was responsible for about 15 percent of the aggregate value of marketed cattle. The export traders, who were typically registered members of a company, had contracts with a private importer, usually from a Middle Eastern country, to supply a specified number of animals at an agreed price.[5] When the Somali trader had written proof of an order, the individual[6] could request a letter of credit from the state-owned Somali Commercial and Savings Bank and receive half of its value in local currency. With the export crisis of the 1980s, cooperation among export traders was minimal, as larger merchants sought to attain a 'bigger slice' of a diminishing trade by forcing out smaller competitors and consolidating their own market advantage.

The local system of procurement for the overseas trade was essentially the same as that used for other markets, with a few important distinctions. First, the overseas traders usually did not purchase animals at local market centers but relied instead on their own chain of middlemen and agents for supplies. Second, export traders often employed full- or near full-time people whose function it was to procure animals. Third, in contrast to other markets, the overseas commerce was restricted to young male cattle aged four to seven years. Female cattle could not be legally exported in 1988 and therefore only the largest males, those that exceeded 275–300 kg live weight, were procured locally. Finally, because of the sheer size of their orders, exporters were forced to procure animals throughout the year and employ hired herders to manage the animals.[7]

The benefits and costs of these different market channels varied considerably. While there were increased risks with the overseas trade, the

---

[5] Some of the individual contracts in the 1970s were for as many as 10,000 cattle over a period of 18 to 24 months. One of the largest traders in Kismayo town exported 47,000 cattle and 18,000 camels to Saudi Arabia between 1971 and 1983. When the Saudi trade was in place, many Somali exporters received private financing from their Saudi Arabian contacts.

[6] While women traders dominate dairy trade and other markets, very few are involved in the cattle or camel trade. In the 1980s no exporters that I interviewed were female.

[7] Exporters usually kept only their head herdsmen employed throughout the year. Other herders were hired as needed. To manage a herd of 100 cattle, one head herder and three other workers were required.

largest net returns for traders took place in the overseas export trade, followed closely by the Kenya trade. Net incomes of traders in the overseas and Kenyan trade were 18 and 17.5 percent of the final sales price, respectively, in 1987–8 (see Little 1996).[8] Although net returns were slightly higher for the overseas trade, the capital outlays and marketing costs were also higher. The overseas export trade involved such marketing expenses as port charges, insurance, and quarantine charges, costs that were not associated with other market channels. On the lower end, the smallest profits were found in the Kismayo regional (8 percent annual return) and Mogadishu trades (12 percent), which were based predominantly on sales of low-value animals. The costs of engaging in the Kismayo regional trade were considerably below those of other markets and, therefore, within the financial capabilities of most small-scale traders.

Effects of the war

The war in southern Somalia had major impacts on the area's livestock markets. Of the four market channels discussed above, only the cross-border trade escaped large-scale devastation. In fact, it has grown considerably as a result of the conflict in Somalia. The regional domestic market in the Lower Jubba still exists, but herders increasingly avoid Kismayo market because of conflict. It is not a reliable market today, unlike the past when it was treated by merchants as a 'fallback' market. To quote a recent journalist's account: 'Kismayo has proved a dangerous place for aid workers in the past. Bitter battles frequently have erupted between the Majerteen [Harti] and Marehan clans during the past few years, killing hundreds of civilians and rendering the port unusable because of poor security' (Sonya L. Green 1998: 1). As a result of this insecurity, markets and food prices in Kismayo demonstrate the greatest volatility in the area.

As mentioned earlier, with the exception of a few isolated cases, overseas exports from the region have virtually stopped. This trend contrasts sharply with that of Somaliland and Puntland (northeastern Somalia) where overseas exports actually grew during most of the post-1991 era. While in 1988 approximately 25 percent of southern Somali traders indicated at least some involvement in overseas export trade, either as middlemen or exporters themselves, less than 4 percent reported export activities during 1991–8. Those merchants who did indicate some involvement utilize the Mombasa (Kenya), not the Kismayo, port.

In terms of the national market, the Mogadishu trade also is at very low levels. Mogadishu used to be a vibrant outlet that drew cattle from

[8] The methodology for examining economic returns and costs in the livestock trade was developed in Evans et al. (1988). It simply breaks down costs and returns (including net returns) at different points in the market chain and for different actors as a proportion of each 100 shillings transacted.

as far away as the Lower Jubba, especially during seasons when the Kenya market slowed. In 1987–8 Mogadishu prices were between 29 to 55 percent higher than prices in other markets of southern Somalia (see Table 5.1), and at that time no sales of cattle were recorded from the Mogadishu area to Kenyan markets. Since the government's collapse, however, cattle from war-torn Mogadishu and the nearby Lower Shebelle Region are being trekked to Kenyan outlets, a distance in excess of 400 km. Price advantages of Mogadishu, in turn, over other Somali markets have been greatly reduced as lucrative trade channels to the city have been violently disrupted. In contrast to the pre-war era, the low cattle prices in locations near conflict-ridden Mogadishu currently attract trader interest from as far away as Nairobi. The reddish-brown cattle, a trademark of Mogadishu animals, one readily observes at Kenyan markets are proof of this trend (author's field notes, July 1998 and June 2001).

A comparison of price data from different time periods helps to evaluate the magnitude of changes during the 1990s. Table 5.1 shows how prices of cattle in Mogadishu (in US dollars) have taken a severe 'hit' since 1987–8, and were actually lower than those in Afmadow and other border markets during the 1990s. In fact, prices have risen in those market centers involved in cross-border trade (Afmadow, Bilas Qooqani, and Libooye), while they have actually declined in US dollar terms for Mogadishu. In the border town, Libooye, prices almost doubled between 1987–8 and 1996, a reflection of the strong growth in cross-border trade with Kenya. Although prices in 1998 showed a slight decline over 1996 prices, a general pattern that was found at the time throughout the African Horn region (see Teka et al. 1999), trans-border commerce kept values higher near the border than elsewhere.

Prior to the conflict there were about 4,000 camels exported annually to the Middle East from Kismayo, and there also was a relatively large

Table 5.1. Average prices of cattle in selected markets: 1987–8, 1996, and 1998

	Mogadishu	Afmadow	(in US $) Bilas Qooqani	Libooye[1]	Kismayo
1987–8[2]	121	94	78	83	80
1996[3]	97	128	154	155	NA
1998[3]	110	117	ND	133	100

Source: Author's data unless otherwise noted.
Notes:
NA = not applicable; ND = no data.
[1] Libooye is located on the Kenya/Somalia border.
[2] Based on analysis of monthly market data collected under the Livestock Marketing and Health Project. The period covered was January 1987 to February 1988, although data were not available for each market every month. Exchange rate for the period averaged approximately 120SoSh = $1.
[3] Based on data from interviews with 84 traders. Period covered was March to July 1996 and June to August 1998, and exchange rates varied from month to month. Cattle were Quality 2 ('medium-quality') animals (cows and bulls older than 7 years).

domestic market for camels in Somalia itself (see Little 1989a). The Somali market was important enough that it attracted relatively large numbers of camels from Kenya, and they fetched considerably higher prices in Somalia than in Kenya.[9] The situation has changed, however, and camel traders bemoan the lack of an export market in the area: 'Export of camels through Somalia was easy because of government assistance and port facilities at Mogadishu, Kismayo, and Merka. We can't export well through Kenya because of lack of government support and port facility' (trader interview, 21 May 1996). As a result of the decline in the export trade and in regional and national trade in Somalia, the cross-border exchange in camels has virtually ceased and camel prices have declined relative to cattle prices.

The cross-border boom

The war has clearly been good for the trans-border cattle trade and the merchants associated with it. It has been less lucrative for the average herder of the region, but even they have benefited from it, especially those located near the Kenya border. As a commodity, livestock has features that make it amenable to cross-border trade even in situations of widespread insecurity. It is a mobile, high-value commodity that can be transported overland rather than on roads, and can easily be moved across borders, a practice that local pastoralists have engaged in since international borders were first demarcated. These characteristics do not hold for most agricultural commodities in the region, which usually require road transport to be commercially viable.

The spectacular surge in cross-border livestock trade with Kenya is reflected in market statistics of the main Kenyan border district, Garissa, and in the findings of trader interviews. The aggregate value of cattle sales in Garissa grew by an astounding 400 percent between 1991 and 1998 and 600 percent between 1989 and 1998 (Table 5.2). In terms of volume, annual sales grew from 24,395 in 1989 to more than 100,000 cattle in 1998. Herders and traders acknowledge that this dramatic increase results from the spectacular growth in cross-border imports from Somalia, which in recent years has accounted for about 65 percent of cattle sold in Garissa.[10] As a result of a debilitating drought and a

---

[9] It should be noted that while the market for camels remains very small in Kenya, it has grown in recent years and as of 1999 about 2,500 camels were being exported annually. There now are markets and slaughter facilities for camels in the Nairobi region.

[10] This figure assumes that about 32 percent or 32,600 cattle marketed in Garissa in 1998 are Kenyan animals, either from Garissa (about 30,000 cattle), Mandera (600), or Wajir (2,000) Districts. Of course, it is very difficult to estimate exact numbers of cattle sales and their geographic origins. The figures for Mandera and Wajir sales are based on unpublished data on marketing and animal movements from the districts' livestock departments, while the estimate for Garissa assumes an annual off-take rate of 7 percent or about 30,000 of the district's cattle population of 422,400 in 1998 (Hendy and Morton 1999: 58).

prolonged closure of the border by the Kenyan government (also see Chapter 6),[11] sales were down in 1999 and 2000 but still well above levels of a decade earlier.

To the casual visitor, the Garissa cattle market, located on the outskirts of this hot, dry town of about 35,000, may seem like anything but an economic 'hot spot.' The market itself is a massive assembly of hawkers and dirty animals converging on an unfenced crowded space one day per week. Swarming flies and clouds of dust add to the market's unkempt appearance, as does the uneven ring of hut-shaped shops that surround it. There appears to be little organization to the market – even chaos – as traders and herders haggle over prices in spirited negotiations, each trying to obtain advantage over the other. In some transactions brokers attempt to mediate and an older, trustworthy broker may work for several parties simultaneously. It is a form of raw agrarian capitalism that has not been seen in the US since the days of the old cattle drives and stockyards of the nineteenth century. Yet, this 'untidy' venue is currently the largest cattle market in Kenya outside the modern urban market of Nairobi, and it is the largest in the country's rangelands.

The activities of Ahmed and Yusuf during June 1996 provide some flavor to how the Garissa market operates.

Ahmed and Yusuf are approximately 35 years old and both come from Afmadow, Somalia. They have been involved in the cross-border trade for about four years and hire trekkers to move animals to the Garissa market up to five times per year. Both are Mohamed Zubeyr Ogadeen, and during this particular week in June 1996 they have hired three trekkers and one armed security person to bring about 105 cattle to Kenya from Afmadow and nearby Bilis Qooqani. Yusuf and Ahmed arrive in Garissa three days before the weekly market day on Wednesday to check out prices and to talk with butchers and market brokers. They stay in one of the many small hotels in town and pay about $3 per night for accommodation. In the small tea shop adjoining the hotel, they meet with other traders over the next few days and with the market broker whose services they will engage. They talk about the cattle trade business and are trying to catch up on recent news from Garissa and Nairobi markets. They learn that because of declining prices in Garissa and excessive supply in Nairobi, there has been about a 15 percent price decline in the past 10 days. Yusuf, in particular, is concerned about what kind

---

[11] From July 1999 to March 2000 the Kenya government intermittently closed the border to halt the illegal flow of weapons from Somalia and stave off a potential threat from General Morgan's forces. The latter had been forcefully evicted from Kismayo by a combined force of Marehan rebels and Hussein Aideed's USC faction (see Africa News Service, 7 July 1999). While the closure lasted just eight months and only partially reduced livestock trade, the scenario did increase risks and transaction costs. The Kenya government reimposed the ban in July 2001, but it is unknown what impact it will have on livestock trade (see Chapter 7).

Photo 5.1   *Garissa livestock market, Kenya* (Peter D. Little)

of market they will find on Wednesday. Only 16 days earlier when they finalized plans to make the 14-day cattle trek from Afmadow to Garissa, prices seemed good, an opportune time to trek animals. They had confirmed this from southern Somalia by speaking with their Kenyan-based market contacts via hand radio. By Tuesday morning their animals finally arrive at a watering area about 5 km from the Garissa market, where the cattle will stay until the morning of the sales. They have arranged with their broker to find a buyer(s), and they need to sell at least 90 of the cattle on market day because the high costs of fodder and water for the herd will steeply cut into profits.

On Tuesday evening about 20 lorries from Nairobi and Mombasa arrive to transport purchased cattle the next day. The large ones hold between 28 to 30 cattle and the small ones between 18 and 22. Traders, like Yusuf and Ahmed, had been hoping for 40 trucks. Another 5 or 10 lorries are likely to arrive in Garissa on the market day. Traders usually can tell what kind of business day it will be by the number of trucks that arrive. When the buying begins on Wednesday, Yusuf and Ahmed are confronted with the bad news that prices will be about 10 percent less than their least optimistic scenario, which means that after their transport and purchase costs they will barely break even. They expect to earn a return after costs of less than 2 percent. The good news is that their broker has been able to sell all 105 cattle: approximately 70 to Nairobi and Mombasa traders; 25 to local traders who will trek the cattle to Garsen near the Kenyan coast or to nearby Kitui District; and 10 to local butchery owners and herders who will fatten the animals near Garissa, slaughter them, and then sell the meat in town.

When I saw Yusuf and Ahmed back at their hotel that evening, they were pleased to have sold their animals and would be heading to Nairobi the next day to convert some of their earnings to dollars. They also planned to purchase consumer products there, like plastic sandals, to sell back in Afmadow. One of the traders owns a small retail store in the Somali town. Yusuf and Ahmed indicated their good fortune of being able to sell all their animals, because in a week or two it will be difficult to do so. By then the market will be flooded with animals from herders and traders desperate to unload their cattle, especially if there is no rain. Because of a lack of surface water along the trekking routes, they did not expect to bring animals again to Kenya for at least another three months. By that time they hoped there would be rain.

Yusuf and Ahmed perceive Garissa as a dynamic town of widespread opportunity, where fortunes can be made as well as lost. In contrast, the town is considered a 'punishment' for most Kenyan civil servants. A government employee who is posted there from outside of the district usually interprets it as a harsh form of demotion, inhospitable, and too close to the borders of warring, ungovernable Somalia with its 'primitive' nomads.

Garissa is increasingly a Somali town, with a marked resemblance to the towns of southern Somalia. Recent migrants boast of its similarity to former Somalia: 'it feels like Somalia – tea shops and all' (author's field notes, June 2001). Open-air tea shops and restaurants, with names and menus that one might find in Mogadishu or Kismayo, are filled with talkative customers. They enjoy the sweetly spiced teas and massive portions of pasta and boiled camel meat (*eleso*), culinary trademarks of Somali culture, that one cannot find in other parts of Kenya. The same customers might have patronized food establishments in stateless Somalia just five to ten years earlier. Similar to Mogadishu, a recent impressive development in Garissa is the proliferation of foreign exchange bureaus and informal communication exchanges (telephone, fax, and internet)[12] that facilitate the movement of goods and money throughout the region and beyond (see discussion in Chapter 6). Brightly painted pictures of $100 notes and the latest computer technologies adorn shop walls in an almost surrealistic way. Crowds of youth can be found around Garissa's street corners at night chewing the mildly narcotic stimulant, *khat*, and occasionally abusing the pedestrian who mistakenly illuminates their activities with a flashlight. Merchants like Yusuf and Ahmed, in turn, crowd into the town's small hotels and discuss the prices of livestock, exchange rates of different currencies – US dollars, Kenyan shillings, and Saudi riyals – and regional politics. The Kenyan state never had more than a minimal influence over the area, but with its emaciated administration its

---

[12] In June 2001 I counted four of these in only a two-block area of downtown Garissa.

control now is even less. This has allowed the town to attract large amounts of capital from southern Somalia and to develop a particularly Somali ambiance, one that has grown since a 1986 visit.

In 1997 the Garissa market generated 659,880,500 Kenya shillings (KSh) or US$11,783,580 in cattle sales alone (Table 5.2). The aggregate value of the cattle market declined in 1998, although the volume of cattle sold was actually 14 percent higher than in 1997. The reason for the decline was the drop in average cattle prices (for all-quality animals) from KSh 8,500 in 1997 to KSh 5,900 in 1998 (Umar 2000: 15). Revenues also dropped in 1999 and 2000 because prices continued to be low and, as noted earlier, drought and border closures affected the cross-border trade. The recent trend of poor prices (1996–2000) throughout the Horn of Africa has reduced pastoral welfare during an especially difficult period of multiple natural disasters (floods and droughts) (see Chapter 2). Despite these constraints, annual revenues in Table 5.2 compare favorably with some of Kenya's major coffee- and cash crop-producing districts, a phenomenon that is rarely acknowledged in Kenya's official economic reports (Kenya

Photo 5.2   Informal telecommunications business, Garissa, Kenya (Peter D. Little)

Table 5.2. Cattle sales in Garissa, Kenya: 1989–2000[1]

Year	Number	Value (Ksh)	Value (US$)[2]
1989	24,395	51,717,400	2,510,533
1990	32,664	84,273,120	3,677,640
1991	33,449	99,510,775	3,618,573
(Somalia state collapses)			
1992	65,127	162,229,648	5,038,188
1993	67,076	387,162,670	6,675,218
1994	62,351	436,457,000	7,793,875
1995	80,795	565,565,000	11,003,210
1996	86,400	ND	ND
1997	90,701	659,880,500[3]	11,783,580
1998	101,593	599,693,700	10,272,307
1999[3]	65,757	380,334,070	6,338,901
2000[4]	77,633	580,990,875	8,802,892

Notes:
ND = no data.
[1] These data are based on annual reports (1989–2000) from the Livestock Marketing Department, Ministry of Agriculture and Livestock Development, Garissa.
[2] Exchange rates for each year were obtained from the International Monetary Fund (1999: 560–1). The decline of values in US dollar terms partly reflects annual devaluations in the value of the Kenya shilling.
[3] Based on Umar 2000: 15.
[4] Annual sales were affected by a devastating drought and an official closure of the border with Somalia.

1997). Most policy directives undervalue and neglect the importance of the pastoral sector to the national economy, since it is poorly understood and does not contribute directly to the state's foreign exchange coffers.

What is particularly noteworthy about the high revenues and sales numbers in Table 5.2 is that they reflect only official market transactions. Because of Kenyan government restrictions, all cattle at the Garissa market must be inspected and cleared by a veterinarian before being transported by truck to down-country markets. Only animals that have been cleared for sale are recorded in the market statistics, since there is no central body to collect all types of market transactions. The permit requirement is an important point of contention among small-scale traders who claim that it greatly increases transport costs, a point that is verified by my own research (see Table 5.5 below). The ban on trekking livestock by foot to markets outside of northeastern Kenya is a colonial 'layover' that was meant to protect European herds from diseases transmitted by African herds (see note 3). Trekking animals by foot tends to be about three to four times cheaper than motor transport, although it takes about 25 times longer and can result in animal weight losses. Certain strategies that include sales outside government market grounds and nightly movements of cattle can circumvent these constraints, but their prevalence is difficult to estimate.

Cattle production and trade spurs other commerce and business activities in the region as well. As was pointed out earlier, the vast majority of revenues associated with the cross-border trade remain in the region, with a large proportion being returned to southern Somalia. Based on available census figures, the population of Garissa town and its suburbs is about 43,000 (1996) (Kenya 1996: 18). This means that the per capita value of cattle trade in the Garissa area was about $275 in 1997, which is sizable for a country with a per capita gross national product (GNP) of only $340 (Europa Publications 2000: 2107). Growth in Garissa's commercial activities since 1991 is largely due to increases in cross-border trade and the arrival of capital and merchants from neighboring Somalia. In the town self-employed businesses (i.e. trading enterprises) have grown much faster than any of the district's other economic sectors (Kenya 1996: 49). From 1989 to 1996 urban self-employed commercial operators and employees in the area increased from 5,723 to 8,428 (ibid.). Probably an additional 20 to 30 percent of petty traders and hawkers are not captured in these official figures, which means that about one out of four Garissa residents are involved in some kind of commercial operation. In addition, between 1995 and 2000 an entire street of downtown Garissa grew up around wholesale trade (with eight large new enterprises), and at least five hotels of 15+ rooms were built during these years (author's field notes). The growth in business activities is evidence of Garissa's thriving commercial sector and the role that trade with Somalia has played.

The genealogies of the town's businesses often share a common heritage: owners first start in livestock trade and then use the profits to invest in other activities. For example, Fasil, the owner of one of the largest hotels in Garissa, used profits from a livestock trading operation to finance its construction. Despite his hotel and other investments, he remains active in livestock trade. Although it is difficult to estimate the number of businesses in Garissa owned by Somalis from the other side of the border, it is widely acknowledged that many traders who left southern Somalia in 1991 and 1992 established businesses in Garissa town. 'This whole section [of wholesalers] in town did not exist before the Somalis came,' remarked Mohamed, an Arab trader whose family has resided in Garissa since colonial times (author's field notes, June 2001). The movement of traders from southern Somalia to Garissa facilitates cross-border trade, because these merchants usually maintain their linkages to suppliers in Somalia. In addition to cattle, food aid, pasta, and electronics from southern Somalia find their way into Garissa's retail sector. Several merchants made it very clear to me that their businesses suffered terribly during the border closures imposed by the Kenyan government in 1999 and 2000. In fact, it was reported that an estimated 100 Kenyan merchants were trapped inside Somalia when the border was closed in July 1999, a strong indication of the area's dependence on trans-border trade (Africa News Service, 25 August 1999).

Most of the cattle sold at Garissa are destined for Nairobi and Mombasa. Together these towns, the two largest in Kenya, account for more than 90 percent of the market, with Nairobi alone accounting for about 70 percent. Prior to its closure in 1994, about 35 percent of Garissa cattle were sold to the government-owned Kenya Meat Commission (KMC) abattoir on the outskirts of Nairobi. Private slaughter houses in the Nairobi region have assumed some of the slack left by the KMC's closure (see Zaal 1998), but traders complain that its absence is particularly felt during droughts when supplies of low-quality, weakened cattle greatly increase and market bottlenecks are common. At these times numerous animals from the range areas, including the border region, flood the market and the private sector's demand for fresh meat can handle only a part of this volume. It is estimated that the Somali rangelands, including animals marketed through Garissa and Mandera, account for about 16 percent of the estimated 375,000 cattle consumed annually in the Nairobi region.[13]

Markets and price relations
Prices for cattle in Somalia generally increase in relation to proximity to the Kenya border. This is a pattern that even existed before 1991, but has been amplified in recent years. On the Kenyan side, regional prices generally reflect proximity to Nairobi and Mombasa, the main terminal markets. Reference to a key market channel, the Afmadow (Somalia)–Garissa–Nairobi market, is helpful as an illustration. Along this route the lowest average cattle prices are at Afmadow, followed by the border town of Libooye where prices are about 25 percent higher (see Table 5.3). On the Kenyan side, prices move in the opposite direction: they are lowest near the border and increase as one moves to the interior. When the animal reaches Garissa, the major transit market in Kenya, cattle prices are about 45 percent higher than at Afmadow and about 20 percent higher than at Libooye. The distance between Garissa and Afmadow and Garissa and Libooye is about 240 km and 150 km, respectively, and there is a seasonal road that connects them. In the final stages of the market chain, the animals are transported from Garissa to Nairobi and sold at prices up to 200 percent higher than at Afmadow. Based simply on the economics of this example, it is hardly astonishing that flows of cattle from Somalia to Kenya increased in the 1990s.

[13] This estimate is based on available slaughter house figures and government statistics from the Veterinary Department, Kabete, Kenya for 1997–8; unpublished statistical data on livestock marketing and movements from the livestock departments of Mandera, Moyale, and Garissa Districts, 1997–8; and data from Kenya (1997 and 1998). It likely also includes purchases in Nairobi by surrounding traders and ranchers that may not actually end up in the Nairobi meat market. Nairobi has three main slaughter facilities for cattle, which are Dagoretti, Njiru (Dandora), and Ngong. Annually they slaughter about 150,000, 35,000, and 21,000, respectively, or a total of about 206,000. Prior to its closure in mid-1990s the Kenya Meat Commission factory slaughtered an annual average of 100,000+ cattle during 1984–94, but this slack has been taken up by these three facilities or the numerous smaller private facilities that have opened in and around Nairobi since the mid-1990s. The liberalization of the meat market in 1990 resulted in a rapid growth in small private meat processing houses, which account for the slaughtering of an estimated 100,000+ cattle per year.

Table 5.3. Cattle prices in the Afmadow–Garissa–Nairobi market chain, 1996

| | Prices (US $) | | |
| | | Cattle[1] | |
Market[2]	Quality 1	Quality 2	Quality 3
Afmadow (Somalia)	198	128	71
Doble (Somalia)	205	141	77
Libooye (border)	225	163	86
Garissa (Kenya)	270	190	115
Nairobi(Kenya)	333	231	156

Source: Author's data.
Notes:
[1] Quality 1 = Highest-quality animals (bulls and steers, 4–7 years)
  Quality 2 = Medium-quality animals (cows, older bulls)
  Quality 3 = Young or very old animals.
[2] Markets are listed in descending order by distance from the terminal markets of Nairobi and Mombasa.

Between 1988 and 1998 price differences in US dollar terms between Kenyan and Somali markets grew by about 20 percent, which implies a slight increase in risks and transaction costs on the Somalia side. With few options, Somali traders are largely restricted to selling animals in the trans-border markets, which partially explains why their animals' prices have not grown as fast as their Kenyan counterparts who have several marketing opportunities. In terms of transaction costs, added expenses include new fees (4–6 percent fee) for currency transactions[14] and slightly higher transport costs because of the need for additional security personnel to accompany transit animals. Security is a special problem between Mogadishu and Dinsoor and Baidoa and between those towns and the Kenya border. On the Kenyan side risks are high between Mandera, Wajir, and Garissa. Although levels of violence are much lower in Kenya than in Somalia, security risks are also very high in northeastern Kenya. What is surprising, however, is that price differences between Kenya and Somalia are not greater under current conditions, a point that is treated in more detail later in the chapter.

Table 5.4 shows price differences at several important market places, both Kenyan and Somali, involved in trans-border trade. For the most part the table is based on information from trader interviews in 1996 and 1998, but not all markets had data (designated by 'ND') and/or sold all three types of cattle. As noted earlier, average prices declined from 1996 to 1998. Table 5.4 displays annual averages, although livestock prices can fluctuate seasonally (and monthly) by as much as 50 to 60 percent. Livestock prices in the border region, however, show much less volatility

[14] For example, many Somali traders convert their Kenya shillings into US dollars at informal money houses in Nairobi. They are then charged up to 6 percent of the transaction's value to have the dollars 'wired' to Somalia. To avoid traveling with large amounts of dollars, many cattle traders convert the bulk of their earnings to dollars and then wire them to Somalia, where they or an associate collect them (the process of informal banking in Somalia is described in more detail in Chapter 6).

Table 5.4. Cattle prices in the cross-border trade, 1996 and 1998

Market[3]	Quality 1	Cattle[1] (US dollars) (1996 price/1998 price)[2] Quality 2	Quality 3
Somalia markets			
Mogadishu[4]	ND/124	99/110	60/38
Baidoa	212/ND	121/117	89/50
Dinsoor	204/164	89/108	49/54
Sakow	243/172	71/ND	57/ND
Bualle	243/200	71/ND	57/ND
Bardera[4]	179/136	89/86	36/ND
Kismayo	243/200	71/100	57/ND
Hagar	214/200	179/117	143/ND
Afmadow	198/200	128/117	71/ND
Dhobley (border)	205/ND	141/ND	77/ND
Kenya markets			
Mandera (border)	268/221	205/143	84/71
Hulugho (border)	210/ND	163/167	88/58
Libooye (border)	225/ND	163/133	86/ND
Moyale[5]	ND/245	ND/165	NA/109
Marsabit[5]	ND/231	ND/133	NA/76
Garissa	270/292	190/176	115/93
Isiolo	232/225	152/121	89/85
Garsen	256/283	208/ND	131/ND
Mombasa	328/300	244/263	168/183
Nairobi	333/303	231/233	156/183

Source: Author's data unless otherwise noted.
Notes:
ND = no data.
[1] Quality 1 = Highest-quality animals (bulls and steers, 4–7 years)
  Quality 2 = Medium-quality animals (cows, older bulls)
  Quality 3 = Young or very old animals.
[2] Based on author's survey, except where indicated.
[3] Listed in order of its geographic distance from the terminal markets of Nairobi and Mombasa.
[4] Prices for 1998 are based on secondary data collected by NGOs and assembled by the Food Security Assessment Unit (FSAU) of the Food and Agriculture Organization and the FEWS project.
[5] These markets were indicated as buying areas for a few traders in the 1998 survey, but are really part of the southern Ethiopia/northern Kenya border trade, not the Somalia/Kenya border trade. They are included here mainly for comparative purposes. It should be noted that animals from the Boran areas of southern Ethiopia are usually large, Boran specie cattle, and fetch a higher price than other cattle types. That is an important reason why markets along the Ethiopia border – Mandera and Moyale – reveal slightly higher prices than other markets.

than prices for grains and cereal products, which are mainly imported from outside since the border areas are grain-deficient. Prices for imported wheat flour and rice can vary monthly by as much as 250 percent in high-risk markets, like Kismayo or Dinsoor. Unlike the livestock trade that often avoids roads and major markets, food trade can be easily disrupted by road blockades, looting, and armed conflict.

Catchment areas for the cross-border trade
Afmadow, the bonanza area of cattle pastoralism, assumes an especially prominent role and accounts for about 20 percent of cattle supplies in the 1996 and 1998 samples. There also are a relatively high percentage of cattle supplied from distant Mogadishu and the Bay region (i.e. Dinsoor and Baidoa), which together account for more than 20 percent of total sales at Garissa market. To quote one experienced Garissa trader, 'until the government collapsed we never used to see these big red-brown animals from Bay Region' (trader interview, 20 June 2001). However, with the decline in domestic and overseas markets, the prime cattle-producing areas near Mogadishu and Baidoa (including Dinsoor) are important participants in the cross-border trade.[15] By contrast, the politics and prolonged fighting around Kismayo town inhibits that area's supply of cattle to Kenyan markets and has reduced its role in cross-border commerce since the 1980s. In the words of another Somali merchant involved with the trade, 'There is not much trade with Kismayo now because of security and problems ... but it is safe going from Afmadow to Kenya' (trader interview, 22 May 1996). Thus, while the catchment area of the border market has constricted in the case of Kismayo, it has greatly expanded in other directions (see Fig. 5.1).

The operations of a major Kenya-based livestock trader highlight the profits that can be made when cattle are procured from distant, but conflict-prone areas like the Bay Region.[16] According to Abdullahi Haji, who works out of both Garissa and Isiolo, Kenya, cattle (called *lo' dafed*) from the Bay Region are especially preferred, because they are bred for plow agriculture and, therefore, are unusually large. Baidoa [Bay region] cattle are recognized as superior to most breeds in Somalia and, according to some traders, were once considered the favorite cattle type of the late President Barre (trader interview, 20 June 2001). Abdullahi acknowledges that because of past conflicts in the Bay region cattle supply can be erratic. He works with three middlemen from the area and occasionally advances cash to them, in order to insure favorable prices and supplies of good-quality cattle. For Abdullahi Haji, a monetary advance is a way to solidify a market relationship and insure that the middleman supplies him with animals rather than sells to others once the cattle reach Kenya. In 1998 they procured about 120 cattle for him at a cost of about US$115 per animal. He was able to resell them in Kenya at a 35 percent mark-up. The risks of theft and disruption to supply increase the further one moves into the interior of Somalia, but potential profits also rise as the case of Abdullahi illustrates.

[15] Similar extensions of the catchment area occur in parts of the Middle Jubba Region (including Sakow) that previously supplied very few animals to Kenyan markets.
[16] Since 1999 Baidoa and the Bay Region generally have experienced much less insecurity and have established a relatively stable regional administration. In 2000 the Bay Region even had its own internet Web site where it highlights news and political events.

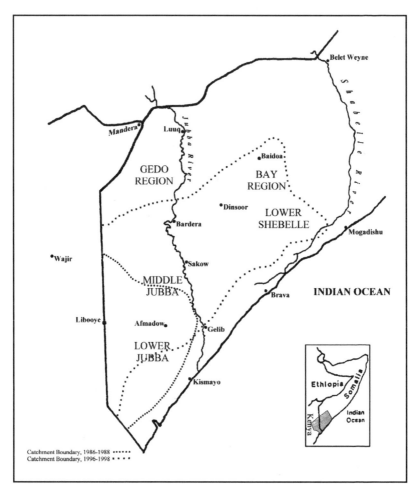

Fig 5.1   Market catchments in cross-border cattle trade, southern Somalia, 1986–98 (Source: Based on Besteman and Cassanelli (1996: 5) and author's data)

Transaction costs

Traders incur various costs in the cross-border cattle business and some of these are quite unique to the activity. They must pay off a range of different actors, including middlemen and trekkers, and cover the expenses of different services, such as veterinary and transport. The higher up in the market chain the merchant works, the greater the business costs s/he incurs. For the small-scale trader unexpected costs due to delays in a sale or theft of a few animals can mean a 'bust' year. Large-scale traders, in turn, can absorb these unanticipated losses and frequently shift such costs on to actors lower down in the market chain. They often do this by delaying payments to other traders and middlemen. Despite the hard work required and the prevalence of insecurity in the 1990s, the costs of conducting cross-border trade in the border region have not grown much since the 1980s and the commerce continues to attract new participants. As will be shown later, actual losses due to cattle theft and insecurity are relatively low, especially when compared to outside perceptions of insecurity.

Transport
One of the most significant and intriguing costs in the cross-border trade involves the transport of cattle, which can take up to several weeks from distant locations. It requires trekking the animals on foot, an age-old profession that dates back to the time of the caravan trade (Dalleo 1975). The cattle are moved overland with normally three trekkers and an armed security person for every approximately 100 cattle. There is a designated 'head trekker' who is directly responsible to the trader and who may be employed on a fairly regular basis. He must make payments to pass through territories controlled by different factions and lineages and, like the position of *Abbaan* (protector) in the days of the caravan trade (see Lewis 1994: 115), he is responsible for the safe passage of the herd. The head trekker or protector usually comes from one of the main lineages or sub-clans whose territory the market animals must traverse.

The Kenyan-based trader is likely to have a young relative accompany the animals on the trek, because of the physical rigor involved and to safe-guard his property. In some cases it can take almost one month to reach the Kenyan market from certain locations in Somalia, and substantial animal weight loss can occur.[17] One of the trekkers usually is responsible for procuring rice, flour, sugar, and tea for the trip and serving as the cook. The trader normally covers the cost of food, and on long treks an entire sack of flour or rice (50 kg or more) will be purchased and transported on a pack animal (donkey).

All traders involved with cross-border commerce incur some transport costs, and more than 50 percent pay cash for transport services. Prior to the follow-up study, it was assumed that transport costs in the region would have risen exorbitantly throughout the past decade because of insecurity. This has not been the case for many of the key routes, where movement costs per animal rarely exceed US$0.01 to 0.18/km and only modest increases took place since the government's collapse. There also were not substantial differences in transport costs between the Kenyan- and Somalia-based circuits. In fact, if anything the costs of transport increased more on the Kenya side in the 1990s, where traders indicate high incidences of banditry.

---

[17] It was virtually impossible to estimate weight loss from trekking, although herders pointed to it as a problem. The amount of weight loss will depend on range conditions, the number of trekking days, the herding skills of the trekkers, and other factors.

There are well-known watering and grazing points along the main trekking routes, but rarely do transit herds stay long at any single place. Some locations do not have sufficient resources to support large numbers of cattle for more than a day or so, and most communities are reluctant to allow 'trade herds' (which can be dominated by large male animals) to remain very long in an area. The goal is to move the animals as fast as possible to Kenya, and work days of 10–12 hours, seven days a week, are the norm. The Kenyan-based trader may go across the border to purchase the animals and arrange the hiring of temporary trekkers, but usually does not stay with the animals during the trek. As they near the border trekkers may receive information on market conditions in Kenya and be instructed to continue on to Kenya or delay until the market improves. For a lengthy trek this is especially crucial because market conditions may have deteriorated since its start. A trader always wants to avoid bringing animals on to a depressed market. Because pastures and water are more plentiful on the Somalia side, it is advantageous to wait out the market there rather than in Kenya. If a decision to wait is taken, then arrangements for grazing and watering must be made with the local community and some additional costs are incurred.

In the majority of cases, cross-border treks are 14 days or less. Animals are usually moved no more than 20 km per day and then watered and grazed at the end of the day. On the Kenyan side, cattle are initially trekked and then trucked from Garissa to a terminal market. The use of motorized transport explains in part the higher transport costs for the Kenyan than Somali routes (see Table 5.5). In the table the costs of transporting one head of cattle via different trekking routes are presented both for 1996 and 1998. As the data show, the length of market routes in the Somalia-to-Kenya trade varied from about 730 km in the case of Sakow-to-Mombasa, which takes about 30 days at a cost of $8.33/head of cattle, to 160 km for the Dhobley-to-Garissa trek, which takes 8 days at a cost of $2.03/animal. However, an animal from Somalia that is moved to Garissa market via the Mandera, Kenya border route will involve an even longer trek than the above. The Mandera–Garissa route alone is 650 km (Table 5.5), and that does not include the Somali part of the route, which could add an additional 150+ km.

Based on the data in Table 5.5 there appears to be a functioning market for cattle trekking in the region. As would be expected, transport costs per animal generally correspond with distance to market and type of transportation involved, except where insecurity is particularly problematic. The Baidoa–Garissa and Dinsoor–Garissa routes are examples of the latter and they experience relatively high transport costs. Both Baidoa and Dinsoor are occupied by a Somali group of Af-May speakers, called the Rahanweyn, who were major victims of the 1991–2 famine and repeatedly attacked by Mogadishu-based factions until the late 1990s. In 1998 traders usually hired one or two extra security persons to trek animals from risky areas like Baidoa and Dinsoor. While traders note that

Table 5.5. Transport costs in cross-border cattle trade, 1996 and 1998

Market route	Estimated distance (km)	Number of days[3]	Cost head (US $) 1996/1998	% Change 1996/ 1998	Cost per km 1996/1998
Garissa–Mombasa[1]	470	1–2	16.15/27.83	+72%	0.34/0.059
Garissa–Nairobi[1]	420	1	13.29/20.15	+52%	0.032/0.048
Mandera–Isiolo[2]	620	3	ND/16.67	—	ND/0.0269
Wajir–Mombasa[1]	650	3	ND/33.33	—	ND/0.046
Afmadow–Garissa	240	14	2.32/3.00	+29%	0.010/0.013
Baidoa–Garissa	550	28	4.59/5.92	+29%	0.010/0.010
Dinsoor–Garissa	490	23	4.03/2.08	–48%	0.010/.004
Dhobley–Garissa	160	8	2.03/ND	—	0.012/ND
Kismayo–Garissa	350	ND	ND/2.92	—	0.010
Libooye–Garissa	150	6	1.60/2.50	+56%	0.011/.017
Mogadishu–Afmadow	300	15	3.27/ND	—	0.011
Mogadishu–Garissa	540	28	4.15/4.92	+19%	0.0100/.010
Moyale–Garissa	590	36	ND/7.00	—	ND/.012
Moyale–Isiolo	500	28	3.91/3.32	–15%	0.007/0.007
Wajir–Garissa	250	ND	1.90/11.67[1]	–	0.008/0.047
Isiolo–Nairobi[1]	250	1	ND/14.17	—	ND/0.057
Mandera–Isiolo	600	36	ND/2.63	—	ND/0.004
Dinsoor–Moyale	540	32	ND/6.00	—	0.011
Mandera–Garissa	650	38	3.84/4.00	+4%	0.006
Marsabit–Isiolo	260	1	ND/2.63	—	ND/0.011
Marsabit–Nairobi[1]	520	2	ND/36.36	—	0.070
Moyale–Nairobi[1]	730	3	15.63/43.45	+178%	0.058/.060
Sakow–Mariakani (Mombasa)[4]	730	30	ND/8.33	—	ND/0.011

Source: Author's data.

Notes: ND = No data.

[1] These prices reflect the use of motorized transport (truck).

[2] This price was mainly for motorized transport but included some trekking on foot.

[3] There is considerable variation in this category depending on environmental and security conditions at the time, the particular motivations of the trader, and the skills of the herders. These numbers represent estimated averages based on trader interviews.

[4] The last part of this trek (100 km) often involves motorized transport.

security risks are partly responsible for the increased transport costs, they also indicate that wages in Somalia have grown particularly fast since 1991. Despite these cases of higher costs, increases in transport rates are not as large as would be expected under current conditions in the region.

Of the 11 market routes where I have data both for 1996 and 1998, transport rates increased by an average of 35 percent. Eight out of the 10 routes had positive changes in rates, ranging from 4 percent to over 170 percent. By a substantial margin, the highest annual increases in rates were for Kenyan routes that involved motorized transport. For example, rates along the Garissa–Nairobi and Garissa–Mombasa routes grew by 52 and 72 percent, respectively. Even with the near completion of an asphalt road

Photo 5.3   *Trucks waiting to transport Somali cattle* (Hussein A. Mahmoud)

between Garissa and Nairobi in 1998, rates for this route still increased substantially between 1996 and 1998. Traders note that security risks are partly responsible for the increased transport costs, but also indicate that truck availability is a problem. While this study did not investigate the transport sector in detail, indications are that certain large traders and companies control transport on these routes and limit the number of lorries. They monopolize the route and are known to restrict entry by outside entrepreneurs who might want to participate in the lucrative transport business.

Photo 5.4   *Somali cattle being loaded for transport to Nairobi* (Peter D. Little)

Procurement

The highest cost for cattle traders, of course, is the price they pay for animals. And this is the activity that Somalis take the most pride in and show an uncanny ability to accurately gauge animal weights, quality, and prices. This is where an experienced trader holds an advantage over younger merchants and explains why many of the major cattle brokers have been in the business for several years. Early attempts by both the Kenyan and the Somali governments to 'rationalize' the system by introducing scales for weighing animals proved futile, as traders had little use for such expensive devices. The large, rusty scale in Garissa market serves as testimony to such misplaced interventions. Rather than used for its intended purpose, the device currently serves as a market stand for women traders and their colorful fabrics and milk containers, as well as a source of shade for young goats during the midday heat.

Most traders (called *jeeble*)[18] who are involved in the cross-border cattle trade utilize middlemen based in Somali market towns.[19] The Somali term *jeeble* roughly equates to the concept of a middleman but also is used to refer to a general trader. By definition, a middleman in the cattle trade is not involved in final transactions and often works with another trader. In the border region the term can actually be applied to most traders, except for brokers and export traders, who are engaged in commerce on a full or near full-time basis. For present purposes I use the terms *jeeble* and middleman interchangeably.

The number of middlemen that most livestock traders dealt with changed very little during the 1990s. On average traders currently work with about two or three different middlemen during the year, and about one-third of them (i.e. the most experienced traders) have dealt with the same middlemen for more than five years. Once a trader builds up a relationship of trust with a middleman, the merchant is likely to stick with that individual. In contrast to the earlier period, it now is common for a Kenyan-based trader to receive price quotes by hand radio or telephone (via Nairobi) from Somali-based middlemen and to adjust buying strategies accordingly. Hand radios are found in most settlements of southern Somalia, including a public 'pay radio' in the small town of Bilas Qooqani, where calls to Mogadishu and Nairobi can be made. In larger cities, like Kismayo and Mogadishu, satellite-linked phone systems provide international connections that are considerably cheaper than in neighboring countries and help to disseminate market information.

On the Somalia side the middleman who procures animals for a trader either charges a fee per animal, sells the animal outright to the trader, or, in a few cases, shares in profits with the trader in a partnership arrangement.

---

[18] The term *jeeble* often is used interchangeably with another Somali term for livestock trader, *gedisley* (see Janzen 1988: 22).

[19] All middlemen and traders interviewed were males, although one female livestock trader (out of 120+) was observed in 1996. She was involved with buying cattle near Mogadishu and reselling them in Garissa.

The relationship between a trader and a middleman is based on a great deal of trust, since many unknowns exist and large sums of cash are transacted. These relationships are increasingly reinforced through clan and sub-clan ties, a tendency that was less apparent in the 1980s before the government's collapse. As noted in Chapter 3, militia-enforced clan boundaries currently restrict the kinds of social and economic interactions that help to reinforce trust, good will, and familiarity among members of different clans. Since many Kenyan-based traders are reluctant to enter southern Somalia, they greatly rely on Somali-based clansmen and friends to serve as middlemen. This is especially the case for large-scale traders, who have annual sales of 600+ cattle and who strongly depend on middlemen to procure animals. While normative statements from traders indicate a sole reliance on their own clan – and in many cases, their sub-clan – the reality of the situation is more complex and some work closely with middlemen of different clans.

The work of a middleman is difficult, as s/he must move among homesteads, grazing camps, and small bush markets looking for good-quality animals to purchase. Only by piecing together multiple purchases of a few animals can orders be filled. A middleman may negotiate with a particularly resistant herder for several days to encourage him to sell one large bull. In northern Kenya I observed a middleman who haggled over price with a wealthy pastoralist for almost four days before the herder relinquished and sold him two big bulls. Because herders are generally suspicious and 'untrusting' of middlemen and traders, merchants often rely on social means to reinforce buying relationships. These strategies may include contributing a gift for a local ceremony, such as a wedding, or providing veterinary supplies to the herder's homestead. These practices remove the buying activity from the strictly commercial realm and create an aura of good will. However, they can be very time-consuming and costly for the middleman. Merchants usually know those homesteads with large enough herds to sell surplus animals, and pursue long-term social relationships with them.

Very little seems to have changed during the past two decades in terms of the use of cash in market transactions. As was the case in the 1980s, smaller merchants usually advance little credit to middlemen but, instead, rely on cash transactions. By receiving credit the middleman is closely tied to the trader's activities, and has a vested interest in the operation's profitability. In such cases, middlemen are advanced money by traders who must have faith that the middlemen will not abscond with the funds, will negotiate the best possible price, and will honestly report sales and market conditions in Somalia. At the upper end of the market chain it is not uncommon for the trader to sell an animal to a wholesaler or butcher on short-term credit and then be repaid when the meat is sold. Traders complain about providing animals to Nairobi-based butchers on credit and then not receiving payment for several weeks or, in a few cases, not at all. Ironically, while meat wholesalers and Nairobi residents generally adhere to rigid cultural stereotypes about Somalis and their aggressive behavior, it is actually the latter who are vulnerable in the market place and sometimes exploited. This is an important reason why merchants from northern Kenya frequently utilize Nairobi's Njiru market where there are some Somali buyers, rather than the larger, Dagoretti market which is dominated by non-Somalis.

Market and broker fees
In all of the markets, including Nairobi, there are brokers (called *dilaal*) to match sellers and buyers and negotiate prices on their behalf (for descriptions of brokers elsewhere in Africa, see Dupire 1962; Cohen 1969; Manger 1984). A *dilaal* is an individual who works in the market and can represent buyers, sellers, or both. As was shown in the case of Ahmed and Yusuf, they assume very important roles in the cattle trade. The broker insures the validity of the sale by certifying that the animal is not stolen. The fee is usually around 1–2 percent of the animal's price, or about $2.00 per animal. In some cases, the cost is shared equally by buyer and seller, while in other instances one party may cover the entire charge. When the two parties are working with different brokers, they each will be paid separately. For the seller these arrangements remove the dual burden of finding a buyer and negotiating a price. In the Nairobi marketplace, Somali traders almost always deal with Somali rather than non-Somali brokers. In Somalia the role of the *dilaal* is so significant that they are officially registered by the local administration and prior to the state's collapse they paid a small tax to local government.

The fees of brokers changed very little from 1988 to 1998. As a percentage of livestock prices, average broker fees at most markets in 1988 and 1998 were about the same. This finding might seem surprising given the security situation in the region. Since a broker is paid to insure the legitimacy of a transaction and is responsible if a stolen animal is sold, greater insecurity should translate into higher broker fees. A higher broker rate would provide some insurance against losses. Yet, brokers' fees have not risen very much, which would imply that either transactions in stolen animals are rare or dishonest sellers avoid brokers.

Risks and losses
Broker fees are actually slightly higher in Kenya than in Somalia, an indication that market risks may be as great (or greater) in Kenya. This paradox confirms what many traders emphasize: livestock thefts are actually higher on the Kenyan than Somali side of the border. They claim that in Somalia areas of hostility are well known and avoided, or 'passage' fees are paid to traverse them. Moreover, one group, the Mohamed Zubeyr, controls most of the territory along the main cross-border route between Afmadow and the border. It is viewed regionally as a relatively safe territory for Ogadeen traders to move cattle. On the Kenyan side of the border, however, the clan structure is heterogeneous, consisting of

rival Ogadeen groups like the Abdwak and Aulihan, and sporadic police posts manned with officers who have little interest in controlling raiding. Recent accounts highlight the widespread banditry and conflict on the Kenya side, even quite near to Garissa town (*Daily Nation*, 13 December 1999, p.1). In short, attacks in northeastern Kenya are difficult to predict and bandits can quickly transport stolen animals outside the area and sell them with little difficulty.

In the 1990s cattle losses from theft increased but the numbers are still relatively low. In 1996 less than 10 percent of traders indicated any cattle stolen during the previous year, but in 1998 the corresponding figure was 33.3 percent. The mean number of cattle stolen in 1998, however, was relatively low at 2.71, or less than 3 animals per trekking herd of 100.

Other transaction costs
Other transaction costs are associated with the cross-border trade. In both the 1980s and 1990s most traders incurred annual expenses for water, hired labor, and veterinary inputs. As with herders (see Chapters 2 and 3), traders frequently purchase drugs on the informal market to protect against trypanosomiasis, as well as chemical sprays to reduce tick infestation. While traders did not complain about shortages of veterinary drugs in 1996 and 1998, they do lament their high costs and use them less frequently than they did in the 1980s. Without a government, animal vaccination campaigns are virtually non-existent. Those few NGOs that have implemented them provide only partial coverage. Chapter 2 highlighted the inefficiency of the past government's veterinary services, but at least at that time an institutional context for animal health campaigns existed. The disease-related market embargoes during 1998–2002 highlight this deficiency and threaten the country's dynamic pastoral sector.

At Garissa merchants occasionally buy fodder to feed their animals when they cannot find a buyer and the herd must remain in the area. Brokers reduce the chances of these kinds of bottlenecks, but even *dilaal* have little control over external events. For example, when there is an unexpected glut of animals on the Nairobi market from neighboring countries, such as Tanzania and Ethiopia, traders may have to wait several days in Garissa before transporting cattle down-country. When this happens, the trader often has little recourse but to purchase fodder or to move animals into surrounding range lands.

Who benefits?
Do the increased price differentials between Kenya and Somalia mean that traders earned considerably higher profits in the 1990s than in the 1980s? The answer is complex and depends greatly on the merchant's position in the market chain, the type of animal traded, and the particular year. Because of the high risks (e.g. insecurity, drought, or floods) of trade in certain years, it is difficult to talk of returns in a 'normal' year. Nonetheless, based on certain assumptions (discussed below) it is possible

to calculate the costs and returns to traders at different levels in the market chain, and to determine where profits are highest (Table 5.6). It also is possible to assess the amount of the trade that is captured by pastoralists, as well as the amount of income that actually stays in the border area. Recall that for the overseas export trade most of the revenues accrued to towns and actors outside the region.

Table 5.6 is based on the same cross-border market route, Afmadow–Garissa–Nairobi, that was discussed earlier in the chapter. A common traded animal, 'Quality 2 cattle,' is used in the calculation of returns. The table assumes that there are two traders involved in the market chain; one based in Garissa who buys from a Somalia-based middleman, and one based in Nairobi who purchases from the Garissa trader. The estimates

Table 5.6. Trader returns in the cross-border trade, 1998–1999

ITEM	Amount US$ per cattle	% net return
Initial purchase price from herder	108.00	
Purchase price from middlemen, Afmadow	128.00	
Transport cost (Afmadow–Garissa)	3.00	
Hired herd labor	1.60	
Security/transit fees	0.40	
Water (50 days @ .08)	4.00	
Medicine/dips	1.82	
Fodder (Garissa market) (dry season only)	0.60	
Risk from loss (theft, drought, etc.) (6%)	7.6	
Broker fee (Afmadow)	1.25	
Broker fee (Garissa)	1.67	
Council tax (Kenya)	1.33	
Currency transaction/conversion fees	5.28	
Trader 1 costs	156.63	
Sale price, Garissa	176.00	
TRADER 1 RETURN		15
Transport cost (Garissa–Nairobi)	20.15	
Movement permit/fees	1.33	
Hired labor	0.33	
Water	1.00	
Fodder (Garissa and Nairobi)	0.60	
Market/municipal tax (Nairobi)	1.33	
Broker fee (Garissa)	1.67	
Broker fee (Nairobi)	2.50	
Trader 2 costs	204.91	
Sale price, Nairobi	233.00	
TRADER 2/MIDDLEMAN RETURN		16
Gross difference between original purchase and final price	105 (82%)	
Trader return if one trader only and purchases from Somalia and sells in Nairobi		31

Notes: Based on sample of 84 traders, author's data.

include other assumptions that will vary from year to year. For example, the figures in the table are based on a non-drought, non-flood year, and a period without conflict and border closures, all of which can disrupt trade and trader profits. In the 1998 survey, pastures were plentiful near marketplaces and animals sold quickly, so there were few expenditures on fodder. In very dry months or in times when animal sales are especially slow, considerable costs can be allocated to fodder and to water – as much as five to six times the figures in Table 5.6.

As would be expected, the highest risks and costs in cattle trade involve the initial purchase and transport. The net return for the trader (Trader 1 in Table 5.6) who buys directly from Somalia and sells at Garissa is 15 percent. The return is almost the same at 16 percent for the trader (Trader 2 in Table 5.6) who purchases at Garissa and then resells in Nairobi – the high cost of transport between Garissa and Nairobi (about 12 percent of the Garissa purchase price) accounts for most of Trader 2's marketing costs. As Table 5.6 shows, if Trader 2 purchases an animal directly from Somalia rather than at the Garissa market, then the net return per animal can be as high as 31 percent. If the livestock trader owns his/her own transport, the profits can be even higher than this figure. Thus, while the risks can be excessive in some years, the returns in the cross-border trade are also very high – well above profits in other types of agricultural trade and higher than returns in 1987–8 (see Little and Dolan 1994).

Benefits from the trans-border trade also accrue to herders, but at lower levels. Since there is no production cost data to utilize, the best means of calculating the extent to which herders have – or have not – captured the benefits of increased cross-border trade is to look at their price shares in the different markets and for varied types of animals. In 1996 a herder at Afmadow whose cattle were eventually sold across the border in Garissa received between 62 and 73 percent of the price depending on the quality of the animal. These percentages are about 10 percent lower than in 1987–8, when herders had more marketing options and received better prices. Pastoralists who sell high-quality animals receive a higher proportion of the Kenyan sale price than those who supply other animals. The difference probably reflects the higher demand for and limited supplies of high-quality cattle in northern Kenya. Generally herders who sell the highest quality animals also tend to be the wealthiest herders. They are the pastoralists who have reaped the bulk of benefits from the increased cross-border trade with Kenya, although as discussed earlier the overseas trade favored wealthy herders even more.

The price data also reflect the advantages of residing near the Kenya border. Generally those pastoralists who reside closest to the border benefit most from the Kenya trade. For example, a Mogadishu herder receives only 52 percent of the Garissa sale price for both Quality 2 and 3 animals, but the Afmadow herder receives more than a 60 percent share. In short, locational advantage vis-à-vis the Kenya border strongly affects the extent to which Somali herders benefit from the cross-border trade. Of the $10+ million in cattle sales at Garissa (see Table 5.2 above), herders are receiving no more than 60 to 70 percent of that revenue regardless of residence. A herder's share of the terminal price in Nairobi is even lower than these figures, about 46 percent or less than half of the final price. In 1987–8 the proportion was about 13 percent higher than this, which indicates that benefits from the growth in cross-border trade have been captured more by livestock traders than herders. Yet, as indicated earlier, without this commerce the prices that herders receive would have been markedly lower than the figures presented here.

In terms of the gendered dimension of the market, it is clear that women have reaped very few direct benefits from the booming trans-border animal trade. Indirectly, they probably have gained from sales of cattle in cases where the cash was used to purchase foodstuffs for their families. As noted earlier, women are rarely involved with the cattle trade (see note 6) and the kind of petty trade – for example, milk – that they control does not involve trans-border exchanges. Even for related occupations – butcheries, transporters, and brokers – very few women participate in the cattle business. In fact, it is likely that the increased trade in cattle could actually compete with their own income-earning activities, such as milk trading and dairy production. If male herders are selling dairy animals (females) to take advantage of cross-border opportunities, their market transactions could be having a negative impact on women's incomes.

Traders and trader relations

Social relations underlie vital business ties and permeate all levels of cattle markets in the region, including the cross-border trade. They are increasingly based on clan, but among larger traders patron–client relationships also are found. So far in this chapter, discussion has centered on the geography of different markets and the transaction costs associated with them. To complete the picture, the rest of the chapter is devoted to the role of traders, their social characteristics, and their responses to different political and economic crises. They are the actors who have played such important roles in the economy and politics of stateless Somalia.

The rapid expansion in cattle exports from 1970 to 1983 resulted in two momentous changes for merchants that had major implications for the direction of political struggles in the 1990s. First, it inserted into the border region a class of very large export traders from Mogadishu and other areas to the north.[20] These traders, who were de-linked from the pastoral sector of the Lower Jubba, depended on large brokers and middlemen to procure their animals. Many of the exporters were Harti

---

[20] In 1988 there were more than 100 registered companies in Somalia involved with livestock exports, but none were from the Lower Jubba area.

but there also were Marehan, some of whom had strong ties to the corrupt Barre regime. Second, the growth in cattle exports altered local and regional market relations, as certain local middlemen and brokers began to serve as agents for the large export traders. In the border region this resulted in a scale of trading enterprise and specialization not characteristic of earlier periods. In the case of the overseas commerce, three large traders alone accounted for more than 70 percent of overseas cattle exports from Kismayo in 1987.

At the time of the follow-up study there were few active export agents or exporters to interview since the overseas export trade had virtually collapsed. While a few traders still engaged in overseas trade but from a Kenyan base, its prominence was significantly less than in the 1980s. Yet, as will be shown here, the lasting impacts of the trade on social and political relationships were still very evident in the 1990s and accounted for some of the major political alliances that were to become so important.

Part-time bush traders
The smallest traders in the region, called 'bush traders', are the most numerous, and prior to 1991 were more likely to be involved in the regional domestic and Kenyan trades than in the Mogadishu and overseas markets. They are distinguished from other local traders (*jeeble*) and middlemen by (1) scale of enterprise – frequently they buy only 20 to 25 cattle a year – and (2) their lack of full-time commitment to trade. Many of these traders started in the livestock business by first trading in goats, accumulating some capital, and then moving into the cattle trade. They frequently buy from small- and medium-scale rather than wealthier herders, and pursue a pastoral lifestyle that is usually indistinguishable from local herders. Many of these traders are young, often under 30 years of age, and use profits earned from livestock trade to build up their own herds, marry, or move on to a larger scale of trade. Their position in regional livestock trade has improved as the trans-border market has grown. The account of Abdulcadhir illustrates how this type of trader operates in the rural areas:

> Abdulcadhir lives in Bilas Qooqani and in the late 1980s he was buying animals from Mohamed Zubeyr herders near Afmadow and from a few Aulihan herders near Bualle. His sister had married an Aulihan and he had relatively good social ties to that area. Because few homesteads are likely to sell more than a few animals at any one time, a bush trader like Abdulcadhir has to purchase cattle from up to 10 homesteads before he has sufficient animals to take to market, or to sell to a larger trader or middleman. To pursue potential sellers, Abdulcadhir moved to the seasonal grazing areas, where herders congregated, often traveling up to 100 km between seasons. He preferred to buy animals in the dry season when prices are low and hold on to them until the rains came and prices

improved. During 1996 it took him about four months to accumulate 12 cattle, which he then sold at Dhobley to a middleman working on behalf of a Kenyan-based merchant. While he has been involved in cattle trade for about 10 years, he has only pursued the cross-border trade since 1994.

Some part-time bush traders, like Abdulcadhir, who were interviewed during 1987–8 are now engaged in cross-border trade. Approximately 45 percent of the 69 livestock traders interviewed in 1996 had indicated that they started trading only within the past five years. This would imply that the growth in cross-border commerce has attracted a growing number of traders, who perceive it as a viable means to accumulate quick profits. Bush traders are in excellent positions to capitalize on this trade, since they have direct ties to the cattle-rich areas of southern Somalia.

Agents of large traders
Agents of large traders are middlemen who have attached themselves to a large trader (or group of traders) on a full- or near full-time basis and are referred to as *wakil* in some areas (see Abdullahi 1990: 180). This practice was first associated with the overseas trade, but in 1998 some of the largest Nairobi-based traders also had agents in the border region. The agent position is a direct result of the growth in the export trade, first the overseas and later the cross-border trade. It reflects a degree of organization and specialization not witnessed previously in the area. During the Saudi export boom of the 1970s and early 1980s, agents profited more than other local traders. It was less costly for export traders to buy directly from an agent than to pay a fee to a broker, and it was in the interest of the exporter to force his client to be responsible for buying and caring for the cattle. As profits were increasingly squeezed in the overseas trade, export traders delayed purchases from their agents to oblige them to incur more of the production costs. It was only after the exporter received his money that the agent was paid in full and then finally paid off the herder. Because these outlays were costly, only the larger middlemen could afford to become agents for overseas exporters.

Most middlemen who became full-time agents in the overseas trade were from the major towns of Kismayo District. While there were important exceptions, many of those agents were Harti, the same clan group as many exporters. In an activity as risky as overseas export trade, family and clan-based ties help to reduce transaction costs and disseminate market information among different actors. As has been suggested here, regardless of clan affiliations, costs and risks were increasingly passed down the market chain, from exporter to agent and then to herder. A large middleman or agent may have dozens of credit relationships outstanding at any given time, supported by few or no formal credit instruments. Because of the absence of formal contracts, credit also is reinforced through clan ties and explains why Ogadeen herders usually work with

Ogadeen traders, and Harti deal with Harti agents. The informal system works because these trust-based relationships are not founded on financial exchange alone, but involve multiple obligations that can be invoked if an agreement is violated. Prior to the war the overseas export trader tapped into such relations by working through a small number of local agents and middlemen, who then invested in community relationships and activities to ensure a regular supply of cattle.

Overseas export traders

As discussed earlier, the overseas export traders usually were not from the Kismayo region and operated procurement systems based on their own networks of agents. In some areas they were referred to as *Ganacsato* (see Abdullahi 1990: 180). In terms of livestock trade their operations essentially collapsed in 1990, and some moved into other types of commerce, such as food import activities and charcoal exports. Some traders moved out of the region altogether, re-establishing businesses in Bossaso, Mombasa, or, in some cases, Garissa, Kenya (see examples later in this chapter). Those who were Harti were forced to move to Bossaso and other towns of Puntland (northeastern Somalia), where many of their clan members are found.

Prior to 1991 export traders employed three to four agents on average, as well as several middlemen on a part-time basis. Those exporters who resided in the area lived in Kismayo town, the only regional center that provided some of the banking and communication facilities necessary for the export trade. They did not maintain strong links to the nomadic sector nor to smaller traders. When interviewed at their bases in Mogadishu, many exporters showed poor familiarity with the actual day-to-day operations of their enterprises and relied heavily on managers and hired herders.

The special case of cross-border merchants

Unlike overseas exporters, traders who dealt with the Kenya market were (and still are) from the smaller towns of the border region and directly involved in cattle trade. The logistical requirements for this trade are not exorbitant, differing very little from the domestic trade in Somalia. These markets require trekking and attract a range of cattle types, from older steers and cows to young (4–7 years) bulls and cows. Thus, a cross-border merchant based in Somalia in 1988 was not likely to be much different from other local traders and usually oriented a portion of the business to regional and national markets as well.

More than 60 percent of the 84 traders interviewed in 1996 and 1998 were engaged in procuring cattle for the cross-border trade and, as was the case for the 1980s, most (> 85 percent) were from Ogadeen sub-clans – especially the Mohamed Zubeyr and Aulihan sub-clans. Most non-Ogadeen involved in the cross-border trade operate from the Kenya side and at upper levels in the market chain. As I have pointed out elsewhere, all types of trade have become increasingly clan-based as a result of the recent instability and the blatantly clan-based tactics of different militias. As one non-Ogadeen trader explains: 'Animal prices were low in the past but now are very expensive because clan borders are existing now and, therefore, the Borana, Degodia Somali, and others have decided to keep their animals in their area. It is only Ogadeen who stay here now that participate in the trade on the Kenya side' (trader interview, 28 May 1996). Thus, unraveling the cross-border trade routes and supply chains in the region exposes different strata of ethnic, clan, and sub-clan structures.

Differentiation and scale

By the 1990s cross-border traders demonstrated greater scale and organization than I had observed in the 1980s. The numbers of actors and complexity of enterprises grew and some operations moved away from conflict-ridden Somalia to Kenya's large and middle-sized towns. Unlike in the past, their current operations generally are larger than those of other traders in the region. In Table 5.7 the average sales associated with trader operations confirm this point, while the excessive standard deviations suggest a high degree of variability and differentiation. Analyses of the different data sets in the table show the extent to which the research in the 1990s captures large-scale traders. More than 60 percent of the sample had annual sales of more than 600 cattle. By contrast, in the 1987–8 study only 20 percent of merchants reached an equivalent status, while a relatively large number of traders (50 percent) had annual sales of only between 1 and 300 cattle.

The information from the 1990s also shows that merchants who mainly focus on the largest market, Nairobi, have considerably larger operations than other traders. While average annual sales in 1996 were 943 cattle, they reached 1,133 for traders who sold directly to Nairobi. In many cases

Table 5.7. Annual sales of cattle by traders

Range of annual sales	Percentage of total		
	1987–8	1996	1998
1 to 300	50	17	34
301 to 600	30	18	26
601 to 900	–	20	5
901 to 1,200	5	28	22
1,200+	15[1]	17	13
Total	100	100	100
Average sales (mean)	434	943	855
Standard deviation:	606	760	883
	N = 17 traders	N = 84 traders	

Source: Based on author's data.

Notes:

[1] Traders in this category were all overseas exporters, with the largest having annual sales of 6,000 cattle.

these entrepreneurs are based in or have partners in Nairobi and their enterprises approach the scale and capitalization of the overseas export operations described earlier. In short, those actors with direct access to the Nairobi outlet, the largest market in the whole of East Africa, clearly hold advantages over other traders.

Diversification
The scale of cattle trading among the wealthiest merchants requires a relatively full-time commitment, although many traders (large and small) have investments in other sectors. They engage in such activities as (in order of importance): (1) retail stores; (2) butcheries; (3) hides and skins trade; and (4) grain trade. This pattern of diversification was also found in the 1987–8 study, but on a smaller scale. Only 47 percent of traders engaged in more than one economic activity then, while 68 percent did so in the 1990s (author's field notes). The increased diversification in the past decade is a response to an environment of heightened volatility and risk.

What is apparent about diversification, as we have seen in the earlier case of Fasil (the hotel owner), is that livestock trade often generates the initial capital for other activities. Some of these ventures, such as the hides and skins trade and the butchery business, closely complement livestock trade; others have little to do with livestock. Since a certain number of cattle perish annually en route from Somalia, the hides and skins business is a way to recoup at least some revenue from herd losses. Grain trade also partially complements the cross-border livestock trade, in that traders can bring Kenyan grain and flour back to Somalia on their return. It is a relatively recent cross-border activity that some traders pursue, partially in response to opportunities created by large-scale food aid and grain availability in Kenya. Food aid often finds its way into private markets, where it is bought and sold by merchants and occasionally bartered directly with herders for livestock. Merchants usually await word on the status of World Food Programme (WFP) shipments of grain to southern Somalia before making decisions about transporting grain across the border from Kenya. Traders are well aware of the dampening effect that food aid can have on local prices and markets.

On the other side of the border consumer electronics, used clothes, and other goods are imported 'duty free' from Dubai through Somali ports and find their way to Kenyan markets via border towns like Mandera and Libooye. As many Kenyans will acknowledge, the country's cheapest prices for consumer electronics (televisions, stereos, and satellite dishes) are found in Mandera town, the small remote border town located more than 1,000 km from bustling Nairobi. Large-scale traders in Somalia have partners in Dubai to facilitate this trade. Discussions with traders and NGO personnel reveal that while this commerce is very important, it also suffers from banditry and sporadic border closures. The occasional government confiscation and impound of a truck in Kenya that is laden with electronic goods attests to the significance of this trade (*The People*, 25 June 2001, p. 3). On a smaller scale, a reverse type of trade occurs: Somali livestock traders use Kenyan shillings to purchase small amounts of Kenyan trade goods, such as plastic products, tea, and other small consumer goods, for resale in southern Somalia. This strategy was very common in the 1980s, but now it is more profitable for Somali retailers and wholesalers to buy Asian goods imported through 'tax-free' Somalia.

Dealing with crisis

As a social category, in Africa and elsewhere, traders are especially exposed when national economic and political indicators decline (Clark 1988; Ring 1989). This is particularly the case for so-called 'stranger' traders, who operate outside their home regions and thus cannot easily draw on support from kin and others. Instead, such merchants frequently use clientelism to build up relationships that can be mobilized during periods of crisis and uncertainty, but can be turned against them in particularly extreme cases like in Somalia.

The disintegration of the export trade and the subsequent collapse of the Somalia state especially exposed outside export traders and their agents. Prior to the 1990s a number of export traders had diversified into urban real estate and other business, using revenues accrued from animal exports. These investments were additional buffers against the vagaries of the export business, but proved to be inconsequential as these assets were visible targets in the chaos of 1991–2. Those traders and local brokers who had put most of their social capital into maintaining market channels for the export trade suffered the most. Because their alliances, including relationships with herders, were geared to the overseas trade, most benefited little from the burgeoning trade to Kenya.

In the initial period after the state's collapse, Kismayo-based merchants were among the most vulnerable in the region, especially during 1991 to 1992. Recall the urban attacks discussed in Chapter 3 that targeted the Harti elite of Kismayo. Further indication of the city's precarious situation at the time was its disproportionate representation of displaced victims at Kenya's refugee camps (see CARE 1994). As the following accounts portray, the effects of the different crises have been uneven but generally negative for Kismayo traders.

> Umar is about 55 years old and was among the largest middlemen in the overseas export trade of the 1970s and 1980s. He resided in Kismayo District and acted as an agent for an export company owned by town-based relatives. He supplied cattle directly to them and had business relationships with six small middlemen (*jeeble*) in Kismayo and Badhaade Districts who purchased animals for him. These trade relations endured throughout most of the 1970s

and early 1980s. He often advanced money to middlemen and would delay full payment to them until after the animals had been exported. With the decline in cattle exports after 1983, he continued to export a small number of camels. During 1986 to 1988 he neither bought nor sold cattle, and traded less than 10 camels per year during that period. In 1990 he had almost completely withdrawn from the livestock business and, instead, concentrated on his small retail store in Kismayo. By the time of the follow-up study, Umar no longer had any involvement in the livestock trade and seemed to have suffered considerably from the turbulence in Kismayo. Few traders in 1996 and 1998 were able to provide information about him, other than to say that he no longer engaged in business activities.

Abdi Saed, 50 years of age, concentrated his efforts on the overseas trade during the 1970s and early 1980s, but also kept his hand in the domestic trade of Kismayo town. He served as an agent for five export traders, of which three were based in the Mogadishu area. When the export trade was good, he worked with four small middlemen in Kismayo District who supplied him with cattle. His revenue was hurt by the loss of overseas markets, but not to the extent that Umar's was. From 1986 to 1988 he bought and sold only 40 cattle, but traded more than 300 goats on local markets in Kismayo. Unlike Umar, he has maintained ties with middlemen and herders oriented toward the Kismayo domestic market and, thus, has been able to avoid the full effects of the catastrophic downturn in overseas trade. When information was sought about Abdi Saed in 1996, it was unknown if he still focused on trade in the Kismayo area, but he was not one of those merchants who had been able to shift his business to Kenya.

Neither Umar nor Abdi Saed, both of whom were Harti, have been able to capitalize on the booming unofficial trade to Kenya. They did not have the kind of relationships – with traders in Kenya or with Ogadeen middlemen and herders – to take advantage of opportunities in the Kenyan trade. Moreover, both men were older traders, unlikely to want to endure the rigors of the cross-border trade. They also have not been able to relocate to Kenya and to establish businesses there, and as of 1996 were maintaining a precarious existence in the Kismayo area. With the decline in the overseas export trade in the 1980s, Abdi Saed and Umar were already hurting when the 'shocks' of 1991 further jeopardized their livelihoods.

In contrast to Abdi Saed and Umar, the dramatic changes in the cattle trade placed many small-scale 'bush' traders and middlemen in favorable positions despite the collapse of the official economy and state. As was pointed out earlier, many Afmadow middlemen participated in the Kenya and Somalia domestic trade, even if they occasionally sold to agents of overseas exporters. They established themselves in the late 1980s and benefited immensely from the recent growth in cross-border trade. Some of these individuals were interviewed in the late 1990s and were found to have annual cattle sales in the 400+ range (see Table 5.7). Profiles of two traders who have benefited from the Kenyan trade provide an informative contrast to the previous cases.

Ali is one of the 'new' entrepreneurs who has taken advantage of the growth in cross-border trade. He has only been in the cattle business since 1993 but together with a partner he already has annual sales of around 550 cattle. He is from Afmadow but frequently stays at a small town near the border, especially at the end of the wet season (July to August) when the volume of trade is high. He and his partner are both from the Mohamed Zubeyr sub-clan and have many market contacts in Garissa, Kenya. For Ali the boom in commerce has brought many economic benefits and he described himself as relatively poor until the last few years. After selling his cattle in Garissa he often boards a bus for Nairobi and deposits his money with a currency trader who then wires US dollars back to Somalia. He also buys consumer goods in Nairobi (medicines and clothes) and if grain prices are favorable in southern Somalia he arranges to ship small amounts (400 kg or less) to border markets. In many respects he is a regional citizen with a Kenyan identification card that allows him to reside in Kenya as well as Somalia. When queried about market constraints and changes since 1991, he provides the usual litany of problems about low prices, insufficient demand, and exorbitant transport costs, but generally feels business is better now than before.

Dahir is a merchant who was fortunate enough to flee the conflict in Kismayo and to establish a business in Garissa. He is approximately 60 years of age and his clan affiliation is not known. Born in Kismayo, his family has ties to the city dating back to the 1890s. Prior to the war he owned a wholesale store, butchery, and livestock trading enterprise. He exported animals to the Middle East until 1988 and also sold livestock at the Kismayo and Mogadishu markets. When the conflict in Kismayo worsened in April 1991, some of his family members moved to Kenya and sought refugee status at camps near Libooye and Dadaab, Kenya. In late 1992 the situation in Kismayo had become unbearable and fearing for his life Dahir transited to Mombasa, Kenya on an overcrowded boat. By this time he had already sent most of his cash out with family members who had exited earlier. He took his remaining funds with him and headed for Mombasa where a trusting business associate lived. From Mombasa he made his way to Garissa after about one year. There he established a small retail store and butchery. By 1996 Dahir was in possession of one of the town's largest wholesale stores and his business seemed prosperous.

The latter two entrepreneurs were able to survive the economic and political problems of the 1980s and 1990s and both were able to capitalize on the thriving cross-border trade. Clearly, the high costs of war were also felt by Dahir, but unlike Umar and Abdi Saed he was able to flee the country and re-establish a viable enterprise in northeastern Kenya. The middlemen who became involved in the cross-border trade profited more than most other traders, as is evident from Ali's story. Somali-based traders who are either Ogadeen themselves or who have maintained strong ties to them are able to capitalize on the Kenya trade. In the next chapter we learn more about how Somalis like these have gone on with their lives despite the absence of a government and most public institutions.

6
Life ▌ Goes On

While Somalia today is stateless, it is not anarchic. Although repeated efforts to revive a central government have failed, local communities have responded with a range of strategies to establish the minimal essential elements of governance. What has emerged in Somalia are fluid, localized polities involving authorities as diverse as clan elders, professionals, militia leaders, businessmen, traditional Muslim clerics, Islamic fundamentalists, and women's associations (Menkhaus 1998b: 220).

It is difficult to state with any conviction that local herders or rural populations generally benefited much during the 1980s when Somalia had a government. They acquired little of the actual value of the livestock and other commodities they produced and only received minuscule investments in infrastructure, schools, and health clinics. One estimate is that the pastoral sub-sector, which accounted for more than 80 percent of annual exports, 'received only about 6 percent of public expenditure, corresponding to 1.2% of GDP annually during 1974–1988' (Mubarak 1997: 2029). When the state actually intervened in the pastoral areas, it often was with punitive force, as in the late 1980s, or with half-hearted interventions that heightened ambiguities and risks rather than reduced them. In terms of providing basic human services and support, the state had failed miserably in the rural regions of southern Somalia. For most residents of the border areas, therefore, 'life goes on' and the challenges of herding and surviving in a risky environment still dominate daily practice.

The Somalia of the 1990s represented for some observers 'one of the purest laboratories for capitalism' (Fisher 2000: 4). Indeed, the 'laboratory' aspect has attracted its fair share of attention from libertarians and radical free market advocates who see any government controls as inherently bad and admire the way that Somalis have resisted the centralization of authority (see MacCallam 1998). They enthusiastically praise the manner in which the business sector has survived – even prospered – in the absence of government. To quote one extreme observer (Graham Green 1998: 1–2), 'Business is booming in this unusual country where taxation and government regulation used to destroy almost all private business ventures ... its sin is that it defeated the UN army that came to restore the central government that the Somali nation had abolished in 1991.' However, what this and other anti-statist positions fail to appreciate is that the 'free trade' environment of Somalia has not benefited all parties equally (see Chapter 5) and that even businessmen seek a return to some form of government as evidenced by their support for the newly created Transitional National Government (TNG).

The 'ungoverned' nature of Somalia and its economy, heralded by some as a triumph of the free market, are currently the country's own worst enemies. Now sadly associated with global terrorism and shady economic practices in some international quarters, their territory is claimed to have hosted terrorist networks, such as al-Qaida, and actions against Somalia have been taken recently. Indeed, it is now assumed by the US and its allies that Usama bin Laden himself and his al-Qaida network may have had a hand in the Mogadishu debacle of October 1993 that so badly humiliated the US and UN interventions.[1] It also is thought that the innovative informal banking system, which evolved in response to Somalia's collapsed finance sector, has generated profits and laundered funds for noted terrorists, although firm evidence of this has never been presented. As a result of these accusations, one of Somalia's key financial institutions was closed by the US and its allies in November 2001 as part of the 'global war against terrorism' (see discussion later in this chapter). Thus, almost overnight the global significance of Somalia and its politics, which already greatly challenged scholars and policy makers, increased in complexity by at least tenfold. After a long absence Somalia was back on the front page of major international newspapers and publications! The implications of these accusations, as well as the renewed global concern for Somalia – a country that was generally forgotten after 1995 – are discussed in more detail in the next chapter.

This chapter mainly explores what has happened in selected sectors of Somali life – business and economics, food security, education, and local governance – since the government's collapse. The discussion avoids depicting an overly rosy portrait of local life, since there is much to be pessimistic about: (1) a generation of students without formal education; (2) widespread discrimination and attacks on vulnerable minorities and clans; and (3) the collapse of most public institutions for health, emergency services, and welfare. Despite the fact that some aspects of the business sector have done fairly well in recent years, it is still a region marred by widespread social and economic problems and an appalling lack of public institutions. Rather, the intention here is to counter popular perceptions

---

[1] In light of the recent terrorist attacks in the US, the US and UK have claimed publicly that there is some evidence that Usama bin Laden and his network were at least partially responsible for the downing of the US helicopters in Mogadishu and for training Aideed's militia.

that daily life has collapsed because of the downfall of a moribund government or the departure of UNOSOM in 1995. What is amazing about the border region and other parts of Somalia and Somaliland is the degree to which life goes on and the extent to which populations have weathered instabilities along all fronts – political, economic, and climatic. In fact, in an era when affluent Western consumers bemoan high fuel costs and energy shortages, Somalis get on with their lives under far more trying circumstances, taking care of their families and herds, and trying to make the best of a situation for which most hold little responsibility. I would venture to say these same elements of persistence hold true for other areas of Africa, where states are in various stages of collapse or ineffectiveness and where physical security is a daily concern.

Local perceptions

During fieldwork in 1996 and 1998, a set of open-ended questions about current social and economic conditions was asked of 84 traders. These queries were designed to gauge traders' perceptions of problems and changes that have occurred since the state's collapse in 1991. They were centered on three related themes: (1) the major problems with current livestock trade in the region; (2) the major differences in cross-border trade during the past five years; and (3) how the war (conflict) and general insecurity in Somalia affected livestock trade. The responses of traders were quite extraordinary in many respects and provide a good indication of changes and problems during the 1990s (see Tables 6.1 to 6.3).

From the perspective of traders, several issues affect their welfare but consensus is far from uniform. Although security remains a major dilemma, they point to prices, transport, and excessive competition as equally compelling concerns. In fact, anxiety over insecurity is less than what one would have expected, although as a concern it increased slightly from 1996 to 1998. As one trader remarked, 'Now we have to arrange for security men with arms when we trade. Buying cattle from Somalia is a security risk for money and person' (trader interview, 18 May 1996). Another trader in 1996, who had just arrived in Kenya from Mogadishu, acknowledges insecurity as a problem but emphasizes the positive aspects of trade: 'Since the fall of the government we have been doing well in livestock trade' (trader interview, 24 May 1996). Identification of conflict and security-related issues grew from about 15 to 24 percent of total responses during 1996 to 1998 (Table 6.1), but about one-third of all traders in 1998 indicated that insecurity did not have a major impact on trade.

The survey results in Tables 6.1 to 6.3 highlight four prevalent sets of constraints. These are, in order of importance: (1) price and marketing problems; (2) insecurity; (3) water and grazing shortages; and (4) transportation. Problems (1) and (4) are issues of importance for most traders,

Table 6.1. Problems with current livestock trade

Category	Percentage of responses	
	1996	1998
1. No problem	4.5	0
2. Price problems/low demand/marketing system is a problem	17.4	24.1
3. Security – cattle rustling/banditry	15.5	24.1
4. Transportation/no trucks/high transport cost/long trek from Somalia	12.3	6.9
5. Animal disease – lack of veterinary drugs	6.5	6.9
6. Water shortage/drought/lack of forage/lack of grass between Libooye and Garissa	15.5	20.7
7. No holding ground/have to buy grass at market/lack of pasture at market	5.2	0
8. Shortage of animals	3.2	0
9. High tax/license fee (Kenya)	3.2	0
10. Pay 'tip' to government police	1.9	0
11. No credit/not paid by Nairobi traders and butchers	6.5	10.3
12. Lions on trekking routes	1.3	3.4
13. Clanism/tribal hostilities	1.3	6.9
14. Need movement permit to transport cattle	1.9	0
15. Other	3.9	0
TOTAL	100	100
	n = 84 traders	

Source: Based on author's data.

Table 6.2. Major differences in cross-border trade since 1990

Category	Percentage of responses	
	1996	1998
1. No difference/no problem	6.5	13.0
2. Increased security problems	9.7	13.0
3. No information/do not know	7.5	0
4. Livestock trade is good/increased cattle from Somalia/ cattle prices are cheaper now	8.6	13.0
5. Big differences	1.1	0
6. Trade is better now	15.1	9.5
7. Trade better before/cheaper animal prices before	20.4	33.3
8. Clan conflict worse now/clan affects trade more now	1.1	0
9. Market prices now are not good in Garissa/prices have gone up but profits are down	10.8	4.3
10. Fewer animals now	3.2	0
11. Somalia traders charge us more now	2.2	0
12. No government now	1.1	0
13. Drought has worsened/low prices because of drought/less animals from Somalia because of drought	8.6	0
14. Other	6.2	13.9
TOTAL	100	100
	n = 84 traders	

Source: Based on author's data.

Table 6.3. Major effects of conflict on livestock trade

Category	Percentage of responses 1996	1998
1. More animals coming from Somalia/high population of livestock at Garissa market	12.6	0
2. Better prices now/better profits/prices have gone down in Somalia	3.6	0
3. No transportation system in Somalia/animals die because of long trek/increased transport problems	6.3	0
4. Security risk/cattle theft	36.0	50.0
5. Not much trade with Kismayo now	1.8	0
6. No effects/no major differences/trade has not been affected by war	11.7	33.3
7. Hurt trade for Kenyan traders/increased competition with Somali traders	8.1	5.5
8. War has decreased trade/not as many cattle traders/ negative effects	3.6	5.5
9. Somali animals are in good condition now	2.7	0
10. Lost best grazing lands because of war – cannot move freely to grazing lands	1.8	0
11. Clanism has spread/have to trade with own clan	3.6	5.7
12. Reduced number of cattle/decreased number of camels coming to Kenya	2.7	0
13. Market contacts now are not reliable/we lose our animals to middlemen	1.8	0
14. Other	3.6	0
TOTAL	100	100
	n = 84 traders	

Source: Based on author's data.

whether in Somalia or elsewhere. Studies of traders in other parts of Africa confirm this point (see Little 2000; Little and Dolan 2000). The security issue (2), on the other hand, may appear unique to the Somali borderlands, but actually is a significant problem in several African border areas where a lack of state controls provides both opportunities and safety risks (see Richards 1996; Ellis 1999b). Additionally, the lack of transport and infrastructure in southern Somalia, as well as the Kenyan government's requirement that cattle must be trucked from the border zone to urban markets, are widely acknowledged as constraints. One trader indicated that 'they wish they could trek cattle to Mombasa and Nairobi markets because it is very expensive to truck cattle' (trader interview, 23 May 1996).

As Table 6.1 shows, water and grazing shortages also impede traders' activities and, as was discussed earlier (Chapter 5), dictate the seasonal nature of cross-border trade. Somali herders who trek their animals the 150+ km to Garissa, Kenya are often forced to sell immediately upon arrival. 'There are no good water facilities and grass in the Garissa market,' one elderly merchant laments (trader interview, 6 June 1996). The rangelands around Garissa town are heavily exploited by local herds and therefore cannot sustain pasture-starved cattle for more than a few days. In a drought year migrating herders and traders are forced to purchase riverine fodder at relatively high prices. The lack of a holding ground and adequate water infrastructure at Garissa aids large-scale traders who can negotiate favorable prices from stockowners who are desperate to sell their animals.

Other problems emphasized by traders include the lack of veterinary and credit services. In terms of veterinary inputs, earlier chapters (2 and 3) showed how herders used to rely on Kismayo town for supplies but because of its continued violence they currently purchase them elsewhere. The credit problems, in turn, relate to (1) trader difficulties in collecting debts from Nairobi wholesalers and butchers (see Chapter 5); and (2) the fact that small-scale traders cannot procure animals in bulk because of the unavailability of capital. One is a problem with how credit is provided (or not provided) by traders, the other stems from traders' lack of access to financial markets. Whenever possible, Somali traders try to contract with Somali-owned butcheries to minimize credit problems, but outside of Eastleigh neighborhood there are few in Nairobi.

When queried about changes in cross-border trade, many traders point to positive transitions, including greater supply and higher prices. 'Cattle trade has been good because we can get animals in good condition from Somalia more easily now,' says one trader (trader interview, 18 May 1996). Another remarks that 'the effect of the war is good for livestock supply to Kenya because of the lack of an export trade in Somalia' (trader interview, 28 May 1996). Others claim that business has been good without the Barre government around: 'During the government of Barre trade was worse, but now ... it is a sort of free business' (trader interview, 5 July 1998).

Certain merchants, however, feel that business is not so favorable and profits have plummeted because of the increased competition associated with cross-border trade and the flood of Somali cattle. One bemoans the fact that: 'These days livestock trade is not very good. The market is flooded with cattle from Ethiopia and Somalia' (trader interview, 18 May 1996, author's field notes). Indeed, more and more small-scale traders from Somalia are involved in the trade, and this has created some resentment among Kenyan traders. Some Garissa traders say that this has led to 'low cattle prices' and other unfavorable market conditions (trader interview, 29 May 1996). As depicted in Table 6.2, traders are almost evenly split between those who say trade is better now and those who claim that it was better in 1990. Large-scale cattle traders with easy access to transport and the Nairobi market are more likely to favor the increased cross-border trade than small traders in Kenya who confront considerable competition from the throngs of other petty traders.

While important changes in Somalia have occurred since the civil war of 1991–2, there have been significant continuities as well. In 1996 information was sought on 27 traders of Afmadow and surrounding areas who had been interviewed in 1987 and 1988. Surprisingly, the location and current activities of 22, or 81 percent, of them were obtained and only two of these had explicitly stopped their business activities because of the regional conflict. One had migrated to Garissa and another had moved closer to the Kenyan border to take greater advantage of the cross-border trade. Two had become involved in local politics as members of elder reconciliation councils but had continued to trade. Their political roles were to resolve conflicts between clans in the region. The vast majority of the traders from 1987–8, however, were still involved in trade, either as suppliers of cattle to Kenyan-based traders or as merchants who brought their own animals across the border. As was explained in Chapter 5, those businessmen who were based out of Kismayo have been seriously affected by the war and most have little role in trans-border trade.

Market trends

Market trends for key commodities generally are good indicators of social and economic welfare in Somalia, because of the population's high dependence on markets. Without trade, herders could not attain needed cereals and merchants and their employees would be jobless. As noted in Chapter 1, relatively reliable marketing data are gathered weekly by a network of NGOs with support by the Famine Early Warning Systems (FEWS, now called FEWS-Net) project and the Food Security Assessment Unit (FSAU) of the Food and Agriculture Organization (FAO). These data are critical for understanding trends in the wider economy of Somalia and Somaliland, rather than just the southern Somali borderlands. The information is used to supplement my own data, which are based mainly on observations of cattle trade at a select number of key border markets.

As was explained in Chapter 5, livestock prices in the border region are less volatile than prices for grains and cereal products. The southern and central Somalia border areas are strongly grain-deficit, and prices for imported wheat flour and rice can increase astronomically in only a few months. In risk-prone Kismayo, for example, the price of maize more than doubled during February to April 2000 (FEWS 2000c: 3). Insecurity and conflict can create artificial shortages and high prices.

There is sufficient secondary data to explore price relationships along three important border routes in Somalia and Somaliland that have not been discussed so far. One of these, the Mandera (Kenya)/Bulla Hawo (Somalia) route, traverses the Gedo Region and lies about 550 km north of the Garissa trade channel that was analyzed in Chapter 5. The different trans-border routes for which there are secondary data include:

1. Southern Somalia/northeastern Kenya circuit centered on Mandera, Kenya and Bulla Hawo market, Somalia;
2. Central Somalia/eastern Ethiopia border focused on Belet Weyne town, Somalia;
3. Somaliland/eastern Ethiopia route centered on Togwajale, Ethiopia and Borama, Somaliland.

These three cross-border routes represent very different market orientations: (1) the Bulla Hawo-to-Mandera channel is for local distribution of food and consumer goods and, similar to the Garissa trade, for export of cattle to Kenyan markets; (2) the central Somalia/eastern Ethiopia border market is geared to local and regional markets, but some Ethiopian small stock transit en route to ports in the regional state of Puntland; and (3) the Somaliland/eastern Ethiopia trade mainly is for exports of small ruminants from Ethiopia to the Middle East (via Berbera, Somaliland) and imports of foods and other products through Somaliland ports. All three trade routes, however, show similarities to the trans-border markets discussed in Chapter 5 in their importance to local economies and food security.

The Bulla Hawo-to-Mandera border trade is particularly volatile, and wide variations in prices can occur within only a few days when conflict erupts. The latter occurrence was quite common in the 1990s, and armed conflict exploded again in early 2002. Figure 6.1 shows just how unstable prices can be for non-livestock goods at the Bulla Hawo border market. The price of imported wheat flour, for example, more than doubled within a few months during 1997 to 1998. Generally prices for imported foods (rice, pasta, and wheat flour) are strongly shaped both by local and external political factors, since they must be brought in along roads controlled by different militias. As will be shown later in this section, a different pattern of market volatility is found in parts of Somaliland, the independent state of the north. In this region, food prices are generally stable but livestock prices experience wide swings because of the state's dependence on uncertain international markets. Recall that livestock trade in Somaliland is geared to Middle Eastern markets and thus subject to a range of contingencies, including debilitating bans due to perceived animal health problems (see discussion in Chapter 2).

In terms of the second trans-border (2) route, that of central Somalia/eastern Ethiopia, the cattle market is particularly thin and prices are especially low. Located 25 km from the border, the town of Belet Weyne suffers from the lowest cattle prices of any of the border markets discussed so far. The settlement is more than 400 km north of the Kenya border and even more distant from the lucrative Middle Eastern trade to its north. While Belet Weyne is very near to Ethiopia, that country also is a net exporter of animals to Kenya and cattle prices there are very low (see Teka et al. 1999). In contrast to the southern borderlands, including Bulla Hawo, cattle trade along the Belet Weyne corridor

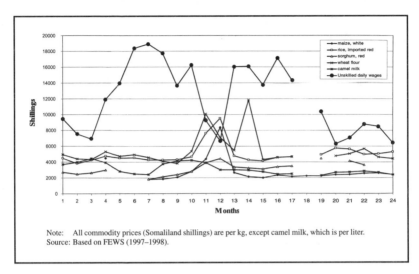

Note: All commodity prices (Somaliland shillings) are per kg, except camel milk, which is per liter.
Source: Based on FEWS (1997–1998).

Fig 6.1   Food prices in Bulla Hawo, 1997–8

moves in the opposite direction, from Somalia to Ethiopia rather than vice versa. Its geographic disadvantage accounts for the appallingly low cattle prices at Belet Weyne, an average of less than $60/head during 1997 to 1998 (FEWS 1997–1998).

In comparison to the other two market routes discussed here, trade between Somaliland and eastern Ethiopia is significantly different and global in scope. A vibrant livestock export trade from Somaliland to the Middle East exists, with an estimated 50 to 60 percent of exportable animals originating from across the border in Ethiopia (Steffen et al. 1998; Ahrens 1998). As was noted earlier, the overseas trade in small stock (goats and sheep) from Somaliland and neighboring Puntland was larger in volume in 1999 than before the government's collapse. In the 1980s Somalia was one of the largest exporters of live animals in the world (see Woodward and Stockton 1989), which makes the recent commercial achievements that much more astonishing. In 1999 the northern ports of Bossaso and Berbera exported about 2.9 million head of small stock (FEWS 2000c: 2–3). Moreover, the two Somali ports accounted for 95 percent of all goat and 52 percent of sheep exports from the entire eastern Africa region (Zaal and Polderman 2000: 17–18), an amazing accomplishment for a 'stateless' society. Since an estimated 2 million head annually are exported from Berbera alone, it means that about 1 to 1.2 million animals are sourced from cross-border trade with Ethiopia.

Somaliland and its border areas achieved relative economic stability and peace during much of the 1990s, in spite of the fact that they remain unrecognized by the UN and by most of the international community (see Prunier 1998). Neighboring Puntland, in turn, also attained stability within a few years of Somalia's collapse, but recently (2001–2002) has been embroiled in internal political divisions that jeopardize its relatively secure environment. The breakaway state of Somaliland has government ministries, carries out development planning exercises, collects minimal taxes and fees, and – as mentioned above – is the leading exporter of livestock among eastern African states and among the world's leaders in live animal trade. This picture is in marked contrast to southern Somalia, where politics remain highly localized, administrative functions are minimal, and overseas livestock exports are at a standstill. In comparison to the southern border areas, food prices based on data from the state capital, Hargeysa, also show less volatility in Somaliland. Located about 50 km east of the Ethiopia border, food prices in the Hargeysa market varied no more than 20 percent during 1997 to 1998 (cf. Figure 6.2).

In sum, the three different trade routes discussed here provide further proof that the economy of Somalia goes on, even 'booms' in some cases, despite an environment of risk and uncertainty. Traders do business and consumers buy products, and through it all markets generally follow principles of supply and demand. Conflict disrupts commerce but, like droughts and floods, it becomes just another risk element for which the trader, producer, and consumer must adjust. With the exception of the Somaliland trade, the dominance of the Kenyan trade looms heavy in

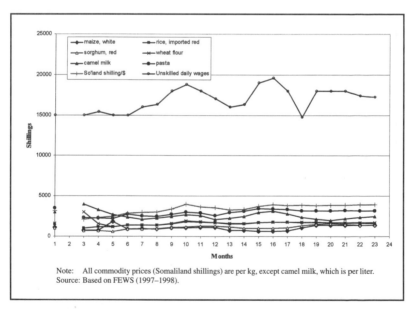

Note: All commodity prices (Somaliland shillings) are per kg, except camel milk, which is per liter.
Source: Based on FEWS (1997–1998).

Fig 6.2   Food prices in Hargeysa, 1997–8

determining livestock prices in most of the cross-border corridors. As will be shown in the next section, changes in livestock prices and in cross-border trade patterns have important impacts on herder welfare.

Sufficient food?

Even before the war Somalia was a massive recipient of international food aid. It was among the world's highest food aid beneficiaries on a per capita basis and among the countries with the lowest per capita food intake during the 1980s (Farzin 1988). When assessing the current food situation in Somalia, therefore, it is important to remember that the country has always been a major client of the global food aid system and suffered periods of widespread food insecurity both in the 1970s and 1980s. If anything, Somalia's recent isolation from the world community has greatly decreased dependence on official food aid, with private imports and trans-border trade making up part of the deficit.

As was pointed out in the previous chapter, the growth in cattle trade has not resulted in a marked improvement in producer prices since herders in southern Somalia are increasingly limited to only one viable market outlet, Kenya. Prices for livestock, in particular for camels, stagnated during the 1990s, especially when compared to grain prices, but they would have deteriorated further had it not been for the cross-border trade. In short, without this commerce herder welfare would have declined considerably, but instead it stabilized during 1995 to 1999.

Since herders depend heavily on grain in the dry season, the commodity's price has a major effect on pastoral well-being. Important reasons why grain prices and marketing are so critical for understanding pastoral food security include: (1) income from livestock sales is used to procure cereals and, therefore, grain price increases force herders to sell additional livestock; and (2) grain purchases allow herders to withstand periods of low herd (milk) productivity. Combined purchases of grain and flour account for the largest cash expenditures for herders in the border region and these expenditures are highly seasonal (author's field notes).

Similar to prices for grain, livestock prices also experience seasonal fluctuations, at times varying as much as 50 to 60 percent. Animals lose weight during dry months, and herders, often desperately in need of cash to buy food, flood the market with emaciated cattle. At such times they sell their animals at the nearest market center and during particularly devastating droughts, such as 2000–2001, cattle literally perish en route to markets. These harsh factors, coupled with the dry season slowdown in the border trade to Kenya, result in strong price fluctuations during the year. For example, in Garissa town prices for three different qualities of cattle and goats dropped an average of 40 percent between May and July 1996 (author's field notes). These fluctuations increase the economic vulnerability of herders, especially the poorer ones, as well as allow

considerable profiteering by those traders who are able to make specu-
lative purchases when prices are low in the dry season.

A critical indicator of pastoral food security in Somalia is the terms of
trade between what herders receive for their products (livestock) and
what they pay to purchase grains and flour. The terms of trade for local
pastoralists show strong seasonal and annual changes that often disadvantage the herder. Disruptions to cross-border trade also affect this
process, as prices are especially volatile during these times. While there is
little doubt that the events of the 1990s affected food security, the terms of
trade for Somali herders are not markedly worse than in other parts of
East Africa (see Little 1992b; FEWS 1999b). As was argued in the previous
chapter, livestock prices throughout the region generally have stagnated
since the mid-1990s, while grain prices have skyrocketed – especially in
drought years. For example, during 1996 to 2000 swings in monthly
maize prices of up to 175 percent were recorded (FEWS 1996–2000).
During one sequence, January 1999 to April 2000, the same source indicates that maize prices varied from US$ 0.16 to 0.42/kg, with the lowest
prices correlating with months of high food aid imports and the highest
with periods of natural disasters and/or localized violence. From 1995 to
1996 exceptional increases in food prices occurred in Baidoa and
Kismayo, two battle-weary towns that are very prone to market 'shocks'.
There also have been periods of up to three months when severe grain
shortages occurred simultaneously in several regional markets. The situation was particularly desperate immediately after the government's
collapse, when local grain prices surged to more than $1.50 per kg, an
astronomical amount for already vulnerable populations (FAO 1994: 56).

Thus, herders have lost some ground during the past decade as cereal
prices grew at a rate faster than livestock prices. In most markets this has
meant that price increases for grain outpaced animal prices by as much as
20 to 25 percent. This difference has meant that herders during the late
1990s sold more of their animals to purchase the same amount of grain
that they did in the late 1980s. Nonetheless, a border herder can still
consume far more in caloric terms by selling an animal and purchasing
grain with the cash than by consuming the animal. In exchange terms
'medium-quality' cattle fetched the equivalent of about 470 kg of maize in
1988 but on average only 350 kg during 1996 to 2000. A similar pattern is
found for imported rice and wheat flour, which are more expensive
commodities than maize. By selling an animal and buying cereals, a
pastoralist almost always fares better in energy (caloric) terms than if s/he
withdrew from the market (see Zaal and Dietz 1999).

Pastoral food security is such a dynamic process and so strongly shaped
by trans-border trade, that short-term (even daily or weekly) market observations are necessary. Assessments of the two border areas with the most
significant amount of cross-border trade, (1) Somaliland/eastern Ethiopia
and (2) southern Somalia/northeastern Kenya, highlight the trade's short-
term impacts on food security. The most graphic illustrations deal with

extreme events, such as warfare, drought, and floods or, in the case of Somaliland, the loss of a key export market like Saudi Arabia. In the Somaliland example the export of animals, an activity that heavily finances food imports, decreased about 50 percent during 1997 to 1998 owing to the trade embargo, and this strongly affected pastoral food security. As one FEWS report highlights, 'there is a clear and positive correlation between livestock exports and food imports in Somalia' (FEWS 2000b: 1). In this case, a reduction in cross-border trade adversely affects pastoral consumers along two fronts: their livestock prices decline and prices of imported foods increase. As Ahrens, who surveyed the area during the first Saudi Arabian ban, notes:

> The cessation of livestock exports has had a serious impact on the economy of the visited area of Somali Region [Ethiopia]: cash income from livestock exports, on which prior to the ban the large majority of the population depended, has stopped. No more goods are coming across the border. Goods available in the local shops represent old stocks and by the time of the mission's visit had started to become more expensive. Terms of trade are deteriorating with animal prices going down and grain prices increasing. Due to the people's significantly reduced purchasing power, the general trade in the towns has already suffered drastic cuts. According to local informants, in Harshin about 25 percent of the shops are closed, in Camoboker about 30 percent and in Rabasso and Daror up to 50 percent (1998: 5–6).

Table 6.4 shows the exchange value of livestock during this time in three different Somaliland markets, all of which are important in cross-border trade. It captures the effects of the export embargo on exchange rates between livestock and food products. Local currency equivalencies are used, and five key foods that figure prominently in cross-border trade are tracked: maize, wheat flour, rice, sorghum, and pasta. As the table demonstrates, the terms of trade between livestock and food commodities worked against the herder at every market. In some cases, the food value from the sale of one small stock declined by almost 40 percent during the ban. For a herder in Borama, Somaliland a goat or sheep bought 79 kg of wheat flour in 1997, while it only purchased 49 kg in 1998. The border market of Togwajale suffered the worst trade terms among the three markets, especially relative to local prices for imported foods. It is located about 230 km southwest of Berbera port along the Ethiopia/Somaliland border, where prices for import foods are high and livestock prices are generally low.

While the disruption in livestock trade impacted on the entire region, it particularly affected border locations, which experienced the steepest declines in small stock prices and highest increases for imported foods. The lifting of the export sanctions in 1999 improved food security, and by January 2000 the terms of trade for herders were even better than before

Table 6.4. Terms of trade between small stock and foodstuffs in Somaliland markets, 1997–8

Food item	Exchange equivalencies from sale of one small stock (export quality)						Range of change 1997–98
	Berbera (in kg)		Borama (in kg)		Togwajale (in kg)		
	1997	1998	1997	1998	1997	1998	
Maize	67	53	89	66	68	52	−21 to −26%
Wheat flour	54	54	79	49	37	30	0 to −38%
Rice	55	55	54	39	37	30	0 to −28%
Sorghum	60	51	69	58	88	55	−15 to −38%
Pasta	28	28	25	16	19	15	0 to −36 %

Notes: Analysis by author based on data from FEWS (1997–1998).

the restrictions. Unfortunately, the ban was reimposed in the summer of 2000 and although Yemen and the United Arab Emirates (UAE) rescinded it in 2001, the largest buyer of Somali animals (Saudi Arabia) still maintains it (see Chapter 7).

Ironically, the recent American attention to Somalia following the September 11 terrorist attacks has some officials talking about possibly intervening with Saudi Arabia on Somalia's behalf to lift the trade embargo (Lake 2002). Such an action would represent a major departure for US policy, which has generally shunned Somalia since the Mogadishu episode in 1993, and would show just how much the world has changed in only a few months. Yet, while the US is raising the specter of increased assistance for Somalia, the US and its allies (including England, France, and Germany) also are patrolling its coastlines and using sophisticated air and satellite surveillance techniques in anticipation of a possible attack against the country as the next phase of the 'war against terrorism' following the Afghanistan campaign (see Vick 2002). Thus, the volatility of Somalia itself is increasingly matched by an unstable global environment, where questions of 'who are allies' and 'who are enemies' remain uncertain (also see Chapter 7).

The El Nino floods of 1997–8 are another catastrophic shock that highlights both the uncertain nature of pastoral food security and the key role of cross-border trade (see Chapter 2). In this case, the example is drawn from the Bulla Hawo border market in the south that was discussed earlier in the chapter. A bundle of key commodities, including maize, wheat flour, and rice, are used to calculate changes in the pastoral terms of trade during this disaster (see Table 6.5). Table 6.5 documents the negative impact that El Nino had on local food markets and prices, including those paid for livestock. From September 1997 to December 1997, the livestock equivalencies for maize, wheat flour, and rice declined 79, 53, and 61 percent, respectively, during the floods (see Chapter 2). A herder who sold a head of cattle in September 1997 could purchase 298 kg of maize, while in December the figure was only 64 kg. With the disruption to cross-border links, the price of cattle (and other livestock species) had declined to pitifully low levels. For

Table 6.5. The effects of El Nino on food/livestock terms of trade, Bulla Hawo border market

Food item	Exchange equivalencies from sale of one head of cattle (medium quality-2) (Kg) 1997				(Kg) 1998			Range of monthly change
	Sept	Oct	Nov	Dec	Jan	Feb	Mar	
Maize	298	221	133	64	238	256	369	26 to 272%
Wheat flour	162	115	58	76	115	47	170	31 to 262%
Rice	143	132	77	56	131	129	176	2 to 134%

Notes: Analysis by author based on data from FEWS (1997–1998).

an average family of eight members who depended on animal sales to finance grain needs, food availability decreased from about 37 kg to 8 kg per capita. It was a major blow to already impoverished households of the region who desperately needed food assistance.

As the rains subsided and international food aid was delivered, food prices started to decline in early 1998, but not before hundreds of individuals had perished. By March 1998 the terms of trade in Bulla Hawo had improved to the point that the food equivalency ratios for cattle were actually better than before the floods. During the torrential rains, however, changes in monthly food equivalencies were as high as 272 percent for certain foods. These wide swings in prices show how unsteady the market is when trade is disrupted.

Nutritional data also serve as indicators of food security, especially for desperate populations. Unfortunately, the availability of nutritional information for southern Somalia during the 1990s is sporadic at best. It is often restricted to refugee camps and settled populations, where the nutritional situation is vastly different from what is found in the pastoral areas. Nonetheless, existing data depict a situation that is not too discrepant from what has been emphasized throughout the book: pastoralists have fared better than other rural groups. The earliest post-1991 surveys showed that on a nutritional scale of 1 to 3, with '3' being the worst nutritional state, pastoral populations had vulnerability rankings of '1' and '2' (ICRC 1992; WFP 1993). Sedentary farmers of the Jubba Valley and Baidoa, in turn, had the most severe cases of malnutrition with ratings of '3'. Famine conditions in these areas were startling, even for such an exceptional period. In 1992 at the height of the famine – a catastrophe that, as stated earlier, killed an estimated 300,000 people – Baidoa and Bardera (Jubba Valley) reported malnutrition rates among displaced farmers as high as 70 percent. This extraordinarily high level is almost unprecedented in the twentieth century and 'rarely documented in famines' (Hansch 1993: 5; also see Prendergast 1993).

After 1993 the nutritional status of most population groups improved throughout the country, except in local pockets of conflict. Nutritional surveys during 1994 to 1997 'reported generally low rates of malnutrition in most areas of the country (e.g. 3–10 percent)' (UNDP 1998: 21); and among nomadic groups the same source reported that global rates of malnutrition were similar to pre-war levels. According to these findings, pastoralists are usually only vulnerable at the end of the dry season when milk and meat production is low. In the same report it is noted that Somali pastoralists are 'generally healthier than other groups because they are more adaptable, have ready sources of milk and meat (except during periods of drought), and usually take water from sand-filtered water' (ibid: 42). The FEWS program, in assessing a potential famine in the Jubba Valley, reaches a similar conclusion 'that the nomadic population seems not to suffer hunger as the sedentary farmers' (FEWS 1996: 3).

It should be noted that the nutritional situation on the Kenyan side of the border is probably equivalent to – if not worse than – the condition in southern Somalia. Global rates of malnutrition along the border in Mandera District, Kenya have been recorded as high as 57 percent during the most recent drought (FEWS 1999b: 3). In other pastoral areas of northern Kenya, such as Turkana and Marsabit Districts, nutritional and food security problems also are probably as bad as – if not worse than – in southern Somalia. For example, child malnutrition rates in Marsabit District (based on anthropometric indicators) during April–June 1997 were more than 30 percent and were above 20 percent for most of 1997 and early 1998 (FEWS 1998b: 2). In Turkana District, Kenya, even higher child malnutrition rates (> 45 percent in some locations) were found in March 1999 (FEWS 1999d), further evidence that Kenyan pastoralists suffer extreme nutritional and food security problems even when compared to herders of stateless Somalia. In contrast to southern Somalia, mobile pastoralism is threatened in Kenya, where debilitating herd losses are not unusual during droughts (see Chapter 4).

The discussion here suggests that pockets of severe food insecurity remain in the Somali borderlands, but local herders have generally fared as well as – if not better than – neighboring pastoral populations. Even with the devastating drought of 1999–2000, the food situation in Somalia was not markedly different from in other parts of the Horn of Africa, including large parts of Ethiopia and northern Kenya where upwards of 10 million residents were in dire need of food assistance (FEWS 1999c; CARE 1999). What makes the Somali situation unique, however, is that Western agencies are still reluctant to ship cereals to a country that has so badly confused them on the diplomatic front and has not had an internationally recognized government for most of the past decade.

A currency without a treasury

Jamil Mubarak has remarked that in contemporary Somalia 'the domestic economy is literally free of regulations, price and exchange controls, and other interventionist policies that prevailed in the past. The financial market in particular has been very active, and arguably more efficient than it has ever been' (1996: 159). The paradox of market transactions in Somalia is that they are still carried out largely in Somali shillings (SoSh), the currency of the deposed regime, which remains the standard medium of exchange for most daily exchanges. While the value of the Somali shilling declined more than 98 percent during the 1980s, it has lost only a fraction of that worth during the 1990s.

Currency markets in the large towns are especially lively and well-developed. On any given morning in Bakara, the main market of Mogadishu, currency traders sit behind tables loaded with US dollars and SoSh while they follow global markets through radio and satellite televisions. They adjust their exchange rates accordingly, as well as to local conditions of supply and demand. There are some practical factors that help to explain the persistence of the Somali shilling, even in the absence of a central bank or treasury.[2] These include, for example, that the SoSh is: (1) needed to facilitate transactions in the absence of another widely available currency; (2) in limited supply and therefore its demand is high; and (3) well known to local consumers and businessmen.

In a classic article on money, Keith Hart (1986) raises issues of relevance to this discussion. He demonstrates how the demand side of monetary supply is determined by civil society, not by government, and draws a valuable distinction between 'state' and 'public' (civic) aspects of monetary systems. To bolster his argument, Hart presents different examples of currencies that have operated with weak or non-existent states. The Maria Theresa thaler, for example, was widely used in parts of East Africa, including Somalia, long after the collapse of the Austrian Empire. It served as a medium of exchange in Somalia well into the twentieth century.[3] When related to the persistent Somali shilling, Hart's useful dichotomy can be applied to an existing 50-shilling note. On one side of the bill is a modern government factory representing the 'state'; on the other a picture of livestock, the main pursuit of most Somalis that signifies the 'public'. These images remain in circulation, although the government symbol holds little relevance today. The livestock icon, in turn, remains a strong symbol of civil aspirations and resiliency, and it is their owners rather than government who account for the money's current use. In the Somali economy the public or civic dimension of money is the power behind the 'currency without a treasury'.

[2] Debates about the role of states in monetary systems cover the full spectrum, from extreme cases of statist intervention to libertarian views that downplay government's importance in currency systems (see Crump 1981; Friedman 1973; Frankel 1977). The Somalia example provides an excellent 'laboratory' for testing these different positions.

[3] A historical assessment of different monies in East Africa shows other cases where money was utilized without the support of a central state. The currencies of trading companies in the nineteenth century, such as the British East African Company, are examples, although they had indirect support from European governments. In addition, rural areas of Burundi and Tanganyika (Tanzania) continued to use German-issued coins long after the departure of the German government during World War I. In short, there is precedence in modern times for currencies operating in the absence of central states and national treasuries.

Photo 6.1   Businessman exchanging money at a Mogadishu market (© Sven Torfinn)

Money's function as a store of value, a characteristic that the Somali shilling sorely lacked under the predatory regime of Siad Barre, also explains why the SoSh is still in use (see Mubarak 1996; Abdurahman 1998). Throughout the 1980s the currency lost its real market value by as much as 300 percent in some years (see Table 6.6), while in the 1970s it showed real strength. From 1981 to 1990 the exchange rate of the SoSh deteriorated from 18 to 3,800 per 1 US dollar (Abdurahman 1998: 14). By

Photo 6.2   Somali currency note (Peter D. Little)

Table 6.6. Currency exchange rates, Somalia[1]

Year (s)	Somali shillings per US $[2]
1980–83	19 (10–31)
1984–85	68 (57–79)
1986	110 (90–140)
1987	180 (140–220)
1988	350 (220–480)
1989	900 (600–1,200)
1990	2,500 (1,200–3,800)
1991	5,700 (3,800- 7,600) (Government collapses)
1992	4,200 (UN and U.S. enter 12/92)
1993	4,467 (3,945–4,988)
1994	4,725 (4,200–5,250)
1995	6,150 (5,100–7,200) (UNOSOM withdraws)
1996	7,000 (6,500–7,500) (New bills printed)
1997	7,430 (7,160–7,700)
1998	7,250 (6,900–7,600)
1999 (through 3/99)	7,850 (7,500–8,200)
1999 (after 3/99)	9,188 (8,200–10,175) (New money supply)
2000 (through 4/00)	9,925 (9,575–10,275)

Notes:
[1] Based on FEWS 1996–2000, 1999c, 1999d, 2000c; Green 1993: 16; Mubarak 1996: 150; Mishra 1993; WFP 1993; and WFP/FSAU 1995, 1997a–f.
[2] For 1979 to 1985 the average of the official and reported parallel rates are used. The parallel ('black market') values of the currency for these years are reported in Abdurahman (1998: 11). In 1986 the government intervened and officially devalued the exchange rate to close the gap between the official and black market rates. For 1986 and subsequent years, I report the ranges in brackets and an 'average' figure, which is calculated as the mid-point between the high and low exchange value for the year. In some years there are only two to three monthly exchange rates reported for the entire year.

contrast, 'the exchange rate showed a remarkable stability in the period 1991–98, floating between SoSh 6,500 and 8,000 per U.S. dollar' (ibid: 13), when a central government was not in existence.[4] If one compares the period from 1995 to 1999 with the last few years (1986 to 1990) of the Siad Barre regime, the differences in monetary strength between the two eras are especially apparent (see Table 6.6). In the pre-1991 period, monetary policy was hampered by excessive printing of the currency to pay for military expenditures and political cronies, general mismanagement of national accounts (Ekstrom 1993), and widespread corruption (Hashim 1997). Paper money was printed in great supply in the last few years of the Barre regime. Without a corrupt central government in the 1990s, there was little political tampering with the monetary system and pilfering of national accounts, all actions that destabilized the Somali economy in the 1980s. Until the recent printings of currency notes first by the late General Aideed's son, Hussein Aideed, in 1999 and later in 2000 and 2001 by

[4] There was actually more variability in exchange rates during 1991–4 than Abdurahman (1998) acknowledges, but fluctuations were still not as great as in the last four years of the Barre regime.

business supporters of the new TNG, the supply of money was held intact and inflationary pressures were limited. In addition, large influxes of dollars from remittances, exports of livestock, and NGOs and relief agencies further stabilized the shilling after the government's collapse. As a result, the convertibility of the SoSh has been surprisingly steady in recent years despite (or because of?) the lack of a central treasury.

In the Somali borderlands, confidence in the local currency facilitates credit and financial transfers, critical components of commerce because of the risks associated with carrying large amounts of cash. While much of the livestock trade is calculated in SoSh and final payments are made in SoSh or US dollars, the actual handling of cash in large transactions is minimal. Somali border traders – like those discussed in Chapter 5 – can take their earnings to Nairobi, convert them to dollars, and then 'wire' them back to money houses in Somalia, where they can be picked up by associates. This informal practice, called the *hawala* or *hawilaad* system (meaning 'transfer' in Arabic), avoids the need to carry large amounts of cash across the border. In other cases the trader will convert part of his earnings in Kenya into tradable goods, which he will arrange with a wholesaler to be picked up at the border to avoid the risk of traveling in northeastern Kenya with excess money and goods. Credit in this trade is mediated through informal money houses and middlemen, who assume special importance in most forms of long-distance trade, including livestock. Many of these are based in Nairobi, and informal bankers will charge fees of 3–6 percent to 'wire' funds from Kenya to locations in Somalia. Different forms of wire transfers and credit minimize risk and reduce the physical handling of worn Somali notes, which slows their deterioration and helps to keep them in circulation. The system, however, requires considerable trust to operate and, as will be shown below, can function in the idiom of the clan system.

An ethnographic example from the Eastleigh neighborhood of Nairobi, a key hub of Somali business activity in East Africa, illustrates the practice of the informal finance system.[5]

A Somali businessman goes to one of the 'money houses' in Eastleigh, in order to pick up a wire transfer of cash (US dollars) from an expatriate relative working in Europe. Upon arrival he is directed to an anteroom where he waits his turn to see a cashier. Clerks check his name on a computer print out to make sure that a money transfer has arrived for the person. When his name is called, he goes to a back room where stacks of US dollars cover a wooden table and three individuals sit behind it. He gives his name to the cashier, shows proper identification, and is required to answer several questions. Because 'official' ID cards and passports are easily manufactured and forged, he is asked about his clan and lineage relations that his European-based relative has provided as security against fraud. Knowledge of

---

[5] The example was given to me in 1999 by a Somali professional who works in Kenya.

one's kinship relations is used as a convenient check on the person's identity and presents a unique twist on the use of 'tradition' in modern transactions. Only after he has answered the questions to the satisfaction of the bankers can he pick up the cash. In this case, the funds will be used to support family living expenses and to buy cattle. In the USA, Europe, and in larger East African cities like Nairobi and Mogadishu, there are several such 'banking houses' from which to choose (author's field notes).

A recent UNDP-commissioned report describes a similar growth in informal money houses related to the remittance business:

A major financial innovation, since the collapse of the State, has been the rise of hawilaad or remittance companies. There are several major remittance companies and innumerable small ones. The large companies handle remittances of funds sent by the Somali diaspora to relatives in country, charging a commission of 3% to 7% (depending on the level of competition and the size of the remittance). Using a mix of telephone, fax, and HF radio, and relying on a worldwide network of agents, the hawilaad companies can instantly transfer money from a Somali in Canada to his family in Bosasso. Increasingly, hawilaad companies also transfer money between businessmen both within Somalia and internationally, allowing merchants to make fast purchases of commodities growing scarce in a local market (UNDP 1998: 15).

The scale of the informal banking system is extraordinary, and at least one of the larger Mogadishu-based enterprises has branches in many cities around the world. Moreover, it is formally registered under the banking regulations of at least one state, Dubai, United Arab Emirates [UAE]. The recent growth in private commercial airline connections between Dubai, Somalia, and Kenya strengthens these financial networks as well as facilitates trading relations (for example, Somali merchants can easily shop for goods in Dubai). In Eastleigh the branch of the large money house is easily recognizable and accessible; its large signpost is known to local residents and visible from a prominent commercial avenue.

Unfortunately for many Somali families, the largest of these *hawala* banks, al Barakaat, abruptly closed in November 2001 over speculation that it laundered funds and generated profits for the terrorist network, al-Qaida (Vesley 2002; IRIN 2001h). Based on a US-led initiative the indictment also claimed that at the highest levels the bank was controlled by key al-Qaida supporters. Thus, what had evolved as a viable institution in such a short time following the collapse of Somalia's finance sector, and depended upon by literally thousands of Somali families in the region and around the world, is now tragically closed. While it remains so, some recent entrepreneurs have started another private bank in the country and there is acknowledgement by some Western nations of how crucial it is for the Somali economy that the *hawala* transfers continue. (see IRIN 2002a; UNDP 2003). While average Somalis who depended on *hawala* services know little of global terrorism, the events of September 11 nonetheless have unfairly impacted on them.

In Somalia other aspects of informal finance are equally pervasive. Numerous money traders openly exchange the Kenyan shilling, Ethiopian birr, Somali shilling, and the US dollar at different markets. A recent issue of the *New York Times* nicely captured the role of money traders in northern Somalia, lined up with their stacks of different currencies, in a colorful article (including a photo) about an urban market (Fisher 1999: 1). The use of the Somali shilling unites an enormous regional network of Somali traders that encompasses Somalia and parts of Djibouti, Ethiopia, and northeastern Kenya. It is a trading diaspora that in some areas, such as the Somali coast, has existed for centuries.

Another ironic twist is that the Somali shilling seems to have greater geographic range and convertibility inside parts of Ethiopia itself than Ethiopia's own government-backed money. Because Somalis occupy both sides of the Ethiopia/Somalia border, the SoSh is widely used in parts of the Somali Region of Ethiopia, one of the country's regional states, to purchase goods imported cheaply through Somalia's ports. The geographic extent of its coverage within Ethiopia's interior is up to 50 km from the border. So while the use of the Ethiopian birr hardly penetrates into the Somali interior, the SoSh is used in markets inside Ethiopia. Merchants from Kenya, in turn, prefer to buy local currency (SoSh) once they enter Somalia and rarely use the money in Kenya.

Thus, while a resident of Somalia still has little access to formal banking and financial institutions, access to other financial facilities actually has improved with the collapse of the state. To quote again from the UNDP report: 'One ironic aspect of the collapse of the state in Somalia is that telecommunications and money-wiring services are now significantly better today than in the past' (UNDP 1998: 15). The growth in telecommunication facilities in Somalia, including expensive satellite telephone systems, facilitates the transfer of remittances from abroad and helps the financial system generally (Sabriel 1997). Al Barakaat, the company whose finance services were recently shuttered, also controlled the largest telecommunication company in the country, offering internet, fax, and telephone services to more than 40,000 subscribers under a contract with a joint-venture firm affiliated with US telecommunications giant, AT&T, and British Telecom (IRIN 2001i). Its communications business was also shut down, a fate that has further isolated Somalia from the rest of the world and crippled cash remittance flows from abroad that are so vital to Somalia's poor (described later in the chapter). Prior to November 2001 what was happening in this sector had been described as nothing short of a 'telecommunications revolution' (see IRIN 1999b: 6). Now, like the *hawala* system, it is unduly tainted by accusations of terrorist links.

Photo 6.3   Shop on a Mogadishu street (© Sven Torfinn)

The SoSh showed particular strength after 1995, even when compared to government-supported currencies in neighboring countries. From July 1995 to February 1999 the value of the Somali shilling declined from about 6,500 to 8,200 SoSh per US$1, or about 26 percent. By contrast, the Kenyan Shilling (KSh) declined from about 45 to 61 per dollar, or about 36 percent, during approximately the same period (IMF 1999: 561), while the Ethiopian birr depreciated about 27 percent (ibid: 423). From January 1996 to March 1999 changes in the value of the SoSh rarely exceeded 5 to 10 percent per month. While exchange rates differ slightly among different markets in the country, currency markets are generally integrated and differences explained by distance and costs of transport (see UNDOS 1999). Because of its relative stability, the SoSh has facilitated cross-border trade and international commerce generally by providing a reasonable store of value and convertible medium of exchange.

The integrity of the SoSh has recently been damaged by a combination of local politics and misplaced interventions. During March to April 1999, Hussein Aideed, the Mogadishu-based warlord, brought in a large shipment of new currency notes for his faction, and as a result the shilling depreciated about 25 percent within a few months. Inflation for key foods and other consumer items sky-rocketed (FEWS 1999c). Fortunately, the currency stabilized – and actually strengthened – within four months. More recently (2000), local actions in support of the Transitional National Government (TNG) resulted in additional imports of SoSh that further devalued the currency and had an even more serious destablizing effect on the economy than Aideed's actions (see discussion later in this chapter).

With a relatively consistent currency during the latter part of the 1990s, barter trade in the border region of southern Somalia has been rare. In fact, commodity-based barter has been more common in northern Somalia

(Somaliland), where the currency was unstable and inflation rampant during the mid-1990s. Herders of that administration occasionally accept imported rice and wheat flour in exchange for their exportable small stock (Stockton 1996). After all, these are key import items that they purchase anyway after they sell animals. In other economically volatile parts of the world, barter trade also is practiced and, in many cases, is far more important than in Somalia. In Eastern Europe and the former states of the USSR, for instance, barter trade and commodity-based monies took hold as economic conditions and currency values deteriorated (Carlin et al. 2000; Humphrey 1999).[6] Russia is probably the country of the region where the practice is most pronounced and where 'the country's impoverished industrial enterprises turned increasingly to barter' (Woodruff 1999: 83), but it also is common in Bulgaria and elsewhere (Cellarius 1999). In southern Somalia, however, barter exchange has not been very important even during 1991 to 1992. The stability of the SoSh has been an important reason for this, as has the Somali trading diaspora in the region that facilitates currency conversions and makes a barter economy generally unnecessary.

As noted earlier, the stability of the Somali currency was recently threatened by massive imports of new notes. With the establishment of the fledgling TNG in September 2000, a clique of businessmen imported about 30 billion shillings (US$3 million) of Canadian-printed notes, in order to support the new government (IRIN 2000). The strategy provoked a rapid collapse of the currency that undermined rather than instilled confidence in the frail government (note that the TNG 'state' does not even control all parts of Mogadishu town, let alone the country's vast rural areas and coastline). It resulted in wide-scale demonstrations and protests in Mogadishu. By January 2001, the value of the SoSh was at 13,000 per $1, a decline of about 30 percent in only three months, and by the end of 2001 the currency had plummeted to about SoSh 22,000 per US dollar. Business leaders met with the new government and voiced their concerns about spiraling inflation and economic uncertainty, and many of them are requiring dollars – not SoSh – for many types of business transactions (IRIN 2001a).

Other recent accounts of Mogadishu's Bakara market, the city's largest commercial venue, describe similar chaos with the currency. In February 2001, for example, an additional US$4 million worth of newly printed Somali notes were brought in, and all transactions at Bakara stopped for four days. People rioted at the market when the shilling lost another 25 percent of its value and commodity prices almost doubled overnight (FEWS-Net 2001a). The TNG administration was forced to buy up large amounts of money, with a generous grant from the Saudi Arabian government, to halt its rapid depreciation and the associated havoc and

---

[6] Other circumstances, such as war and disasters, both of which marred Somalia during the 1990s, can lead to barter exchange. Barter was widespread in post-World War II Germany, where prolonged conflict devastated the national economy (Carlin et al. 2000: 1).

hyperinflation. Nonetheless, during a period of only six months when the new government was seeking political legitimacy, the currency's value declined by about 50 percent.[7] This rapid depreciation exceeded the sum of all devaluations during the previous five years when there was no central state. There is speculation that Somali groups opposed to the TNG played a sinister role in this chaos by funneling additional notes into the market (IRIN 2001b). Regardless of its causes, the recent attacks on the currency's integrity seriously destabilized an economy and its monetary system that was working fairly well until 2000.

To conclude, money assumes a key element in the telling of the Somalia story. It not only facilitates transactions and minimizes market risk, but the shilling also symbolizes the persistence of the Somali economy in the face of considerable turmoil. In the pastoral economy of the borderlands, which has always depended on commercial transactions, money provides a good indicator of social and economic welfare. As noted earlier, cash is needed to buy such foods as wheat flour and rice, and thus exchange rate stability has always been critical for pastoral consumers. It goes without saying that the urban, non-food producing segment of the population, which consumes considerable amounts of imported goods, also has a critical stake in the strength of the local currency.

Remittances from the diaspora

A growing Somali diaspora has resulted from the crisis in Somalia and its significance to the regional economy is (was) enhanced by the informal finance system described above. Literally tens of millions of US dollars are remitted annually from cities throughout the world, and there is little question that this flow has had a very positive influence on the country's economy, including its money. The Somali diaspora encompasses growing migrant communities in Europe, Canada, and the US and an increased presence in Kenya as well (see US Committee on Refugees 2000a). After Sierra Leone and the Sudan, the largest number of African refugees in the world originate from Somalia, an estimated 451,500 in 1999 (UNHCR 2000) or about 7 percent of the country's estimated population of approximately 6 million (see UNDP 1998: 18). In an age of global communications, they keep abreast of events at home through one of several internet sites devoted to Somalia and its current affairs.

A relatively significant Somali diaspora existed in neighboring countries and regions even prior to the state's collapse. During the oil boom of the 1970s and early 1980s, an estimated 150,000 to 175,000 Somalis were working in the Middle East alone (Jamal 1988a: 212). The government at the time recognized the economic significance of migrant remittances and

---

[7] It is reported that after intervention by the TNG the SoSh had strengthened to 18,400 SoSh per US dollar, a rate that is still almost double what it was only 15 months earlier (IRIN 2001c).

allowed Somali businessmen to import goods with their own sources of foreign exchange, which meant that they often served as brokers for Somali workers who remitted their US dollars through businessmen. This system of using remittance incomes to finance imports and increase the official flow of foreign exchange into the economy was called the *franco valuta* system and it explains why local incomes were such a poor indicator of welfare at the time (ibid: 211–12). Local income data did not (and still do not) capture the significant role of remittances. Jamal (1988a) estimated that in 1987 there was about $200 million in remittances entering Somalia, which financed a considerable amount of urban consumption. It was said at the time that dollars earned from this practice equaled or exceeded exports of goods and products from the country (Mubarak 1996: 58). With the decline of oil revenues and jobs in the Middle East during the 1980s, the number of Somali migrants working abroad declined and remittances were on the downturn when the civil war erupted.

The Somali communities in Europe and North America, on the other hand, were relatively small until the 1990s. In the US, for example, fewer than 2,000 refugees from all of Africa, including Somalia, were officially resettled during 1989. With the exception of Egypt, Ethiopia, Ghana, and Nigeria, very few Africans without refugee status (less than a few hundred annually) immigrated to the US until the early 1990s (see US Committee on Refugees 2000a; US Census Bureau 1999). After the overthrow of the Barre regime, however, the number of Somali refugees in high-income countries, including the US, grew rapidly.[8] By the latter half of the 1990s, Somali refugees admitted into the US and the UK were increasing significantly, while the Somali refugee population in Canada was already sizeable and estimated in 1993 to be between 60,000 and 70,000 (Farrow 1993: 10). Most did not come voluntarily; rather, they immigrated in response to a deteriorating and violent situation at home. Seeking political asylum and resettlement in Canada and joining its welfare system was relatively easy until the mid-1990s, after which restrictive measures – similar to other Western nations – were imposed (Farrow 1993; McGown 1999). In the US alone, an annual average of about 3,500 Somali political refugees were admitted from 1996 to 2000. In 1997 alone the number admitted was 6,436, a 50 percent increase over the previous year (US Committee on Refugees 1998).

For a Somali to enter the US or most European countries was a daunting task in the 1990s, especially when compared to Canada. S/he had to successfully pass a very rigorous and time-consuming (often two years or more) review process before being awarded political refugee status. Since the official ceiling for admitting African refugees to the US was raised to 18,000 in 2000 (and Somalis are among the largest African group with

[8] The number of Somalis in the US without refugee status during the 1990s was low. The only African nationalities that account for more than 1,000 immigrants (non-asylum seekers) per year are Egypt, Ethiopia, Ghana, and Nigeria (US Census Bureau 1999). Of these, Egypt represents the vast majority of the total.

refugee status), the number of Somalis residing in the US undoubtedly climbed in 2000 (see US Committee on Refugees 2000a). The official number of Somalis in the US in 1998 was about 25,000 (Kempainea et al. 2001), but the unofficial figure was probably at least two to three times that figure. In 1998 more than 50 percent of ethnic Somalis in the US resided in Minnesota (ibid).

Even greater increases in Somali immigrants have been reported for the UK, which has had elements of a Somali diaspora since the 1800s (McGown 1999). In 1999 alone, 7,495 Somalis sought political asylum in the UK and about 40 percent of these were approved for resettlement (US Committee on Refugees 2000b). During 1995 to 1999 Somalis represented one of the largest refugee groups in the UK, a country that now has the largest Somali population among Western nations. One estimate is that as many as 100,000 Somalis reside in the UK, many of whom are from the former British Protectorate of Somaliland (Ahmed 2000). While many immigrants receive welfare benefits in the UK and elsewhere, they also work in low-wage positions that local residents avoid. Only a relatively small number of well-educated Somali migrants have been able to land well-paid, skilled positions, such as engineers and computer programmers. The combined incomes from different sources allow Somali migrants to remit relatively sizable revenues by African wage standards. With the attainment of political refugee status, some migrants have ended up in countries where even menial, unskilled jobs pay 20 to 25 times higher salaries than comparable positions back home.[9] A telling point of comparison: while a PhD-trained university lecturer in some East African countries makes less than $175 per month, an unskilled worker at a 'fast food' outlet in northern Europe can earn that amount in only a few days. Thus, a paradoxical twist to the Somali tragedy is that the chaos and suffering of the early 1990s heightened the growth of an already existing Somali diaspora, with some members dispersing to high-income countries like the UK and US, where the potential to remit incomes is very high.

Accurate figures on the scale of remittances to Somalia (including Somaliland and Puntland) are virtually impossible to obtain, although it is clear that current levels are much higher than before the war. A conservative estimate places the figure at about $350 million per annum (UNDP 1998: 33), a number that exceeds all other sources of revenue including livestock exports and contraband trade but probably captures only about 50 percent of the real value of remittances.[10] A recent UNDP estimate places the annual value as high as between $750 million and $1 billion (UNDP 2003). In terms of distribution, most remittances 'go to family

[9] It also is clear that many Somali immigrants have suffered terribly from widespread racial and religious prejudices in the West, which greatly detract from whatever economic and political benefits they accrue (McGown 1999).

[10] Ahmed indicates a much higher level of remittances at an estimated $500 million annually for Somaliland alone (2000: 384). This estimate is premised on a figure of $4,170 per recipient household in Somaliland, which seems unrealistically high.

members inside Somalia, but some go to Somali in refugee camps, and some to factions and militias, especially when the diaspora is mobilized to support the clan in times of threat' (UNDP 1998: 33). How remittances are utilized once they arrive in Somalia is even more problematic to assess, although there is little question that a marginal amount has financed militia factions, as well as their resistors (McGown 1999: 41).

Remittances usually are transmitted through the kinds of informal finance houses described earlier in the chapter. Until the recent interventions that shut down the largest of the banks, the system worked remarkably well and fraudulent practices were relatively minor. Without receipts or other formal 'paper' proof, in some cases the process worked through a network of trust-based relations that insured funds would reach their intended sources. In London, a city with a burgeoning number of Somalis, two large money transfer houses could guarantee delivery of funds to most towns in Somalia within two to three days. One of these was a branch of the same finance house (al Barakaat) that was described earlier and has since been closed. Its services and those of other informal banks are (were) especially taxed during Islamic holiday seasons, when remittances to Somalia greatly increase. At these times the impact on the Somali economy is immediate. For instance, the FEWS project reports that as a result of the 'increase in remittances from abroad during *Ramadan* ... the Somali shilling gained slightly against the dollar by one percent in January [2000], from Ssh10,163 in December to Ssh10,143 in January' (FEWS 2000a: 1).

Local politics and 'civil society'

Political life in Somalia clearly has not matched the resiliency and accomplishments of the economic sector. Politics in the border region remain volatile in 2002, especially in the Jubba Valley and Kismayo. In the larger towns like Kismayo, youth, called *mooryaan*, make up the majority of the militia and they remain a powerful, well-armed force under different faction heads and warlords. The so-called warlords maintain control over a territory and population through networks of clients, control over arms, and economies that utilize force to generate resources and maintain power (see Reno 1998: 1–3). A warlord's political power is generally based on an economy of plunder and violence. Hussein Adam (1993) probably goes furthest in comparing current faction leaders to 'warlords', a term that is most closely associated with early Chinese strongmen but recently has been applied to autocrats and militia leaders across unstable parts of Africa (Reno 1998). The most organized of the Somali warlords, such as Muse Sudi Yalahow and Hussein Aideed, control important parts of the contraband economy (for example, arms and stolen food aid) and a hierarchy of followers ('lieutenants') who are rewarded handsomely for their loyalty. The current militia heads possess little vision for how Somali civic life and institutions can be rehabilitated, nor do they offer realistic plans for a government that embraces different elements of Somali society. As will be discussed later, the renewed international attention to Somalia in the wake of September 11 has provided a new global platform for some warlords that has strengthened their positions vis-à-vis the struggling TNG.

Warlords recruited followers from among the youthful unemployed and impoverished who roamed Somalia's larger cities in the 1980s. Their numbers were supplemented later on by pastoral youth who moved to towns to help their clans. According to Ahmed, the term, *mooryaan,* 'is from classical Somali and refers to the have-nots or to a group of people who are robbed of their property' (Ahmed 1995a: ix; also see Marchal 1993). Similar to Sierra Leone (Richards 1996), Liberia (Ellis 1999a), and other war-torn African states, these disenfranchised youths were easily recruited by militia leaders. The *mooryaan* are heavily armed and often serve as security escorts for the larger merchants and development agencies. Their prominence and control of weapons has eroded the authority of elders in certain areas (Menkhaus 2000: 191) even though their significance is minor in the pastoral areas of the borderlands. In the large towns and agricultural areas of the Jubba Valley, the influx of armed youth from non-local clans constrains customary enforcement methods. Often 'local clan elders found themselves attempting to negotiate with young militiamen and bandits from distant clans rather than with "peer" elders' (Menkhaus 2000: 191). As in several West and Central African countries, well-armed youths remain a serious impediment to any lasting national reconciliation in Somalia, but they are the actors who have the least visibility in the country's current peace talks.

In Africa warlord politics and the role of armed youth in economies of plunder have probably been best documented in Sierra Leone and Liberia, where there are important similarities (and differences) to the Somali situation (see Ellis 1999a; Reno 1998; Richards 1996). In the West African cases similar patterns of unemployed youth recruitment, control of valuable circuits of trade, and relations with trans-national business interests are also found. Yet, warlord politics have been more unified, rural-based, and 'visionary' in Sierra Leone and Liberia than in Somalia, where mini-factions proliferate, alliances are particularly fractious, and leaders spend little time 'leading' as opposed to plundering. Moreover, while there was some international business involvement in Somalia during the 1990s, the scale and economic stakes were far less than in mineral-rich Liberia and Sierra Leone. While control of the food aid industry, banana and livestock trade, and contraband commerce (including arms) provided revenues for Somali warlords, these circuits of trade were less valuable than the diamond, mineral, and illicit drug trade of the West African states (Ellis 1999a and 1999b). Consequently, the global interest in resource-poor Somalia by multinational firms was less significant than in West Africa where rich deposits of iron ore (Liberia) and diamonds (Sierra Leone) are found. Earlier in the book it was suggested that conflicts between General Mohammed Said Hersi 'Morgan' and Colonel Omar Jess were grounded in long-standing political and economic tensions in the borderlands (see Chapter 3). These divisions were accented in the 1980s by the rapid expansion of export trade, the creation of a privileged urban-based merchant class, and the previous regime's favoratism to members of certain clans. The discussion here focuses on the post-war period and how local communities have governed themselves despite these endemic conflicts and the absence of a central government. The issue of political leadership in southern Somalia remains unresolved, but nonetheless some degree of local governance exists and a modicum of services is being delivered without a state (Menkhaus 1998b). Certain warlords, such as Colonel Jess and the late Mohamed Farah Aideed, helped to stimulate popular opposition to the repressive Barre regime but then failed to provide any sustained political platform or compromise after the government's collapse. Intent on accumulating personal wealth and power for themselves and their clique of followers through terror, theft, and contraband trade, they have extended few political and economic benefits to the majority of Somalis.

Thus, in this context of political uncertainty local governance in the Somalia borderlands has involved different segments of civil society that include elements of the previous administration, Islamic clerics, local clan elders, women's groups, and livestock traders. Because livestock trading is a lucrative profession in Somalia, it always has attracted local leaders and elites. Livestock traders, in turn, often negotiate multiple agreements with communities and militias to insure safe passage across vast expanses of territory, as well as to procure animals from conflict-ridden territories. As a result, they have a vested interest in reducing conflict. As one trader remarked, 'it is to our advantage to have no conflicts because it helps our business' (trader interview, 8 June, 1996). It has been observed that 'in more than one instance, merchant pressure for open roads has been instrumental in forging peace accords' (Menkhaus 1998a: 7).

With vast networks of contacts and experience in negotiating local agreements, some traders have assumed leadership positions and – as stated above – important roles in peace negotiations. As noted earlier, two of the 27 traders from the 1987–8 study are active in local politics. Other businessmen also are involved in political negotiations and governance. For example, an association of *khat* traders formed the Somali Business Association's party in 1998 to help lobby for peace and agreements to allow their commodity to be moved without harassment; and businessmen and traders have covered the costs of security services for the public in the larger towns. Additionally, part of the costs of the recent peace conference in neighboring Djibouti, as well as the startup activities of the new TNG, have been covered by businessmen and merchants.

In southern Somalia political structures can be markedly different from community to community, from region to region, and from town to countryside. As Novisi remarks in a recent article, 'the operation of politics at the local level is haphazard and varies from region to region. The legitimacy and effectiveness of different local governments varies as well, as do the members of the political bodies in the different regions' (Novisi 1996: 41, 71). Although the so-called warlords and their militias mainly rule the large urban centers, in some border areas powerful clan leaders (called *ugaas* or *sultan*) work together with other notables to provide some context of order and a modicum of services in the rural areas and small towns. In this sense, 'power itself has devolved over the past eight years to radically local levels. Most meaningful political authority today exists at the village, district, or (in large urban settings) neighborhood level' (UNDP 1998: 58). For example, in Afmadow the local council of elders recently confronted the local Sultan, a powerful Mohamed Zubeyr leader with several armed followers, to help reconcile tensions with the neighboring Aulihan (author's field notes, 1998). The disputes had disrupted cattle trade in the area and forced traders to seek alternative border routes to Kenya's lucrative markets. The community was keen to reach a settlement, and within a month an agreement was reached between the two groups that enabled the normal market channels to resume. In this case the negotiations never moved beyond the local communities that were affected.

In other border areas, the elements of local political life are equally diverse. In at least one location a new district administration, complete with a District Commissioner and District Council, was established in 1994 and has been maintained up to now. Other political actions have taken place that include important roles for women. In Kismayo town women's groups have been vocal supporters of peace talks and strong critics of warlord politics, and have staged a number of very visible demonstrations that include exposing their breasts in public to embarrass men and provoke political action (see Women's International Network [WIN] 1998; Farah 1996).[11] Women from southern Somalia have also assumed important functions in the latest round of peace talks (2000) in Djibouti and are especially well-organized in Mogadishu where they play key roles in the business sector as well (Brons 2001: 220).

Islam as an identity and way of life also has provided a modicum of unity and security in a divided Somali society. The religion's increased influence has mainly been felt in small towns and urban centers, but a renewed adherence to its principles has also occurred among herders, most of whom have never been as strictly attached to Islam as their urban

---

[11] Nuruddin Farah describes this vivid example of political agency and protest among Kismayo women just prior to the collapse of the Barre regime. He notes: 'A few dozen women, defying the conviction that enjoins female sartorial modesty, bared their breasts in public in front of a crowd of men. Fists raised, voices harsh, they shouted "Rise, Rise!", challenging the men to action, reproaching them for their failure to confront the excesses of dictatorship' (Farah 1996: 18).

counterparts. Islamic religious leaders have helped to organize security and other services in conflict-ridden towns, such as Mogadishu, and their efforts have been appreciated by groups of businessmen. The establishment of Islamic sharia law outside the border region, for example, has received support from merchants, especially in Mogadishu, where the rule has reduced security problems and cash outlays for security guards. As Barise notes, 'businessmen have worked on uniting the Islamic courts to create one giant security organization for the capital [Mogadishu]' (Barise 2001: 22). In other sectors, such as education, Islamic organizations have helped to reopen schools and have received financial support for these ventures from Saudi Arabia and other Middle Eastern states (ibid: 23). In short, there is little doubt that Islam has helped to fill certain social and emotional voids following the government's collapse in 1991, a point that even harsh critics of Somalia in the current political environment have admitted (see Lake 2002).

Post-September 11 assessments suggest that radical Islamic political movements in the country have made significant impacts on Somali society and represent cells of global terrorism. However, there is little evidence that a current threat exists or that religious identity has supplanted clan and other forms of loyalty. The Islamist group, al-Itihaad al-Islami, which is currently on President Bush's list of terrorist organizations, was prominent in one part of southwestern Somalia immediately after the 1991–2 war, but was crushed by Ethiopian forces in 1997 and currently has little power or a viable network of supporters (Vick 2002). As noted Somali expert Ken Menkhaus explains, it has made few inroads in the local political structures of Somalia and 'the group as a whole is in no way a subsidiary of al-Qaida' (Menkahus, cited in England 2002: 2).

How do these different institutions and innovations described above relate to customary forms of political process? Customary law (*xeer*) and the *diya* principle remain important in the pastoral areas and serve as critical institutions for maintaining order in the absence of a state. The *diya* principle defines compensation for death and injury between different groups and sanctions against misconduct and violence; while *xeer* covers laws – as interpreted by respected elders – involving marriage, war, land and natural resources use, and other practices (see Bihi 2000; Lewis 1961). *Diya*-paying groups serve important functions in resolving local conflicts and are headed by groups of elders. They have helped to fill the gap left by the state's collapse and are respected by most of the new political initiatives in the region. As noted in Chapter 1, large numbers of livestock (up to 100 head of livestock) have to be paid by a *diya*-paying group if one of its members kills or injures a member of another *diya* group, or if they destroy another's property. The Barre government did much during the 1970s and 1980s to undermine the influence of *diya* groups and the customary *xeer* law (see Chapter 1). The regime did so by enforcing its own form of modern governance through appointed administrators and committees at the local level, and by banning the public expression of clan identities, customary law, and *diya*-paying groups (see Ahmed Samatar 1994a). Despite these constraints, *xeer* and *diya* groups continued to operate and still remain important jural and political forces in Somalia.

One of the important mistakes of the UN effort in Somalia was to underestimate the diversity of local social groups. By focusing their efforts on the warlords and their militia and on clans and their leaders, they excluded many other elements of Somali society, including associations of *dilaal* (brokers), traders (male and female), women, religious leaders, and technicians (veterinarians and water technicians). Nor did they recognize the dynamics of local clan identities and their complex relationships with militia, NGOs, and other groups. Instead, clans were treated as fixed entities, with rigid structures and rules of membership. The emphasis on working through clan structures also received support from other groups, which bolstered their roles in political discussions (see Hassan 1995). After all, clans are 'indigenous,' a term that usually finds a receptive audience among community development practitioners and human rights groups. If it is indigenous, it is seen as 'truer' to local culture, and, thus, more appropriate than other forms of social structure, even though identifying what is truly indigenous is a particularly unwieldy task. The emphasis by outsiders on the indigenous did not go unnoticed by Somali communities, who utilized the term in local disputes about land rights in the region. As was shown in Chapter 3, once the United Nations and others privileged clan as the critical 'traditional' (indigenous) identity, especially with regard to territorial claims, new identities and forms of discourse emerged.

In practice, clan identities in the border region have proven to be in different stages of fragmentation and/or consolidation, often responding to the actions of external organizations. The process of fragmentation evolved as groups jockeyed to gain UN support and the resources associated with it. Even NGOs allied with particular clans emerged to take advantage of the favorable environment, sometimes blurring the line between clan and NGO. Without recognizing their potential for fragmentation and/or aggregation, the UN and allied parties may actually have contributed to the proliferation of clan and sub-clan identities and the divisions they represent. They also unknowingly elevated clans to a level of significance that they never held in the 1980s. Not surprisingly, some of these groups, including clan-affiliated NGOs, disappeared as soon as external resources dissipated.

The UNOSOM intervention, however, helped to establish 58 District Councils in the country that were to be 'responsible for managing the affairs of the district' (Addis Ababa Agreements 1993: 108). Yet, even here struggles occurred over the composition of councils. When elders were asked to appoint council members on the basis of clan allocations, a tactic that UNOSOM encouraged in its promotion of distict councils, disputes erupted (Helander et al. 1995: 6–7). Not surprisingly, each clan 'had fairly

inflated notions of the "piece of the pie" to which it was entitled'
(Menkhaus 2000: 198). Additionally, in order to gain the maximum representation, clans would fragment into as many sub-clans and lineages as
possible. The performance of district councils varied markedly in the
border region and some became just another vehicle of local division and a
means for former civil servants and elites to return to authority (see
Prendergast 1997: 133–4). Others simply disappeared as the UN withdrew
in 1995; while a few became administrative links between the local population and outside parties, such as donor agencies (see Eikenberg 1995: 4).

As noted above, the record of district councils has been mixed in
Somalia. In some respects the formation of district councils reinforces
negative processes: ethnic territorialism and border conflicts between
certain sub-clans, like the Aulihan and Mohamed Zubeyr. In the borderlands the Aulihan dominate the membership of the Hagar District Council,
but the Mohamed Zubeyr control the council of neighboring Afmadow
District. Both councils have contrasting views over the proper alignment
of boundaries, as well as their political roles vis-à-vis the other. In this
case, the formation of district councils has reinforced sub-clan rivalries
rather than traversed them. On the positive side, the district institutions
have assumed constructive parts in mediating trade conflicts, such as the
one discussed previously in the chapter, and they have helped to recover
confiscated trade goods and animals as well. One of the main cross-border
routes between Kenya and areas west of the Jubba Valley (including the
Bay Region) requires passage through both Mohamed Zubeyr (Afmadow
District) and Aulihan (Hagar Distict) areas. Agreements between the
district councils have allowed safe passage along this corridor.

What about other elements and institutions of civil society in Somalia;
how have they fared?[12] With a few noted exceptions, the short answer is
they have not done very well. Viable public institutions are noticeably
few, which has made the delivery of social services extremely difficult.
The one area where there has been a modicum of success is in the provi-
sions of water for animals and people. As was indicated in Chapter 2,
approximately two-thirds of the major water points (boreholes) in the
Lower Jubba Region were operable in 1999. Other sectors have not fared
as well, and education is one of these. The term 'lost generation(s)' accurately captures the predicament of students in Somalia during the 1990s,
since even the most optimistic statistics indicate 'only 20% of school-age
children (ages 5–14) are enrolled in school, and are heavily concentrated
in the early grades' (UNDP 1998: 6). The participation rates are even lower
in rural areas, especially in the pastoral zones.

The collapse of the educational system, however, was well under way
prior to the civil war; 'primary school enrollment rates were estimated in

[12] This section relies heavily on UNDP (1998), perhaps the only relatively reliable source
available on the country's public and social sectors. Yet even the authors of this report admit that
their data were collected under volatile and hurried conditions and that they often represent estimates. Another 'Human Development' report for Somalia was to be released in 2002.

1987 at 18 percent for boys and 6 percent for girls (one of the lowest rates in the world)' (ibid: 39). In the pre-1991 era, rates of attendance at formal schools were even lower in the border region. In 1987–8 about 12 percent of pastoral children on the Somali side of the border attended school, and about three-quarters of these were boys (author's field notes). These figures are not surprising since by the late 1980s less than 2 percent of the national recurrent budget was devoted to education (Mubarak 1996). Like other aspects of Somali society, it is difficult to gauge the extent to which primary education deteriorated in the 1990s, although there is little question that the situation was much better before 1991.

The predicament for secondary and post-secondary education is even more desperate. Attendance at secondary and post-secondary schools is only a small fraction (probably less than 25 percent) of what it was in the 1980s.[13] Some estimates claim that fewer than 2,000 children attend secondary schools in Somalia (excluding Somaliland and Puntland) and most of these live in Mogadishu, where the majority of high schools are located (UNDP 1998: 52–3). The lack of education and other opportunities partially explains why warlords have been able to recruit extensively from among the youth. Often armed with kalashnikovs ('AK-47s') and attached to heavily armed vehicles, called 'technicals', the Somali youth have lost an opportunity to acquire the skills needed to rebuild institutions and industries and to compete regionally.

With assistance from donors and NGOs, several education facilities were rehabilitated during the UNOSOM period of 1993 to 1995. However, with the decline of school-feeding programs and external assistance generally, rates of school attendance declined precipitously after the departure of the UN program. To counter this trend, women's groups in towns have taken the initiative to start new schools and to help staff them with teachers. For the elite of the country, other options are available. They can hire private tutors, place their children in one of the few private schools in Mogadishu, or send them to Kenya for schooling (UNDP 1998: 52). These options are not realistic alternatives for most of the Somali population and when (or if) a meaningful central state re-emerges a massive shortage of trained manpower will exist in the country. There is even a question as to whether there are enough qualified Somali students from the primary schools to fill even a small number of secondary schools were they to reopen.

Local Qur'anic schools that focus on Islamic instruction have always attracted a greater percentage of Somali children than secular schools, even in the 1980s (see Little 1989b). In a small way they have helped to close the glaring gap in educational opportunities, a point that was made earlier in the chapter and one that has attracted attention in the 'war

[13] The recent creation of a community-funded university in Borama, in northern Somalia, called Amoud University, demonstrates a demand for post-secondary education and a willingness among local communities to go to phenomenal lengths to support schools. Unfortunately, this type of initiative has been the exception in stateless Somalia (see Abdi Samatar 2001).

against terrorism' because of the Islam connection. While memorization of the Qur'an is the principal activity of the schools, a few also teach subjects, like arithmetic. These schools are widespread, especially in the settled and urban areas. A UNICEF survey in northern Somalia in 1998 found the concentration of Qur'anic schools to be very high in urban areas, where they are distributed about every 300 to 500 meters among settled populations (UNDP 1998: 48). In Mogadishu it is estimated that one Islamic community organization alone operates more than 100 primary and secondary schools in the area (Masland 2002: 30).

Somalia also has faced its share of public health problems during the past decade, including in the border zone. The health sector probably suffers as much as any area of Somali society and badly requires significant levels of public investment. At least three times during the 1990s cholera epidemics killed hundreds of Somalis in the border region, and the El Nino storms of 1997–8 created a massive malaria and Rift Valley Fever outbreak that went uncontrolled for more than one month. Public health institutions to confront such hazards are absent. Immunization coverage in the country, including the border region, is also appallingly low, and only 10 percent of infants are currently being immunized (ibid: 28). In the border areas many of the heath-oriented NGOs, such as ICRC and Médicins Sans Frontières [MSF], pulled out in the 1990s because of insecurity. Some of these have since returned. Without public health institutions, the tracking of disease outbreaks and vaccination campaigns are carried out through 'word of mouth,' and often the voices of minority clans and groups are not heard until it is too late. The net result is that life expectancy in Somalia is estimated to be among the lowest in the world (43–46 years), although it was only 48 years in 1990 during the last year of the Barre government (UNDP 1998).

To fill the health services gap, a range of private facilities have opened in towns, including clinics and pharmacies. However, because most of the doctors and other qualified medical professionals left the country during the turmoil of 1991–2, these enterprises tend to be staffed by technicians and nurses and even some individuals who have minimal or no formal training (ibid: 30). These services also are concentrated in urban centers and, as in the past, pastoral health services are usually limited to emergencies (e.g. a drought or epidemic). The situation is particularly lacking in the Lower Jubba Region and the border region generally, even in the larger towns. It should be noted that Puntland (northeast Somalia) seems to be an exception in Somalia in that the region has 'experienced progress in the area of medical services after 1991' (Farah 2000: 15).

During periods of natural disasters, local communities are still dependent on emergency assistance from NGOs and donor agencies, although it usually is late in arriving. Health services were minimal in the border region during the 1980s, but at least at that time there was a government to rally international assistance. Now local populations must confront a fatigued and increasingly unsympathetic donor community from which to seek aid. They also must rely on external assessments to rally international support, and they have little control over the data that is used to assess their own welfare. Such dependencies are glaringly apparent during droughts, when famine conditions can materialize. As the book has emphasized throughout, the maintenance of mobility and resource access are important reasons why herders have not suffered as much from dependency and disasters, as have other segments of Somali society. The next chapter challenges a future Somalia to create a political system that builds public trust and institutions, but does not threaten one of the foundations of the countryside, mobile pastoralism.

7
Conclusions: | Somalia in a Wider Context

At the end of this century it has for the first time become possible to see what a world may be like in which the past, including the past in the present, has lost its role, in which the old maps and charts which guided human beings, singly and collectively, through life no longer represent the landscape through which we move, the sea on which we sail (Hobsbawm 1996: 17).

This book has highlighted the unorthodox but in some respects remarkable economy and resiliency of a stateless society at the start of the twenty-first century. It is a political drama that continues to unfold, as political battle lines are being drawn in almost every part of the country, and an international invasion in the post-September 11 environment remains a possibility. The once relatively stable states of Puntland and Somaliland of the 1990s are challenged by internal divisions and the fledgling TNG still has not incorporated the different factions – including General Morgan's[1] – into a 'new Somalia'. Kismayo as usual remains volatile, the scene of at least two major battles in recent months, and Mogadishu has experienced periodic conflict in the past year (see Denyer 2001). As I cautioned in the first chapter, contemporary events in Somalia quickly become *yesterday's news* and trends are especially difficult to assess. There can be no pithy sentence or phrase to conclude a tale that really has no immediate end in sight.

What is happening in Somalia is of concern to wider audiences in Africa and elsewhere, and not just because of the events and aftermath of September 11. We are living in an era where the integrity of the state is challenged, large pieces of territory are ungoverned, and informal circuits of trade and finance are everywhere. The latter phenomena are

---

[1] In August 2001 Morgan rallied his followers and recaptured Kismayo for a day or so, before being ousted by forces of the Jubba Valley Alliance. The latter are a pro-TNG faction of Marehan, Ogadeen, and Habar Gedir clan members who have had a tentative grip on Kismayo since they expelled Morgan's forces in June 1999 (IRIN 2001g).

almost as likely to be found on the streets of New York City and in the high-rise buildings of Hong Kong as they are among the thatched-roof *dukaan* (shops) of Somalia's border towns. Under these circumstances elements of modernity both are challenged and at times absorbed under the most unlikely contexts. Nowhere are these contradictory processes more apparent than in Africa, especially in Somalia. To place the Somalia story in a wider context, this final chapter focuses on three overriding themes. One is what could be called the 'intellectual' challenges of the Somali experience that have both scholarly and practical implications; another centers on Somalia's comparative lessons both for Africa and other parts of the world where standard political and economic models are challenged. The third topic of the chapter focuses on what the future might hold for Somalia, including its borderlands, and why outsiders should care. The themes are selected to highlight the book's main findings and to confront some of the disciplinary and other biases that limit an understanding of Somalia, as well as other similar cases. The discussion moves between an emphasis on the southern Somali borderlands and the rest of the country.

Rethinking 'wisdoms'

The Somali case challenges a number of widely held ideas about how societies and economies operate. Anthropologists, political scientists, historians, and even economists have found aspects of the Somali case that either validate or refute accepted disciplinary dogma. For example, it was the first test case in the post-cold war era of the 'new world order', an experiment that soured quickly, as the preceding chapters have shown (McCoy 2000). Many observers hoped that the 'rescue' of Somalia could be an example of a new type of internationalism with the collapse of old cold-war animosities. While the multilateral efforts of UNOSOM and the US-led Operation Restore Hope started with such spectacular optimism and helped to reduce famine in Somalia, they bore few tangible outcomes in the long run. Instead, in the words of one scholar, Somalia 'did so much to shatter the hopes of the new world order in the early 1990s' (Menkhaus 1998a: 8). In the post-cold war era, Somalia was a challenge but now is seen by many internationalists as a 'deviant society' (Lauderdale and Toggia 1999: 157), an undeserved reputation that the events of September 11 did little to eliminate.

As the previous chapters have shown, the Somali case provokes other kinds of questions about societies that are considered to be 'ungoverned'. These include, for instance, ideas about how politics operate in the absence of a government; how markets function without legal institutions and currencies; and how communities draw on customary forms of identity and organization to tap markets and weather extraordinary levels of instability.

An anthropological invention?

The manner in which the segmentary lineage or clan system manifests itself in contemporary Somalia also raises important questions about social structure and its resiliency. Does the segmentary clan system blindly dictate Somali social and political allegiances, as some have suggested (Lewis 1994; Schlee 2001), or has its rigidity and importance been overstated – an invention of the anthropologist that is reinforced by Western journalists who enjoy writing about African 'tribalism' (see Abdi Samatar 1992; Besteman 1996)? The arguments around this question have been especially contentious (see Lewis 1998; Helander 1998; and Besteman 1999b), although the real answer probably lies somewhere between the two extremes. While the segmentary system is flexible and actively negotiated (even invented) by individuals, and manipulated by warlords, it nonetheless shapes important aspects of contemporary Somali politics and economy, but not always in predictable ways (see Chapter 3).

Throughout the 1990s the segmentary principle has been evident in local politics, at times uniting ('fusion') and in other instances dividing ('fission') clans and lineages. The recent coalition (called the Somali Reconciliation and Reconstruction Council) of previously antagonistic factions and militias, including those of Generals Morgan and Gebiyo in response to the formation of the TNG, is a good illustration of segmentary fusion. The clan-based splits in the Somali Patriotic Movement (SPM) that were documented in Chapter 3 are dramatic instances of fission (see Chapter 3). Although Somalia's decentralized political structures draw on the segmentary clan idiom, the society has not descended into barbaric lawlessness or tribalism, as some predicted. In fact, there seems to have been a 'retraditionalization' of kinship and clan structures and a reinvention of social structure in general, as Somali politicians now openly incorporate the 'traditional' into political structures. New leaders of the TNG and Puntland, for instance, have done this by utilizing customary clan-based assemblies and forums and carefully allocating political posts among different clan segments, thereby avoiding the biases that plagued the Barre regime (see Bihi 2000; Doornbos 2000 and forthcoming; Farah and Lewis 1997).

Thus, Somali communities have used 'traditional' custom, as well as their segmentary social system, in very pragmatic ways. Some of these are high-lighted in earlier chapters and involved the creative use of clan and sub-clan identities to stake claims to lands and development resources. In northern Somalia, regional states have formed assemblies of clan leaders and elders who hold real power in the new political systems (Doornbos 2000). Tradition is actively engaged, debated, and incorporated at all levels of Somali society, as well as vulnerable to strong political manipulation. A good illustration is the local interpretations of clan relations during the re-emergence of the Absame 'supra clan' as a counter to other clan-based alliances in the border region (see Chapter 3). In another example, an elderly man even explained how considerable negotiation about cultural rules took place after a person recently was elected as a clan leader (*ugaas*). When the community was asked to organize a ceremony for the leader, heated arguments ensued over the correct customs for the ritual and the appropriate role of the new *ugaas* (author's field notes, 18 June 2001). Since 1991 these kinds of events, where culture is openly debated and shaped, have grown in significance along with a heightened political sense of the clan system.

It is obviously difficult for Westerners to understand the logic of a segmentary system, where groups in conflict in one instance can unite almost instantly in another to oppose an outside party. They also fail to acknowledge the way in which political contexts and circumstances shape social relations, including those based on clans. Along these lines how could a brutal warlord, such as the late Mohamed Farah Aideed, draw mass support from the very people and lineages whom he victimized? The US misunderstood the importance of the segmentary principle on that tragic 'Black Hawk Down' day in October 1993 (Bowden 1999), when it was assumed that once they isolated Aideed, the populace of Mogadishu would not challenge their forces. Segmentary political systems, however, aggregate not divide when confronted by outsiders.

Similar to segmentary kinship systems elsewhere in East Africa and the Middle East (see Lancaster 1997), the Somali system is inherently expansionist. Somali pastoralism, for example, has drawn on the segmentary system to expand territorially in the past four centuries, moving and controlling one key resource patch after another and absorbing new population segments along the way (see Chapters 2 and 3). As a livelihood system, it effectively adapts to uncertain circumstances, incorporates occupied populations, and mobilizes social relations over vast territories. No matter where one is in Somalia or outside among the diaspora, the extensive kinship system creates potential alliances, an attribute that nicely complements mobile pastoralism.

The same logic of extension and alliance also accommodates geographically dispersed trading networks as they seek new markets and partners. Indeed, as I have shown in preceding chapters, the segmentary kinship principle is embedded in the regional and international trading diasporas that are so important for Somalia. It has abetted traders in gaining access to markets, finance, and information both during periods of boom and bust. It also has aided the global trade and remittance networks that have helped to keep the Somali economy afloat. Somali traders and transporters are found throughout East Africa and well into central Africa and the Middle East (Dubai, Oman, and Yemen). These networks have grown in significance with the implosion of the Somali state. The segmentary kinship idiom strengthens them by enhancing trust and guarding against deception in business dealings. A 'greater Somalia'[2] of trade and finance networks

---

[2] Ironically, a 'greater Somalia' based on trade and transport has been achieved, while a 'greater Somalia' political state is now more unrealistic than at any point during the past 40 years. A 'greater Somalia' comprising Somalia, Somaliland, and Somali areas of neighboring Kenya, Ethiopia, and Djibouti was an important political ambition of the 1960s and 1970s and resulted in wars with Kenya (1960s) and Ethiopia (1970s).

has expanded beyond the Horn of Africa area to encompass parts of the Middle East and to link numerous international cities to Somalia. While a significant trade diaspora existed prior to 1991, the war has accelerated its growth, with livestock being just one of its important commodities.

Openly informal economy

Throughout the book it has been argued that Somalia is exceptional in many respects, but not qualitatively different from other regions where states are shallow and weak and formal economies are moribund. As Ellis points out in the case of Liberia, the presence of an internationally acknowledged state does not mean that government treasuries and national banks can be any more trusted to guarantee transactions than elsewhere: 'the Liberian central bank has ceased to fulfill the functions expected of it by the international financial system' (1999a: 185). He goes on to provide an example where an expatriate shipper lost more than US$50,000 of his funds in only a few days when he deposited them in a Liberian national bank, despite formal government 'guarantees' in writing that he could withdraw the full amount of his money. The funds simply disappeared and the government was incapable of enforcing the law against its own bank branches (ibid). In environments like this, distinctions between formal and informal or official and unofficial are simply meaningless, even where recognized forms of governance exist. As Hibou convincingly argues, the lines between legal and illegal in weak states are extraordinarily blurred: 'the division into formal and informal spheres is thus not a useful distinction in Africa, since illegal practices are also performed in the formal sector, while so-called informal economic networks operate with well-established hierarchies and are fully integrated into social life' (1999: 80). In short, many African states are officially involved in the 'unofficial' export of commodities, such as diamonds and ivory, while illegal businesses operate in the open, often with the support of the state (ibid: 89; also see Reno 1995).

One needs only to visit Eastleigh, Nairobi to see how the formal (legal) and informal (illegal) merge in complex ways (see Chapter 6). The shopping area itself, which is widely noted to have the busiest commercial avenue in Nairobi, attracts middle- and upper-class shoppers from around the city and other parts of the country. They come to shop for bargains and, in some cases, to purchase counterfeit identification cards and the like. Up-scale brands of fashion, electronics, and other consumer items can be purchased at 20 to 30 percent below prices elsewhere in town and services, such as internet and phone, can be obtained at a fraction of normal costs. One minute of online time, for example, costs about $0.04, while an international phone call to the USA is as low as $1.00 per minute, compared to $3.00 by normal means. Unregistered (illegal) phone services stand in close proximity to official phone booths, and fuel stations selling contraband diesel are found within a few blocks of a licensed petrol station. On a much smaller scale than this, similar scenarios are found in certain border towns. Interestingly, all of this takes place in Kenya, a state that was once heralded as the bastion of modern capitalism on the continent.

Similar to the cross-border commerce in northern Kenya, the prevalence of illegal trade and its tight integration into daily practice serves to legitimize it. Little official effort is made to halt it, in part because many officials who are supposed to control illegal commerce receive 'rents' (bribes) from it. There is an ill-defined, baffling sense about Eastleigh that inhibits categorization, but nonetheless captures the essence of the new kind of commerce. The neighborhood of Nairobi is neither formal nor informal, but rather a location where unsanctioned trade is increasingly out in the open as it is in stateless Somalia. In some respects, it symbolizes a graphic form of resistance to an economic and political system that excludes it. That other openly informal ('illegal') urban-based economies dominated by diaspora trading groups like the Somalis have taken hold in many African cities, including parts of Johannesburg, South Africa (Rogerson and Rogerson 1996; Peberdy and Rogerson 2000), demonstrate its prevalence on the continent. It is a growing phenomenon that has largely gone unexplained and, in many cases, undocumented (Murray n.d.). In this sense Eastleigh is 'openly informal', neither hidden from authorities nor entirely consistent with an official, public place of business. At the same time it is integral to the service economy of Nairobi and its 2.5+ million residents who depend on it for low-cost products and services.

Thus, trade and other informal channels of economic activity characterize large parts of Africa, where 'nothing can be taken for granted because everything is open to parallel negotiation' (Hibou, cited in Chabal and Daloz 1999: 135). On a macro or global scale these informal flows of trade and finance link large areas of Africa, including Somalia, to the world. More politically stable entities than Somalia participate in these commercial circuits. For example, it is estimated that in the West African state of Benin smuggling represents about 90 percent of the country's trade (Reno 1995: 20). In describing cross-border trade in southern Africa, Ellis also suggests that 'Mozambique today has effectively become a free trade area for businessmen and smugglers of every description' (Ellis 1999b: 63). Like Somalia, it has become an entry point for goods and commodities from Asia and the Middle East that are distributed tax-free throughout the region, especially to South Africa.

The lack of a recognized government and of national institutions, such as a treasury or judicial system, does not discourage legitimate international firms from dealing with Somalia, including its breakaway states in the north. As noted earlier, Dole Fruit Inc had investments in Somalia's agricultural sector in the 1990s, as did Italian agribusiness companies. Somalia currently is served by international couriers, such as DHL, and by automobile companies, such as General Motors of Kenya (Africa News Service, 20 April 2000). Moreover, Total Oil Company operates in Somaliland, while last year (2001) the Chinese government sent a trade mission to Mogadishu to discuss investments in the energy sector (IRIN 2001d). Finally, the British Broadcasting Corporation (BBC), the well-known pillar of European journalism, has established a formal affiliation with one of Somalia's new media companies. This involvement of international corporations adds to the complex blend of formal and informal elements in the economy. Their presence in Somalia, as well as Somaliland's recent trade and landing (airline) agreements with neighboring Ethiopia, tend to formalize certain parts of a very unofficial economy. Even British Airways, one of the world's largest airlines, has an affiliate airline that serves Somaliland. In the northern Somali state of Puntland formal agreements also have been reached with a number of fishing fleets from Asian and European countries that further heighten the official aura of its economy (IRIN 1999a). Thus, while their governments and their economies are not officially recognized in international circles,[3] this has not discouraged international business interests from operating there. Through their presence, multinational companies add an element of legitimacy to Somalia and to the regional states of Puntland and Somaliland.

Informal politics

For some observers Somalia 'is interesting precisely because it is an indication of the options available in at least some parts of Africa to replace the orthodox forms of the state' (Ellis 1996: 19). The state remains the main means of international validation, either by governments or international organizations, but as the previous section shows formal agreements are still made with stateless territories. Along with the informalization of the Somalia economy an equally informal type of politics has developed, as the previous chapter indicated. Radical localization is the norm, and even before the state collapsed, most meaningful politics were conducted outside official channels (see Chabal and Daloz 1999: 95). Some scholars suggest this extreme decentralization based on the segmentary lineage system helped to bring about the state's demise and, therefore, represented the success of Somali social structure over bureaucratic hierarchy (Simmons 1998: 57). As this book has shown, while the segmentary system is important, social and economic injustices were the foundation of the state's collapse. Although Somalia has shown a capacity to resolve differences and unify when challenged externally, it has been extremely fractious domestically when competing for political and economic resources. For example, at the country's last real democratic elections in 1969 there were amazingly 62 parties and 1,002 candidates vying for 123 national offices (ibid: 59). And the 2000 Djibouti peace conference that

---

[3] In 2001 the OAU and the United Nations recognized the TNG as the legitimate government of Somalia, but very few countries have followed suit and opened diplomatic missions there. The TNG's control outside of Mogadishu is extremely limited, and even large parts of Mogadishu itself are outside its influence. The IMF and World Bank recently (June 2001) held talks with Somali (TNG) leaders for the first time in more than 10 years.

led to the formation of the Transitional National Government (TNG) drew more than 1,000 Somali clan elders, businessmen, and others representing dozens of different political factions. When focused internally Somali social structure can be almost chaotically democratic and decentralized. For anthropologists like Simmons (1995), Lewis (1994), and Luling (1997), the overwhelming challenge for a future Somalia, once again, is how to accommodate a hierarchical government with a social structure that is so decentralized and inconsistent with it.

What needs to be remembered, however, is that the coup of 1991 was more of an attack on a regime's inequitable policies than a repudiation of the modern state. The story in this book holds an important lesson. As long as government does not overly constrain local livelihoods (especially pastoralism in the Somali case) and trading systems, nor excessively distort the flow of resources to certain groups and regions at the expense of others, it does not make a great deal of difference to many communities what kind of political configuration (democratic, socialist, religious, or other) exists at the top. Life will go on if these critical facets are left alone.

Reconciliation between the modern state and pastoralism, Somalia's key livelihood, is essential if a central government is to be restored.[4] In fact, as the book has depicted, the obliteration of key state investments in the Jubba Valley during the 1990s actually opened up additional resources for local herders (see Chapter 2). The irony is that in rural Somalia pastoral mobility has been maintained, perhaps even strengthened, without a state. Despite the predominance of the pastoral sector in the national economy, the previous regime and its policies and investments – often with World Bank and other funding – were only marginally different from those of neighboring countries where the livestock sector is less prominent. As with Barre's government, few Horn of Africa countries have done anything to benefit pastoralism. Although Barre himself was from a pastoral background and the majority of the country practiced pastoralism, his regime did its best to undermine mobile pastoralism through resettlement schemes, irrigation investments, and subsidized water development for large-scale traders and elites. The state's inability in the 1980s to look beyond the overseas livestock trade, which increased its foreign exchange coffers and 'greased' its patronage machine, contributed to conflict in the southern borderlands and sparked widespread discontent throughout the country (see Chapter 3). Is it surprising, then, that communities have resisted a centralized government model

---

[4] Caroline Humphrey and David Sneath, writing on Mongolia, feel that not only is such a reconciliation possible but necessary in countries that are highly dependent on mobile pastoralism: 'Far from being a practice associated with the most backward herders, highly mobile livestock herding is often the basis for the most efficient, wide-ranging, well co-ordinated and specialized production, and it is compatible with technologically advanced and profit-oriented economic activity' (Humphrey and Sneath 1999: 1). They go on to suggest that where the pastoral sector is the backbone of the national economy it needs to be supported rather than threatened (ibid: 75).

during the past decade and, instead, have opted for decentralized forms of governance (see Bryden 1999: 134)?

Stateless or near-stateless parts of the world have grown immensely since Somalia's demise in 1991. Afghanistan and large parts of central Asia and the troubled Balkan region come immediately to mind. In fact, the so-called tribal areas of sovereign Pakistan near the southern Afghanistan border, where deposed Taliban leaders and al-Qaida supporters are said to have fled during the recent war in Afghanistan, is a noted haven of smuggling. There openly 'illegal' economic and political activities go largely unchallenged by state officials (*The Economist* 1995: 36). It is said that in the northwest borderlands of Pakistan illegal trade is so formalized that there is a shopping centre with an unofficial 'branch' of the British department store, Marks and Spencer, 'selling a range of the retailer's (smuggled) own-label goods'. And all of this takes place in a country, Pakistan, that by African standards has a reasonably strong central government, fairly robust formal economy, and a well-developed military force. In sub-Saharan Africa, one can assume that, with the exception of a few countries – most notably South Africa – the so-called state is 'a relatively empty shell' (Chabal and Daloz 1999: 95). In the final years of the Barre government this was particularly true, thus making the transition to statelessness not as dramatic an occurrence as it might have been elsewhere. Rural Somalis rarely depended on the state in the 1980s, except for a small clique of elite, while much of the Somali economy was based on pastoralism and unofficial trade. As this book has shown, production and market risks remain high for herders, but the destruction of the state only marginally impacted on them.

The same cannot be said of urban and settled Somalis, who, as the book has shown, have been dramatically affected by the state's collapse. Urban services and institutions not only disappeared, but brutal warlords stepped in to fill the political vacuum, as they have in other feeble states. Most of them have acted as viscous warlords who use force and violent means of extraction for economic gain. With the establishment of the TNG in 2001, some weakening of warlords fortunately occurred for a short period but, as will be shown below, all this changed with the events of September 11. The current context (2002) for political reconciliation holds less promise than it did pre-September 11.

Modernity, globalization, and the new world (dis)order

Somalia is the outcast child of the post-cold war era when almost overnight small states no longer seemed to matter. After all, with the demise of the USSR and its perceived threat, economic support for and security alliances with undeveloped African states were no longer foreign policy priorities. It is hardly a coincidence that many of the states, including Somalia, Sudan, Liberia, and the Democratic Republic of the

Congo, which figured so prominently in US-based support in Africa during the 1970s and 1980s, are those very countries that are so conflict-ridden and internationally ostracized today. However, while generally isolated from the international community, Somalia has not been removed from global policies and politics. For instance, it is clear that Dole's investment in the banana sub-sector was at least partially motivated by the so-called Lome Agreement that allowed favorable access by a former colony (Somalia) to the markets of its former European patron (Italy) (Nduru 1996). When this trade policy was revoked later on, Dole's interest in Somalia quickly waned. Likewise, recent pressure on the World Trade Organization (WTO) by major livestock exporters, such as Australia and Brazil, over animal health regulations can be interpreted as an assault on Somalia and its lucrative animal trade with the Middle East. By campaigning for rigid health and export controls, wealthier countries are aware that Somalia (including Somaliland) and its neighbors will face great difficulty in meeting stringent requirements and, consequently, will lose access to international markets.[5]

Other global forces are in play with potentially strong impacts on Somalia, including its southern borderlands. One is the general assault by wealthy countries on immigration policy and the welfare state, including economic benefits for political refugees and low-income immigrants generally. Such actions could have a major impact on Somalia. For example, welfare reform and benefit reductions in places as different as Oslo, Norway, Glasgow, Scotland, and Minneapolis, Minnesota could have as much to do with the future stability of the Somali economy as local development activities and cross-border trade (personal communication, Leif Manger). As was shown in the previous chapter, the impact of remittances on the Somali economy is enormous and at least partially determined – directly or indirectly – by welfare flows. The important role that the Somali diaspora has played in rebuilding the economy is considerable, and despite the recent closure of the al Barakaat bank, remittances remain important and could be jeopardized by reduced welfare benefits for refugees and immigrants in the West. Thus, global linkages between Somalia and wealthy countries and their domestic policies are deeper and more complex than normally assumed, and they affect large numbers of Somalis.

Improvements in communications and air service clearly facilitate Somalia's links with the rest of the world. At present there are at least four airlines that fly from Somalia to neighboring African countries and the Middle East (Barise 2001: 23). Until recently there were also numerous satellite phones, private internet connections, and at least one public internet service that opened up communications with the rest of the world. Recent evidence suggests that in the wake of the closure of al Barakaat, including its communications facilities, the gap

[5] Some Somalis suspected that Australia, which is a major exporter of livestock to the Middle East, was at least partially behind the prolonged export ban of the 1980s.

in telecommunications in Somalia has been partially filled by recent internet and telecommunications startup companies (IRIN 2002b). Finally, there are satellite-based televisions that allow the transmittal of international news services, including the ubiquitous CNN. These new devices are found in Somali hotels and among wealthy individuals and allow residents to closely follow global events.

Thus, Somalis have latched on to many elements of modernity – mobile phones, computers, and pharmaceuticals – taking those desired aspects and incorporating them on their own terms. While they challenge Western development ideas and governments, they embrace certain dimensions of 'free-wheeling' capitalism and its latest gadgets and technologies. The informal finance houses that were described in the previous chapter are good examples of this. The use of computer software programs, which have been modified for these 'banks', is another instance of 'selective modernization'. Ironically, local communities also have reinvented local systems of administration – complete with District Commissioners – that date back to the colonial period, and in territorial disputes have used colonial boundaries to reinforce their claims (see Chapter 6). All of these examples are taking place devoid of any endorsement of modernization and Western-style development and ideologies.

Rejection of a particular form of the modern nation state and orthodox development models is not evidence of an aversion to development. Somalis want improvements in living standards, welfare, and administrative models that work, just like other Africans do. While they seek development, however, they reject the ill-conceived programs and policies that characterized the 1970s and 1980s. (Unfortunately, the latter could re-emerge if donor agencies return to the area without fundamental changes in their approaches.) In the past decade, Somalis have been able to negotiate development on their own terms and incorporate elements consistent with their livelihoods and culture. In this sense, they are no different than other Africans: 'The evidence suggests that virtually everyone in Africa desires the enhanced standard of living which programmes of development are supposed to encourage. But these programmes have been applied in such a form as to create strong resistance in some places' (Ellis 1996: 23). As was discussed earlier in the book, inappropriate livestock development projects provoked some of the strongest feelings of resentment, as well as the most disastrous results.

Why care about Somalia's future?

Some governments and organizations view statelessness in Somalia and other 'ungoverned' spaces as threats to global security, because they harbor threatening diseases, international crime rings, and uncontrolled weapons markets (see Menkhaus 2001: 17). Evidence of the latter are the open-air markets in Mogadishu that sell everything from small arms to large anti-aircraft guns and supply herders throughout East Africa with weapons (see Associated Press 2001).[6] What often is not remembered, however, is that the 'arms culture' in Somalia was initially fueled by massive amounts of US military aid to the country in the 1980s, which totaled more than US$150 million, and by the former Soviet Union's assistance programs in the 1970s (see Rawson 1994: 164). The visual effects of these cold war strategies are still found around the city of Mogadishu. In 2000 civil strife raged in at least 17 African countries (including Somalia), a staggering number that has destabilized large parts of the continent, spurred a major exodus of asylum seekers to the West, and reduced foreign investment to a trickle. If this is not motivation enough, there are other reasons discussed below why the international community should care about Somalia, in particular, and Africa generally.

One sees lots of evidence worldwide of how impoverished populations can lose confidence in states and their 'modern' apparatus, encouraging lots of potential 'Somalias' in Africa and elsewhere. While until the tragic events of September 11 Somalia was of little interest to many wealthy industrialized countries, this was not the case for other states, including Egypt, Ethiopia, Libya, and Saudi Arabia. Some of these countries are of considerable interest to the global community, whether as adversaries or allies. As one example, Egypt, one of the US and Europe's strongest allies in North Africa/Middle East, has official representation in Mogadishu and has been a significant actor in reconciliation talks, even hosting a major peace conference on Somalia in 1997. Indeed, the Egyptian government formally recognizes Somalia, in opposition to most of the international community, and has always had a keen interest in Somali affairs dating back to the nineteenth century.

Ethiopia, another important state on the continent, increasingly relies on Djibouti and the Berbera port, Somaliland for trade, because of the loss of the use of Assab port, Eritrea. The latter was a casualty of the recent Ethiopia/Eritrea war. According to Somaliland's Minister of Finance, Mohamed Said Mohamed 'Gees', 'We do all kinds of trade with the southeastern part of Ethiopia ... our main trading partner is Ethiopia and we are now trying to harmonise our customs, our custom duties and develop the official trade between the two countries' (IRIN 2001e).

Ethiopia also has interests in southern Somalia not related to trade. It has been very concerned about the growing influence of fundamental Islamic movements on its borders and has made military incursions into southern Somalia to silence such groups as the al–Itihaad al-Islami group. Following September 11, Ethiopia has been especially vocal in its claims to the US and its European allies that Somalia harbors radical Islamic and terrorist groups (BBC News 2002). There is a long history of animosity between Somalia and Ethiopia, and in the late 1970s they fought a war over the Ogadeen region of western Ethiopia. Not surprisingly, Ethiopia

[6] It is even said that 'in Somalia's unfettered free market economy, when fighting breaks out, gun prices go up' (Associated Press 2001: 1).

has been strongly opposed to the TNG and is supporting opposition groups and warlords in the country who also have a vested interest in a politically divided Somalia (Denyer 2001). Its cordial commercial and political relationships with Somaliland are at least partial responses to a general disfavor for the TNG and its quest for a unified Somalia.

For better or worse, therefore, the territory of Somalia is not situated in political isolation, either from its neighbors or from the larger international community. As the above examples point out, the motivations of these external parties are not always benign. While the absence of a state has not had a particularly devastating effect on certain segments of the population or economy, without a state the territory called Somalia will have problems protecting its resources and sovereignty along several fronts.

First is the issue of its most precious resource, water. Both of its two main rivers, the Jubba and Shebelle, flow from the Ethiopian highlands and bi-lateral agreements are needed to help insure that a dam(s) or other impediments are not constructed in their catchments. Such pacts are unlikely without a Somali state.

A second important topic related to Somalia's natural resources is the current lack of control on forest products. Since the collapse of the government, there has been a massive increase in deforestation motivated by a growth in charcoal exports to the Middle East (Farah 2000: 25). In northeastern Somalia alone, it is estimated that charcoal production and trade results in deforestation rates as high as 35,000 ha/year (IUCN 1997). Charcoal is commonly referred to as Somalia's 'black gold' and much of it is exported to Saudi Arabia, where it fetches $5 per bag or about 300 percent more than local prices. Conflicts between charcoal makers and camel herders who need trees for their herds, and between the former and militia factions who control the trade have resulted in several armed skirmishes. Clan elders attempt to control the trade and extraction of trees, but have been only minimally successful. Here, as in other cases, there is a need for a government to defend and protect its natural resources, including fisheries, and to defend its borders against potentially hostile states.

Thirdly, some form of government and enforcement is needed to protect external parties from overexploiting Somalia's rich coastal fisheries and to keep wealthy nations from dumping toxic waste along its coast. There is more than a little evidence that wealthy countries have dumped toxic materials along its coast, although this also happened during the Barre period (Bayart et al. 1999: xv).

Fourthly, some external body (state or other) is needed to protect the livestock industry from import bans and devastating diseases like Rift Valley Fever, and to help it find alternative export markets. Earlier chapters showed how Somalia and Somaliland have been vulnerable to import bans imposed by Middle Eastern countries, which have been aggravated by Somalia's lack of quarantine and animal health facilities. Without a unified campaign to confront trade and animal health barriers, Somalia's spectacular growth in animal trade may come to a screeching halt. Actions by competitor countries are already underway to encourage this.

In the south there are other processes that threaten the long-term viability of the livestock sector. For instance, the southern borderlands' increased dependence on the Nairobi market is unhealthy, and there are signs (e.g. low prices and oversupply) that the Nairobi market may be reaching a saturation point. A concerted effort is needed to find alternative markets – either in the region or outside – for Somali livestock. A campaign like this would be facilitated by the presence of a government, which could send trade missions to different countries and help find new markets.

Finally, the Kenyan government continues to intermittently close its border with Somalia, with the latest incident being in 2001. This most recent action could have a chilling effect on that segment of southern Somalia – herders and traders – that has survived the past decade reasonably well. This is the second punitive border closure that the Kenyan government has enforced during the past two years. While there is recent evidence that the closure is being circumvented in some cases, the general impacts are likely to be felt by communities of southern Somalia. Without a state, the Kenyan government holds the upper hand in these matters, and recently has implied that it will not engage in a border agreement until Somalia has a legitimate government (IRIN 2001f).

In closing, the international community needs to realize that increasing parts of the world are in conditions of statelessness or near-statelessness where poverty and despair are endemic.[7] In many cases these 'countries' are casualties of post-cold war neglect when global strategic interests no longer dictated a need to be overly concerned about their social, economic, and political welfare. The cold reality about their importance, however, could not be further from the truth. In these 'ungoverned' areas, including large parts of Somalia, conventional forms of diplomacy and agreements are inappropriate and new approaches need to be devised. This does not mean that there is local anarchy in these places but, rather, normal political units (states) and institutions are absent. Their fluidity and unorthodox forms are what makes them so difficult to understand, but as this book hopefully has shown these areas do matter immensely to different regions and to the rest of the world.

[7] The current 'war against terrorism' led by the US in retaliation for unsuspected attacks on innocent civilians and infrastructure in New York and Washington, DC confronts this anomaly of statelessness. Generally the confrontation is not against a state or group of countries – though the initial target has been Afghanistan – but against a network of powerful individuals and terrorists who operate clandestinely outside normal institutional channels and are only loosely connected citizens of any particular country.

during the pre-September 11 period, most American newspapers have carried at least one story about the informal institution since Bush ordered the closing of al Barakaat. Coupled with the untimely appearance of the Hollywood film, *Black Hawk Down*, Somalia has re-emerged as a noteworthy news story, perhaps even more so than during the busy days of famine and Operation Restore Hope.

The renewed attention to Somalia has clearly opened up 'space' for certain warlords and political actors that were increasingly out of the country's national picture in early 2001. The strong anti-terrorist posturing among warlords and others has been predictable, if not sadly ironic. Employing the dual shields of anti-terrorism and anti-Islamic fundamentalism, some faction chiefs have capitalized on Western suspicions about the TNG by accusing the fledgling government of hosting radical Islamists and terrorists among its ranks. According to one militia head, 'there are approximately 20,480 armed extremists in Somalia' and '85 % of the government (TNG) is al-Itihaad' (*The Economist* 2001: 54). Such gross exaggerations are easily discredited by Somali experts, but these kinds of accusations have not stopped, including a recent letter by one warlord to President Bush asking the US to attack Somalia because of the TNG's support for terrorism (Lacey 2002). These tactics are not surprising and reflect an uncanny understanding of Western sentiments and fears of global terrorism and radical Islam. Thus, the power of warlords and opposition movements has been markedly strengthened since September 11, while political concessions to the anti-TNG groups have increased, as has violence and conflict in Mogadishu and the Jubba Valley. In hindsight none of these outcomes are beyond the unexpected given the fractious national political context, but they nonetheless reflect the extent to which Somali events continue to be shaped by global forces and patterns.

So, Somalia is back on the international radar, not necessarily for the best of reasons, but still some would argue at least there is recognition of its existence and perhaps even a faint acknowledgement of what it has endured since 1991 (Valdmanis 2002). The renewed international interest in Somalia does not mean that the country has stood still since the global community's last extended ventures there seven and more years ago. Indeed, quite to the contrary, the book has shown that the country has dynamically reacted to an environment of statelessness, sometimes responding in predictable and other times in unpredictable ways. For the most part Somalia and its people have changed out of necessity and, thus, the information based on the pre-1991 era when official data were still being gathered is badly outdated. The awkward manner in which the US and its allies currently are maneuvering amid Somalia's shifting politico-economic milieu shows just how weak current understandings of the region are. What tomorrow holds for Somalia is difficult to predict in today's highly charged, militaristic environment. What is perhaps more reliably forecasted is that after what

Somalis have endured since 1991, it would be surprising if they were not able to adapt socially and economically to the post-September 11 environment – one that hopefully will be peaceful.

———1995b 'Daybreak is Near, Won't You Become Sour?' Going Beyond the Current Rhetoric in Somali Studies. In *The Invention of Somalia.* Ali J. Ahmed, ed. Pp. 135–155. Lawrenceville, NJ: Red Sea Press

Ahmed, Ismail 2000 Remittances and their Economic Impact in Post-War Somaliland. *Disasters* 24 (4): 380–389

Ahmed, Ismail and Reginald H. Green 1999 The Heritage of War and State Collapse in Somalia and Somaliland: Local-Level Effects, External Interventions and Reconstruction. *Third World Quarterly* 20(1): 113–127

Ahrens, Joachim D. 1998 *Cessation of Livestock Exports Severely Affects the Pastoralist Economy of Somali Region.* Addis Ababa: Emergencies Unit for Ethiopia, United Nations Development Programme

AHT (Agrar- und Hydrotechnik GMBH) 1987 *Masterplan for Juba Valley Development.* Essen, Germany: AHT

All Africa News Agency, 22 Feburary 1999, 'On the Brutal Murder of Elders and POW's,' www.africaonline.ke

Anderson, David M. and Vigdis Broch-Due, eds. 1999 *The Poor are not Us: Poverty and Pastoralism in East Africa.* Oxford, UK: James Currey

ARD (Associates in Rural Development) 1989 *Jubba Environmental and Socioeconomic Studies: Final Report.* Burlington, VT: Associates in Rural Development

Associated Press (AP), Somalia Gun Markets Continue Trades, p. 1, 9 July 2001. Available on http: // www. hiiraan. com /july /july 9.html

Bailey, DeeVon, Christopher B. Barrett, Peter D. Little, and Francis Chabari. 1999 *Livestock Markets and Risk Management Among East African Pastoralists: A Review and Research Agenda.* GL-CRSP Pastoral Risk Management Project Technical Report No. 03/99. Logan, UT: Utah State University

Barfield, Thomas J. 1993 *The Nomadic Alternative.* Englewood, NJ: Prentice Hall

Barise, Hassan 2001 Money Rules in Mogadishu. *UNESCO Courier* (February Issue): 23

Barkhadle, A.M.I. 1993 The Somali Traditional 'Deegaan' Ecological Classification System, *Rivista di Agricoltura Subtropicale e Tropicale* 87(1): 107–135.

Bayart, Jean-Francois 1999 The 'Social Capital' of the Felonious State. In *The Criminalization of the State in Africa.* Jean-Francois Bayart, S. Ellis, and B. Hibou, eds. Pp. 32–48. Oxford, UK: James Currey

Bayart, Jean-Francois, Stephen Ellis, and Beatrice Hibou, eds. 1999 *The Criminalization of the State in Africa.* Oxford, UK: James Currey

BBC Monitoring Service, 1 March 2001, Somali Warlords call on President Hassan to step down. http://www.globalarchive.ft.com/...ticle.html?= 010301002944&query=Somalia

BBC News, 7 January 2002, Ethiopian Troops 'deploy' in Somalia. http: //news.bb.co.uk/hi/English/world/Africa/newsid 1747000/1747396.stm

Berry, Sara 1989 Social Institutions and Access to Resources. *Africa* 59: 41–55.

Besteman, Catherine 1991 Land Tenure, Social Power, and The Legacy of Slavery in Southern Somalia. PhD Thesis, Department of Anthropology, University of Arizona, Tucson, AZ

——1996 Violent Politics and the Politics of Violence: The Dissolution of the Somali Nation-State. *American Ethnologist* 23: 579–596

——1999a *Unraveling Somalia: Race, Violence, and the Legacy of Slavery.* Philadelphia, PA: University of Pennsylvania Press

——1999b A Response to Helander's Critique of 'Violent Politics and the Politics of Violence'. American Ethnologist 26(4): 981–983

Besteman, Catherine and Lee Cassanelli, eds. 1996 *The Struggle for Land in Southern Somalia: the War behind the War.* Boulder, CO: Westview Press

Bihi, Adam J. 2000 *Building from the Bottom: Basic Institutions of Local Governance.* War Torn Societies Project (WSP). Somali Programme in Puntland. Nairobi: UNDP

Bohannan, Paul and George Dalton, eds. 1962 *Markets in Africa.* Evanston, IL: Northwestern University Press

Boutros-Ghali, Boutros 1994 Report by the Secretary General Concerning the Situation in Somalia. 26 September. New York: United Nations

——1996 Overview. Pp. 3–87. In *United Nations and Somalia, 1992–1996.* The United Nations Blue Book Series, Volume VIII. New York: United Nations Publications

Bowden, Mark 1999 *Black Hawk Down: A Story of Modern Warfare.* New York: Atlantic Monthly Press

Box, Thadis W. 1968 Range Resources of Somalia. *Journal of Range Management* 21(6): 388–392

Brackenbury, Andrew 2001 Gem Warfare. *Geographical Magazine* (January) 73(1): 60–64

Brons, Maria H. 2001 *Society, Security, Sovereignty, and the State: Somalia, from Statelessness to Statelessness.* Utrecht, Netherlands: International Books

Bryden, Matt 1999 New Hope for Somalia? The Building Block Approach. *Review of African Political Economy* 79: 134–140

Burawoy, Michael and Katherine Verdery, eds. 1999 *Uncertain Transitions: Ethnographies of Change in the Postsocialist World.* Boulder, CO: Rowman and Littlefield

CARE 1994 *Refugee Survey Analysis.* Nairobi, Kenya: CARE

——1999 *Regional Overview: Increased Food Insecurity in 1999.* Nairobi, Kenya: CARE

Carlin, Wendy, S. Fries, M. Schaffer, and P. Seabright 2000 *Barter and Non-Monetary Transactions in Transition Economies: Evidence from a Cross-Country Survey.* Working Paper No. 50. London, UK: European Bank for Reconstruction and Development

Cassam, M. 1987 *The Kenya Beef Industry: Prospects for Somali Cattle Exports.* Mogadishu: Livestock Marketing and Health Project

England, Andrew 2002 U.S. IDs Possible Terror Group, 16 February, 2 pp, http: //www.washingtonpost.com/wp-dyn/articles/A20593–2002Feb16. html

Ensminger, Jean 1992 *Making a Market: The Institutional Transformation of an African Society*. Cambridge: Cambridge University Press

Europa Publications 2000 *World Year Book, Volume II*. London, UK: Europa Publications

Evans, Hugh, Michael Cullen, and Peter D. Little 1988 *Rural–Urban Exchange in the Kismayo Region of Somalia*. Worcester, MA, and Binghamton, NY: Cooperative Agreement on Settlement and Resource Systems Analysis

FAO (Food and Agriculture Organization) 1994 *Towards a Strategy for Agricultural Development in Somalia: From Relief, Rehabilitation and Reconstruction to Development*. Mogadishu, Somalia: FAO

Farah, Ahmed Yusuf 2000 *Opportunities for the Improvement of Essential Services: Primary Education, Health and Water*. WSP Somali Programme in Puntland. Nairobi, Kenya: UNDP

Farah, Ahmed Yusuf and Ioan M. Lewis 1993 *Somalia: The Roots of Reconciliation*. London, UK: ACTIONAID

——1997 Making Peace in Somaliland. *Cahiers d'Etudes africaines* XXXVII (2): 349–377

Farah, Nuruddin 1996 The Women of Kismayo: Power and Protest in Somalia. *Times Literary Supplement*, 15 November, p. 18

Farrow, Moira 1993 Welfare Warlords: Somalia Welfare Cheaters in Canada. *The New Republic*, 22 November, vol. 209, no. 21, p. 10

Farzin, Y. Hossein 1988 *Food Import Dependence in Somalia: Magnitude, Causes, and Policy Options*. World Bank Discussion Papers No. 23. Washington, DC: The World Bank

FEWS (Famine Early Warning Systems) 1996 *Juba Valley Trip Report: Sakow and Bualle Districts*. Nairobi, Kenya: FEWS

——1996–2000 *Unpublished statistics and data from selected markets*. Nairobi, Kenya: FEWS

——1997, *Gu Crop Assessment for Lower and Middle Jubba Region*, 1997. Nairobi, Kenya: FEWS

——1997–1998 *Unpublished statistics and data from selected markets*. Nairobi, Kenya: FEWS

——1998a *Food Security Bulletin, 26 February*. AFR 98–2. Washington, DC: FEWS

——1998b *Food Security Bulletin, 22 December*. AFR/98–12. Washington, DC: FEWS

——1999a *Monthly Market Report, April*. Nairobi, Kenya: FEWS

——1999b *Bulletin on Pastoral Food Security in Kenya*. Nairobi, Kenya: FEWS

——1999c *Food Security Bulletin, 30 June*. AFR/99–6. Washington, DC: FEWS

——1999d *Food Security Bulletin, 26 March.* AFR/99–3. Washington, DC: FEWS

——2000a *Monthly Market Report, January.* Nairobi, Kenya: FEWS

——2000b *Monthly Market Report, March.* Nairobi, Kenya: FEWS

——2000c *Monthly Market Report, April.* Nairobi, Kenya: FEWS

FEWS-Net (Famine Early Warning Systems-Network) 2001a Livestock in Somalia. Unpublished field report. Nairobi, Kenya: FEWS-Net

——2001b Somalia Food Security Summary, 15 March. Washington, DC: FEWS-Net

FEWS-Net/CARE International 2001 Greater Horn of Africa Food Security Update, 15 July 2001. Nairobi, Kenya: FEWS-Net

Fisher, Ian 1999 'An Oasis of Peace in Somalia Seeks Freedom.' *New York Times*, 26 November, Pp. 1, 16

——2000 'Somali Business Thwarted by Too-Free Enterprise.' *New York Times*, 10 August, p. 4

Fortes, Meyer and E. E. Evans-Pritchard, eds. 1940 *African Political Systems.* London, UK: Oxford University Press

Frankel, S. Herbert 1977 *Two Philosophies of Money: The Conflict of Trust and Authority.* New York: St Martin's Press

Fratkin, Elliot 1991 *Surviving Drought and Development: Ariaal Pastoralists of Northern Kenya.* Boulder, CO: Westview Press

Friedman, Milton 1973 *Money and Economic Development.* New York: Praeger

FSAU (Food Security Assessment Unit) 1997 *Report No. 12.* Nairobi, Kenya: FSAU

——1998 *Food Security Highlights: Southern Somalia – November 1998.* Nairobi, Kenya: FSAU

Fukui, Katsuyoshi and John Markakis, eds. 1994 *Ethnicity and Conflict in the Horn of Africa.* Oxford, UK: James Currey

Gambetta, Diego, ed. 1988 *Trust: Making and Breaking Cooperative Relations.* Oxford, UK: Basil Blackwell

Gellner, Ernest 1988 Trust, Cohesion, and the Social Order. In *Trust: Making and Breaking Cooperative Relations.* Diego Gambetta, ed. Pp. 142–157. Oxford, UK: Basil Blackwell

Giddens, Anthony 1990 *Consequences of Modernity.* Stanford, CA: Stanford University Press

Gow, Doug 2001 'Mahmoud Wardere launches his mayoral campaign'. *Minneapolis Star Tribune*, 18 July

Green, Graham 1998 Laissez Faire in Africa. Unpublished paper

Green, Reginald H. 1993 *Somalia: Toward Reconstruction, Rehabilitation, Restructuring.* Mogadishu: UNICEF

——1999 Khatt and the Realities of Somalis: Historic, Social, Household, Political and Economic. *Review of African Political Economy* 79: 33–49

Green, Sonya L. 1998 Correspondent Report on Somalia, Voice of America. Washington, DC: Voice of America

—2002a Somalia: New Bank to be Launched. 16 January. http://www. reliefweb.int/IRIN

—2002b Somalia: Second Internet Provider for Mogadishu. 31 January. http://www.reliefweb.int/IRIN

—2002c Horn of Africa: US General Says Evidence of al-Qaeda in Somalia. 19 March. http://www.irinnews.org/report.asp?reportID=26277

IUCN (International Union for the Conservation of Nature) 1997 *Somali Natural Resources Management Programme.* Eastern Africa Programme. Nairobi, Kenya: IUCN

Jamal, Vali 1988a Somalia: Understanding an Unconventional Economy. *Development and Change* 19: 203–265

—1988b Somalia: Survival in a 'Doomed' Economy. *International Labour Review* 127(6): 783–812

Janzen, Jorg 1988 *JESS Report on Pastoral Economy and Seasonal Livestock Movements in the Jubba Valley.* JESS Report No. 33. Burlington, VT: Associates in Rural Development

Jubaland Relief and Rehabilitation Society 1993 *Update Report, September–October 1993.* Nairobi, Kenya: Jubaland Relief and Rehabilitation Society

Kempainea, Robert, K. Nelson, D. Williams, and L. Hedermonk 2001 Mycobacterium Tuberculosis Disease in Somali Immigrants in Minnesota. *Chest* 119: 176–180

Kenya, Government of 1993a *Inter-Agency Drought Assessment of Seventeen Districts in Kenya.* Nairobi, Kenya: Ministry of Agriculture and Livestock Development

—1993b *Inter-Agency Assessment of Drought-Affected Districts in Kenya.* Nairobi, Kenya: Ministry of Agriculture and Livestock Development

—1994 *Kenya Population Census 1989, Volume I.* Nairobi, Kenya: Government Printer

—1996 *Garissa District Development Plan.* Ministry of Finance and Economic Planning. Nairobi, Kenya: Government Printer

—1997 *Economic Survey of Kenya.* Nairobi, Kenya: Government Printer

—1998 *Economic Survey of Kenya.* Nairobi, Kenya: Government Printer

Kenya Standard, 16 August, 1989, p. 10

Konczacki, Z.A. 1978 *The Economics of Pastoralism: A Case Study of Sub-Saharan Africa.* London: Frank Cass

Kopytoff, Igor 1987 The Internal African Frontier: The Making of African Political Culture. In *The African Frontier: The Reproduction of Traditional African Societies.* I. Kopytoff, ed. Pp. 3–86. Bloomington, IN: Indiana University Press

Lacey, Marc 2002 Somalia's Multitude of Factions Hinders Antiterror Efforts. *New York Times,* 6 January, p. 14

Laitin, David D. 1977 *Politics, Language, and Thought: The Somali Experience.* Chicago, IL: University of Chicago Press

Lake, Eli. J. 2002 U.S Weighs Options on Somalia, 6 February, United Press International. News provided by COMTEX (http://www.comtexnews.com)

Lancaster, William 1997 *The Rwala Bedouin Today*. Prospects Heights, IL: Waveland Press

Landa, Janet Tai 1994 *Trust, Ethnicity, and Identity*. Ann Arbor, MI: University of Michigan Press

Lauderdale, Pat and Pietro Toggia 1999 An Indigenous View of the New World Order (A Book's Portrayal of Somalia). *Journal of Asian and African Studies* 34(2): 157–168

Lewis, I.M. 1955 *Peoples of the Horn of Africa*. London, UK: International African Institute

——1961 *A Pastoral Democracy: A Study of Pastoralism and Politics among the Northern Somali of the Horn of Africa*. London, UK: Oxford University Press

——1988 *A Modern History of Somalia: Nation and State in the Horn of Africa*. Boulder, CO: Westview Press

——1993 *Understanding Somalia: Guide to Culture, History and Social Institutions*. London, UK: Haan

——1994 *Blood and Bone: The Call of Kinship in Somali Society*. Lawrenceville, NJ: Red Sea Press

——1998 Doing Violence to Ethnography: A Response to Catherine Besteman's 'Representing Violence and "Othering" Somalia.' *Cultural Anthropology* 13: 100–108

Lexington Herald-Leader. 'Greenspan Touts Honesty in the Economy.' 13 September 1999, p. 10

Little, Peter D. 1989a *The Livestock Sector of the Kismayo Region, Somalia: An Overview*. Working Paper No. 50, Institute for Development Anthropology, Binghamton, NY

——1989b *The Cattle Commodity System of the Kismayo Region, Somalia: Preliminary Analysis*. Working Paper No. 51, Binghamton, NY; Institute for Development Anthropology

——1992a Traders, Brokers, and Market 'Crisis' in Southern Somalia. *Africa* 62(1): 94–124

——1992b *The Elusive Granary: Herder, Farmer, and State in Northern Kenya*. Cambridge: Cambridge University Press

——1994 Contract Farming and the Development Question. In *Living Under Contract: Contract Farming and Agrarian Transformation in Africa*. P. Little and M. Watts, eds. Pp. 217–250. Madison, WI: University of Wisconsin Press

——1996 Conflictive Trade, Contested Identity: The Effects of Export Markets on Pastoralists of Southern Somalia. *African Studies Review* 39(1): 25–53

——2000 *Selling to Eat: Petty Trade and Traders in Peri-Urban Areas of Africa*. Madison, WI: Broadening Access and Strengthening Input Market Systems Collaborative Research Support Program, University of Wisconsin

Little, Peter D. and Irae Baptista Lundin de Coloane 1992 *Petty Trade and Household Survival Strategies: A Case Study of Food and Vegetable*

Menkhaus, Kenneth and John Prendergast 1997 Political Economy of Post-Intervention Somalia. In *Crisis Response: Humanitarian Band-Aids in Sudan and Somalia.* John Prendergast, ed. Pp. 91–107. London, UK: Pluto Press

Merryman, James 1996 The Economy of Geedo Region and the Rise of Smallholder Irrigation. In *The Struggle for Land in Southern Somalia: the War behind the War.* Catherine Besteman and L. Cassanelli, eds. Pp. 73–89. Boulder, CO: Westview Press

Ministry of Agriculture and Livestock Development (MOALD), Kenya 1996–2000 Summary of Monthly Marketing Data. Unpublished statistics, Livestock Production Department, Garissa District. Garissa, Kenya: MOALD

Mishra, Satish C. 1993 *Finance, Banking and Economic Regeneration in Somalia.* Nairobi, Kenya: USAID

Mubarak, Jamil A. 1996 *From Bad Policy to Chaos: How an Economy Fell Apart.* Westport, CT: Praeger

——1997 The 'Hidden Hand' Behind the Resilience of the Stateless Economy of Somalia. *World Development* 25: 2027–2041

Mumin, Ali Mumin 1995 *Crop Production Prospective in Middle and Lower Juba Regions.* Nairobi, Kenya: FEWS

Murray, Martin n.d. Diasporic Peoples and Transnational Communities: The Changing Dynamics of the New Urban Migration. Unpublished manuscript

Nduru, Moyiga 1996 No End in Sight to Banana War. Report of 24 April, 1996. Unpublished paper. Nairobi, Kenya (also available on http://www.netnomads.com/banana.html)

Nietschmann, Bernard 1997 Protecting Indigenous Coral Reefs and Sea Territories, Miskito Coast, RAN, Nicaragua. In *Conservation through Cultural Survival: Indigenous Peoples and Protected Areas.* S. Stevens, ed. Pp. 193–224. Washington, DC: Island Press

Ninsim, Kwame A. 1991 *The Informal Sector in Ghana's Political Economy.* Accra, Ghana: Freedom Publications

Novisi, Aladika 1996 Adapting to Anarchy: The Localization of Somali Government. *Harvard International Review* (Fall Issue): 40–41,71–72

Nugent, Paul and A.I. Asiwaju, eds. 1996 *African Boundaries: Barriers, Conduits, and Opportunities.* London, UK: Pinter

Omaar, Rakiya and Alex de Waal 1993 *Land Tenure, The Creation of Famine, and Prospects for Peace in Somalia.* Discussion Paper No. 1. London, UK: African Rights

Omar, Mohamed Osman 1992 *The Road to Zero: Somalia's Self-Destruction.* London, UK: Haan Associates

Palmer, E.H. 1977 *The Desert of the Exodus, Vols. I and II.* New York: Arno Press

Peberdy, Sally and Christian Rogerson 2000 Transnationalism and Non-South African Entrepreneurs in South Africa's Small, Medium, and

Micro-Enterprise (SMME) Economy. *Canadian Journal of African Studies* 34(1): 20–40

Pierre, Robert E. 2001 'DC Mayor's Longtime Adviser to Depart.' 1 April, *Washington Post*, p. C3

People, The 2001 'Police Impound Lorries,' 25 June p. 5. Nairobi, Kenya

Perlez, Jane 2000 'For 8 Years, A Strained Relationship with the Military.' 27 December, *New York Times*, p. 17

Peters, Pauline 1994 *Dividing the Commons: Politics, Policy, and Culture.* Charlottesville, VA: University of Virginia Press

Prendergast, John 1993 *The Bones of Our Children Are Not Yet Buried: The Looming Spectre of Famine and Massive Human Rights Abuses.* Washington, DC: Center of Concern

——1997 *Crisis Response: Humanitarian Band-Aids in Sudan and Somalia.* London, UK: Pluto Press

Prunier, Gerard 1998 Somaliland Goes it Alone. *Current History* 97(619): 222–225

Rawson, David 1994 Dealing with Disintegration: U.S. Assistance and the Somali State. In *The Somali Challenge: From Catastrophe to Renewal.* Ahmed I. Samatar, ed. Pp. 147–187. Boulder, CO: Lynne Rienner Publishers

Rawson, David, with M.L. Bothwell, T. McKey, and E. Walton 1993 *The Somali State and Foreign Aid.* Washington, DC: Foreign Services Institute, Department of State

Reno, William 1995 *Corruption and State Politics in Sierra Leone.* Cambridge, UK: Cambridge University Press

——1998 *Warlord Politics and African States.* Boulder, CO: Lynne Rienner Publishers

Resource Management and Research 1984 *Southern Rangelands Survey.* Mogadishu: National Range Agency

Reuters, 1998, 'Somali Militia Fight for Southern Town of Kismayu,' 28 October. http://www.reuters.com/news

Richards, Paul 1996 *Fighting for the Rain Forest: War, Youth and Resources in Sierra Leone.* Oxford, UK: James Currey

Ricks, Thomas E. 2002 'Allies Step Up Somalia Watch.' 4 January, *Washington Post*, p. A1

Ring, Moses M. 1989 Dinka Stock Trading and Shifts in Rights in Cattle. In *Property, Poverty and People: Changing Rights in Property and Problems of Pastoral Development.* P. Baxter and R. Hogg, eds. Manchester, UK: International Development Centre, University of Manchester

Rogerson, C.M. and J.M. Rogerson 1996 The Metropolis as Incubator: Small-Scale Enterprise Development in Johannesburg. *Geojournal* 39(1): 33–40

Roseberry, W. and J. O'Brien 1991 Introduction. In *Golden Ages, Dark Ages: Imagining the Past in Anthropology and History.* Jay O'Brien and William Roseberry, eds. Pp. 1–18. Berkeley, CA: University of California Press

Sabriel, Abdi M. 1997 The Performance and Constraints of the Civil War Private Sector in Southern Somalia with Particular Reference to

——1994a Report on the 'Lower Jubba Peace and Reconciliation Conference.' Unpublished paper, UNDOS Documentation Unit, Nairobi, Kenya

——1994b Unpublished papers and notes, 1994–1995, UNDOS Documentation Unit, Nairobi, Kenya

US Census Bureau 1999 *Statistical Abstracts of the USA: The National Data Book.* Washington, DC: US Census Bureau

US Committee on Refugees 1998 *United States of America: Annual Report for 1998.* Washington, DC: US Committee on Refugees

——2000a *Annual Refugees Admitted and Resettled into the US, FY 1987–2000.* Washington, DC: US Committee on Refugees

——2000b *United Kingdom: Annual Report for 2000.* Washington, DC: US Committee on Refugees

Valdmanis, Thor 2002 'Somalis "welcome" U.S. Attack.' *USA Today*, 8 February, p. 6A

Verdery, Katherine 1996 *What was Socialism, and What comes Next?* Princeton, NJ: Princeton University Press

Vesley, Milan 2002 Somalia: US Cuts Net Lifeline. *African Business*, January Issue, p. 44

Vick, Karl 2002 'Al Qaeda Ally in Somalia is in Tatters; only remnants remain of Potential U.S. Target.' *The Washington Post*, 24 February, p. A16

Vigneau, Frederic 1993 *UNISOM-Kismayo, General Report (2 weeks of activities).* 22 January 1993, UNDOS Documentation Unit, Nairobi, Kenya

Villalon, Leonardo A. 1998 The African State at the End of the Twentieth Century: Parameters of the Critical Juncture. In *The African State at a Critical Juncture: Between Disintegration and Reconfiguration.* Leonardo A. Villalon and Phillip A. Huxtable, eds. Pp. 3–26. Boulder, CO: Lynne Rienner Publishers

Villalon, Leonardo A. and Phillip A. Huxtable, eds. 1998 *The African State at a Critical Juncture: Between Disintegration and Reconfiguration.* Boulder, CO: Lynne Rienner Publishers

Watson, Murray 1987 Aerial Surveys of Livestock Populations in the Dry Season, Jubba Valley. Unpublished report

Wedel, Janine R. 1998 Informal Relations and Institutional Change: How Eastern European Cliques and States Mutually Respond. *The Anthropology of East Europe Review* 16: 4–13

Western, David and Virginia Finch 1986 Cattle and Pastoralism: Survival and Production in Arid Lands. *Human Ecology* 14(1): 77–94

WFP (World Food Programme) 1993 *Demography and Distress Survey of Somalia.* Nairobi, Kenya: WFP

WFP/FSAU (World Food Programme/Food Security Assessment Unit) 1995 *Price Report on Southern Somalia.* Nairobi, Kenya: WFP and FSAU

——1997a *Report No. 1* (January): FSAU. Nairobi, Kenya: WFP and FSAU

——1997b *Report No. 2* (February): FSAU. Nairobi, Kenya: WFP and FSAU

——1997c *Report No. 4* (April): FSAU. Nairobi, Kenya: WFP and FSAU

——1997d *Report No. 6* (June/July): FSAU. Nairobi, Kenya: WFP and FSAU

——1997e *Report No. 8–9* (August/September): FSAU. Nairobi, Kenya: WFP and FSAU

——1997f *Report No. 10–11* (October/November): FSAU. Nairobi, Kenya: WFP and FSAU

Wolf, Eric 1982 *Europe and the People Without History*. Berkeley, CA: University of California Press

Women's International Network [WIN] 1998 Somalia: Juba Women Development Center. *WIN* 24: 54–55

Woodruff, David 1999 Barter of the Bankrupt: The Politics of Demonetization in Russia's Federal State. In *Uncertain Transitions: Ethnographies of Change in the Postsocialist World*. M. Burawoy and K. Verdery, eds. Pp. 83–124. Boulder, CO: Rowman and Littlefield

Woodward, David and G. Stockton 1989 *Somalia: A Study of the Profitability of Somali Exports*. Washington, DC: Abt Associates

World Bank 1983 *Project Report: Somalia-Trans-Juba Livestock Project*. Washington, DC: World Bank

Zaal, Fred 1998 Pastoralism in a Global Age: Livestock Marketing and Pastoral Commercial Activities in Kenya and Burkina Faso. PhD Thesis, University of Amsterdam, Netherlands

Zaal, Fred and Ton Dietz 1999 Of Markets, Meat, Maize and Milk: Pastoral Commoditization in Kenya. In *The Poor are Not Us: Poverty and Pastoralism in East Africa*. David M. Anderson and Vigdis Broch-Due, eds. Pp. 163–198. Oxford, UK: James Currey

Zaal, Fred and Annemarie Polderman 2000 High Risk, High Benefits: International Livestock Trade and the Commercial System in Eastern and Southern Africa. Paper presented at the OSSREA Sixth Congress on Globalisation, Democracy and Development in Africa: Future Prospects, 24–28 April 2000, Dar es Salaam, Tanzania

Zartman, William, ed. 1995 *Collapsed States: Disintegration and Restoration of Legitimate Authority*. Boulder, CO: Lynne Rienner Publishers